The Limits
of Realism

Tim Button

OXFORD
UNIVERSITY PRESS

OXFORD
UNIVERSITY PRESS

Great Clarendon Street, Oxford, OX2 6DP,
United Kingdom

Oxford University Press is a department of the University of Oxford.
It furthers the University's objective of excellence in research, scholarship,
and education by publishing worldwide. Oxford is a registered trade mark of
Oxford University Press in the UK and in certain other countries

© Tim Button 2013

The moral rights of the author have been asserted

First published 2013
First published in paperback 2015

Published in the United States of America by Oxford University Press
198 Madison Avenue, New York, NY 10016, United States of America

British Library Cataloguing in Publication Data
Data available

Library of Congress Cataloging in Publication Data
Data available

ISBN 978-0-19-967217-2 (Hbk.)
ISBN 978-0-19-874412-2 (Pbk.)

The Limits of Realism

Tim Button explores the relationship between words and world; between semantics and scepticism.

A certain kind of philosopher—the external realist—worries that appearances might be radically deceptive; we might all, for example, be brains in vats, stimulated by an infernal machine. But anyone who entertains the possibility of radical deception must also entertain a further worry: that all of our thoughts are totally contentless. That worry is just incoherent.

We cannot, then, be external realists, who worry about the possibility of radical deception. Equally, though, we cannot be internal realists, who reject all possibility of deception. We must position ourselves somewhere between internal realism and external realism, but we cannot hope to say exactly where. We must be realists, for what that is worth, and realists within limits.

In establishing these claims, Button critically explores and develops several themes from Hilary Putnam's work: the model-theoretic arguments; the connection between truth and justification; the brain-in-vat argument; semantic externalism; and conceptual relativity. *The Limits of Realism* establishes the continued significance of these topics for all philosophers interested in mind, logic, language, or the possibility of metaphysics.

Vous m'expliquez ce monde avec une
image. Je reconnais alors que vous en
êtes venus à la poésie: je ne connaîtrai
jamais.

You explain this world to me with an
image. I realise then that you have been
reduced to poetry: I shall never know.

Le mythe de Sisyphe

ALBERT CAMUS

Contents

Introduction

Metaphysics longs for magic. I take this thought from William James, who claims that metaphysicians operate in that tradition of folklore, where to know something's name is to control it:

'God,' 'Matter,' 'Reason,' 'the Absolute,' and 'Energy,' are so many solving names. You can rest when you have them. You are at the end of your metaphysical quest.[1]

These particular solving names have fallen out of fashion. But contemporary metaphysicians have found new solving names: 'Causal', 'Fundamental', 'Grounding', and 'Natural'. Added to this, metaphysicians have solving *gestures* (desk-thumping), solving *typographies* ('Really', '*really*', or 'REALLY'), and solving *locations* (the ontology room). These many solutions are so many incantations.

Or so I am often inclined to think. But inclinations are not arguments.[2] I started writing this book with the aim of turning inclination into argument; of *demonstrating* that metaphysics belongs to magic. I finished writing this book with this aim realized in part, but only in part. Indeed, I have come to believe that partial success mixed with partial failure is inevitable. We can show that there are limits to realism, and limits to 'anti'-realism. But most of all, we can show that there are limits to what we can show at all. The aim of this book is to sketch all of these limits.

That aim is realized by considering the relevance of both *semantics* and *scepticism* to the realism debate. Their relevance might seem surprising, given that there is a very direct approach to the realism debate which mentions neither. On the direct approach, you start by choosing some putative entities, such as kitchen appliances, mountains, electrons, virtues, or numbers. Then you simply ask yourself: *should we be realists about those entities?*

That direct question mentions neither scepticism nor semantics. However, it is simply too direct. Until we know what it means to be a *realist* about something, the question has no clear content. Fortunately, there is a way to give the question *some* content, whilst retaining the idea that the

---

[1] James (1907: 28).
[2] Even if James (1907: 8–9) is right that temperament is 'the potentest of all our premises'.

realism debate should be approached directly. We treat the question as asking us: *are those entities constitutively independent of us?*[3]

Often, this question is clear enough. We did not build mountains with our bare hands, and we did not build them with our naked minds either. So, mountains are constitutively independent of us. *Mountains are real.* Of course, this is hardly profound, but the direct approach to the realism debate takes this to be a sign of its level-headedness.

There is, however, a rival approach. Rather than starting with the question of whether mountains, virtues, or numbers are independent of us, we might instead start by investigating our use of the *words* 'mountain', 'virtue', and 'number'. Perhaps this will give us some insight into the role of mountains, virtues, or numbers in our lives. The realism debate thus shifts from considering the world directly, to considering the world by examining our words.

Philosophers who want to approach the realism debate directly are rarely impressed by this semantic turn. They complain: *I don't want to talk about how we talk about objects; I want to talk about the objects!* And this complaint is good, as far as it goes. No one should deny the difference between talking about the world and talking about words.

However, this difference does not establish that semantics is irrelevant to the realism debate. For suppose we can mount an argument with the following conclusion: *By your own lights, you are simply unable to talk about any of the objects you wanted to talk about.* Then the complaint in the previous paragraph will ring utterly hollow. In the face of this argument, a philosopher who wants to approach the realism debate by talking about objects will have to explain *how we can* talk about them. They will have to engage with some semantic questions after all.

We are, then, looking for an argument that forces realists to consider semantic questions. A natural place to look is in the discussion of meaning scepticism that took America by storm in the 1960s onwards, culminating in Hilary Putnam's model-theoretic arguments against a certain kind of realism.[4] This is my entry point to the realism debate.

I begin by outlining an earnest position, called *external realism*. This countenances good old-fashioned *Cartesian* scepticism and, for this reason,

---

[3] This is Devitt's (1984a) recommendation.

[4] Putnam's first full public presentation of the argument was in December 1976 (Putnam 1977), but this was somewhat anticipated during an exchange with Dummett in April 1976 (Putnam 1979c).

Putnam's model-theoretic arguments show that it must countenance incoherent meaning scepticism. (Perhaps I should emphasize right now, given how frequently it is misunderstood, that Putnam does not *embrace* meaning scepticism; instead, he uses it as a *reductio* of opposing positions, such as external realism.) This will prompt a loss of faith in external realism, and the remainder of this book explores how we might reconcile ourselves to this loss. We shall find no particular position that deserves our allegiance, not even *internal realism*, which is defined colourlessly in diametric opposition to external realism. By the end of the book, we shall have little more positive to say than that we must be neither external realists, nor internal realists, but something vaguely in-between.

I have just mentioned Putnam for the first time. During the course of this book, I shall mention him several hundred times more. Putnam has provided some of the most powerful arguments in support of the idea that metaphysics longs for magic, and some of the most interesting criticisms of those arguments. All of these form the central subject matter of this book, and the book is consequently a blend of exegesis, reconstruction, and novel contribution. In the interests of providing an unbroken line of narrative, I have not drawn sharp lines between these components. Nevertheless, I do my best to indicate in the text where I am agreeing with, where I am parting company from, and where I am outright disagreeing with (various time slices of) Putnam. Doubtless I shall prove mistaken on certain specifics, but one thing is absolutely certain: without Putnam, this book could not have existed. I owe him tremendous thanks for the pleasure I have drawn from reflecting on his work, and I hope that the depth of my gratitude comes through in what follows.

There are many more people to thank. For artwork: Helen Macdonald (Figure 2.1) and Lawrence Lek (the cover image). For help with German translations: Maike Albertzart and Christine Tiefensee. For community: the philosophy departments in Cambridge, Harvard, and UT Austin. For comments, corrections, discussions, suggestions, and questions over several years: Sharon Berry, Thomas David Button, Christina Cameron, Adam Caulton, Colin Chamberlain, Elijah Chudnoff, Tim Crane, Matti Eklund, Daniel Elstein, Peter Godfrey-Smith, Peli Grietzer, Alex Grossman, Hallvard Lillehammer, Jon Litland, Christina McLeish, Steven Methven, Adrian Moore, Sam Nicholson, Seb Nye, Alex Oliver, Huw Price, Hilary Putnam, Tim

Storer, Peter Sullivan, Amie Thomasson, Sean Walsh, Lee Walters, Nathan Wildman, and four anonymous readers.

A handful of people are owed very special thanks. First, Michael Potter, who was my PhD supervisor when I began what would become this book. Second, Brian King, who first made me realize that I love philosophy and who keeps reminding me that I do. Third, Adam Stewart-Wallace and Rob Trueman, who have both influenced me more than I can express in mere footnotes. And finally—and always—Ben, who may not care about cherries and cats or brains in vats, but who cares deeply about me.

Part A
External Realism

1

The picture of external realism

The model-theoretic arguments should erode one's faith in external realism. That is the central claim of Part A of this book. The aim of the book as a whole is to learn how to live with this loss of faith, and without much by way of a substitute. But to understand all of this, we must first understand the faith held by external realists, and how it came under attack.

External realism goes by many aliases: *metaphysical* realism; *capital-'R'* Realism; *robust* realism; *desk-thumping* realism; *genuine* realism; the choice of adjective is yours. The purpose of that adjective is to indicate just how *serious* the position is about its realism. I have chosen to stick with 'external' realism, because that adjective is most evocative of the philosophical picture which this position employs. That picture is of reasoning from a 'God's Eye point of view'.[1]

Pictures are often difficult to attack, and philosophical pictures are no exception. Fortunately, Hilary Putnam presents us with three principles that flow naturally from the external realist's picture, and shows us how to attack those. These principles collectively enshrine what I shall call the *Credo* of external realism. The precise interpretation of the Credo is not itself a straightforward task, but the Credo is the only place to start.

1.1 Credo in Independence

Generically, realists believe that *we* do not determine what there is; rather, the *world* does that. Of course, this bold statement needs some caveats. No one can deny that we have built cities, sculpted statues, started wars, and invented Esperanto. *These* things would not exist without us. But *most* of

[1] Putnam (1980a: 100; 1981c: 49; see also 1982a: 38; 1983a: x, xviii).

the universe did, does, and will manage perfectly well without us. In this spirit, then, the external realist advances the first of three principles:

The Independence Principle. The world is (largely) made up of objects that are mind-, language-, and theory-independent.[2]

Belief in Independence is undoubtedly a necessary component of realism. It would be controversial to claim that it is *sufficient* for realism,[3] but I shall postpone discussion of this point.

1.2 Credo in Correspondence

If the objects of the world are (largely) independent of our minds, languages, and theories, we need to know how we are able to think, speak, and theorize about them. An early realist answer to this question was the *copy theory* of truth. This held that true representations must copy reality. But this claim is implausible, as William James noted.[4] There are many different conventions for true representation, beyond mere copying. It is not clear why we should care about copying. And in any case, the world is just too rich to make copying it a plausible enterprise.

The *correspondence theory* endeavoured to accommodate these objections. For the correspondence theorist, true theories do not aim to copy the world, but aim only at some kind of *structural* similarity. In the simplest case, names pick out individual objects and predicate letters pick out properties and relations. (The more nominalistically inclined may prefer to read this, and similar expressions throughout this chapter, as saying that predicate letters lasso certain objects together.) Thus for the correspondence theorist, an atomic sentence of the form '$Rt_1, \ldots, t_n$' is true exactly when the relation named by 'R' holds between the objects named by 't_1', $\ldots$, 't_n'. This view is enshrined in the second principle of external realism:

The Correspondence Principle. 'Truth involves some sort of correspondence relation between words or thought-signs and external things and sets of things.'[5]

---

[2] Putnam (1977: 484–5; 1980a: 100; 1981c: 49; 1982a: 30; 1989: 352).

[3] Devitt (1983: 292–3; 1984a: 3–4, 34–40; 1991; 2010: 52–3) makes this controversial claim.

[4] James (1904: 467–9).

[5] Putnam (1980a: 100; 1981c: 49; see also 1982a: 30; 1989: 352; 2000: 126).

Certain versions of the correspondence theory go further, and insist that each individual sentence must correspond with an individual object of a special sort: a *fact*, or *state of affairs*. The Correspondence Principle takes no stance on the existence or otherwise of such objects. It enshrines only the modest view that names pick out objects and predicates pick out properties and relations.

Certain other versions of the correspondence theory make the extremely strong claim that 'there is just One True Theory of the fixed mind-independent Reality'.[6] That Theory is penned in *Ontologese*, a language which is perfectly suited to limning reality's distinguished structure. Putnam often attributes this doctrine to external realism, and there is probably more explicit support for it now than in any recent time. Nevertheless, at the outset my external realist will treat the existence of Ontologese as a pious legend, rather than as Credo-enshrined orthodoxy. She subscribes only to the much more modest Correspondence Principle.

But perhaps even the correspondence theory of truth is too ambitious, since it insists that there must be a structural similarity between the subject/predicate distinction of some language and the object/property distinction in the world. *Truthmaker theory* abandons this structural requirement. It requires only that true sentences (typically) have some worldly (mind-independent) truthmaker.

In these three successive incarnations—copy, correspondence, and truthmaker—the quintessentially realist theory of truth has steadily sacrificed detail. For the sake of generality, it might be best to pin only a truthmaker theory on the external realist, since she could always add greater detail by postulating that the truthmakers have the structure required for full-fledged correspondence. As it happens, though, the choice between truthmaker and correspondence theory will make almost no difference to our subsequent considerations. (If anything, it makes external realism marginally more difficult to attack, if it adheres to a correspondence theory rather than a mere truthmaker theory.) So it will do no harm to assume that the external realist accepts the Correspondence Principle.

---

[6] Putnam (1989: 352; see also 1979a: 288; 1980a: 100; 1981c: 49; 1982a: 30).

1.3 Credo in Cartesianism

For the external realist, then, truth consists in correspondence. Falsity will consist in a certain failure of correspondence. A worry now arises. Let us imagine that humans have arrived at some scientific theory which is marvellous in every imaginable respect that we can investigate. It predicts all our observations perfectly; it retrodicts equally well; it explains without fault; it is simple to work with; it is harmonious and beautiful; perhaps to learn about and employ the theory gives the sensation of seeing directly into the mind of God. Such a theory is canonically *ideal*.[7] It gives every indication of being true. But if the world really is as mind-, language-, and theory-independent as the external realist believes, then might not appearances be radically deceptive? For example: perhaps the theory tries to talk about hadrons, but there are no hadrons to correspond with hadron-talk. Or perhaps, although the theory says otherwise, the world really came into existence exactly five minutes ago, so that the theory gets everything wrong about the past.[8] Perhaps we are really all just brains in vats,[9] or being deceived by René Descartes's *malin genie*. Such thoughts lead to the third principle of external realism:

> **The Cartesianism Principle.** Even an ideal theory might be radically false.[10]

This captures a kind of anxiety about Cartesian-style sceptical scenarios (hence the name). This anxiety is undoubtedly associated with a certain breed of realism.[11] One way to put the idea is as follows: only God, whose knowledge is not constrained by *mere* science, could say for sure whether any given theory is true or false. For this reason, we might say that the external realist's 'favorite point of view is a God's Eye point of view'.[12]

---

[7] This follows Putnam's (1977: 485) explication.

[8] A worry mentioned by Russell (1921: 159–60).

[9] Putnam (1977: 485, 487; 1981c: 5–17; 1986b: 110–13; 1989: 352) takes this worry as central to external realism.

[10] Putnam (1977: 485; 1980b: 473; 1989: 352; 2000: 127–31).

[11] Since Dummett (1963: 153), several authors have drawn this link between realism and the threat of Cartesian scepticism. Van Inwagen (1988: 95) explicitly holds that 'truth is radically nonepistemic'. This might seem to express the Cartesianism Principle, but van Inwagen (1988: 104–7) claims only that truth is a mind-independent relationship between *propositions* (which are 'necessarily existent, abstract' mind-independent objects) and the (largely mind-independent) world; this is just a little icing on the Independence Principle.

[12] Putnam (1980a: 100; 1981c: 49; see also 1982a: 38; 1983a: x, xviii).

We therefore have three Principles to which the external realist adheres: Independence, Correspondence, and Cartesianism. These together form the Credo of external realism. It is worth noting that many philosophers who self-define as 'realists' will reject elements of the Credo. The most salient example is Putnam himself, who called himself an internal *realist* whilst rejecting *external* realism. Accordingly, it is not worth objecting that the Credo fails to capture *realism*,[13] for external realism is just one denomination within the broad church of realism. Moreover, it is not an irrelevant sect. The three Principles of the Credo have, individually and together, a distinguished line of descent.[14]

1.4 Modelling the Credo

To set up Putnam's attack on external realism, our next task is to offer a model-theoretic treatment of the external realist's Credo. (For those totally unfamiliar with model theory, I offer a beginner's primer in Appendix I.)

Suppose the external realist has presented her favourite theory, which she hopes corresponds to the mind-independent world. We shall assume that this theory is expressed in a formal language containing individual constant symbols ('c_1', 'c_2', ...), predicates ('R_1', 'R_2', ...), and function symbols ('f_1', 'f_2', ...). We are to imagine the external realist's mind-independent world as the intended model, W, of the external realist's theory. W's domain, W, is to be thought of as the objects which make up the world. Each constant, 'c', is mapped to the object c^W in the domain of the intended model. Each predicate, 'R', is mapped to a set R^W of objects (or pairs, triples, etc. of objects) drawn from W; these are to be thought of as the extensions of the predicates. A similar treatment is offered for function symbols.

This model-theoretic treatment sits extremely well with the external realist's Correspondence Principle. The idea of mapping the words of the formal language onto the objects of the world gives us an excellent means for thinking about reference. When the external realist says that the name 'c' refers to some object, a, we can parse this as stating that on our

---

[13] Though Hansen (1987: 95–7) and Van Inwagen (1988: 107–8) make this objection. Putnam (2012b: 62) now acknowledges that it was a mistake to call the position 'metaphysical realism' (rather than, for example, 'external realism'), since one can be a realist and want to do some metaphysics without being (what I have called) an external realist.

[14] As Putnam (1982a: 30) notes.

interpretation, 'c' denotes $c^W = a$. Derivatively, this gives us an excellent way to understand what it would mean for an atomic sentence to be *true*. Where 'R' is an n-place predicate, and 't_1' through to 't_n' are terms of the language, we have the schema:

$$\text{'}Rt_1 \ldots t_n\text{' is true iff } \langle t_1^W, \ldots, t_n^W \rangle \in R^W$$

Similar clauses are used to explain the use of function symbols, and correspondence for non-atomic sentences is explained recursively.

The model-theoretic treatment also sits well with the Independence Principle. On the model-theoretic treatment, the external realist conceives of the world as a particular model. Which model the world happens to be does not depend upon our minds, languages, or theories. There are plenty of models and, a priori, any of them *might* be the actual world. This captures some of the idea of Independence. In turn, this gives us a way to understand the Cartesianism Principle: since it is a mind-independent matter which model represents the world, there is always the possibility of stating a bunch of falsehoods about the world.

The model-theoretic approach therefore validates all three Principles of the external realist's Credo. Unsurprisingly, then, this way of modelling external realism has become firmly entrenched among contemporary metaphysicians. To take one example: in passing, Cian Dorr sketches a three-step recipe for doing *fundamental metaphysics*.[15] First, we describe the '*fundamental ontology*'. Next, we specify the '*fundamental ideology*'. Finally, we lay down 'some *laws*'. This is to appropriate model theory for metaphysical ends: Dorr has called domains 'the fundamental ontology'; he has called the (formal) language 'the fundamental ideology'; and he has called axioms 'laws'.

Dorr describes this three-step recipe as a 'standard approach'.[16] I would go further, and describe it as an *orthodoxy* for post-Quinean metaphysicians.[17] Willard van Orman Quine gave us the division between *ontology* and *ideology* upon which Dorr relies.[18] Moreover, Quine told us that a theory's ontological commitment is determined by its regimentation in first-order logic, since 'to be is, purely and simply, to be the value of a variable.'[19] Of course, Quine was no friend to metaphysics, let alone to 'fundamental'

---

[15] Dorr (2011: 139).   [16] Dorr (2011: 139).
[17] Putnam (2004: 15–16, 78–81) plausibly traces the resurgence of metaphysics back to Quine.
[18] Quine (1951b).   [19] Quine (1948: 32; see also 1951a: 67; 1957: 17).

metaphysics (whatever that might be). But metaphysicians working after Quine have typically embraced the idea that a theory's quantifiers gauge its 'ontological commitment', and have then quibbled (in a non-Quinean fashion) on the exchange rate between ontology and ideology.[20] The three-step recipe is *the* method of contemporary analytic metaphysics, and it enshrines a model-theoretic approach.

Despite the centrality of these ideas to contemporary metaphysics, an external realist might object to the use of model theory. After all, it is unclear why someone who wants to be a realist (of any stripe) about concrete entities, like cats, cherries, and electrons, should be forced to believe in *models*, which are abstract mathematical entities.

An external realist with such qualms should feel free to think of model theory as nothing more than a convenient tool for discussing correspondence between words and world. This will allow her to *use* model theory to model (in the informal sense) her Credo, without committing her to the *existence* of the models themselves.[21] If she digs in her heels and absolutely refuses to employ model theory in any capacity, then she will have to explain what her correspondence relation amounts to with both hands tied behind her back. Bear in mind that model theory was designed, among other things, precisely in order to discuss different ways to make theories true.

This, however, gives rise to a more serious concern. Model theory was developed by mathematicians for mathematical ends. So, whenever we deploy a result from model theory in order to demonstrate something about external realism, we should ask whether that result is simply an artefact of a theory that is appropriate for mathematics but too permissive for metaphysics. This is not a question that can be settled once and for all in advance; we shall simply have to proceed with caution.

In the meantime, model theory gives us an excellent way to think about the philosophical claims of external realism. We are not asking the external realist to *believe* in the existence of abstract models, but only to employ the model theory. And we are allowing the external realist the freedom to argue, at a later point, that model theory is too permissive. In short, there can be no general objection to a model-theoretic approach to the external realist's Credo.

---

[20] D. Lewis (1986: 4) is probably the most famous exponent.

[21] Putnam (1994a: 263) offers a similar thought; thanks also to Sharon Berry for suggesting this.

2

The model-theoretic arguments

In Chapter 1, I explained the external realist's Credo: Independence, Correspondence, and Cartesianism. I then explained why model theory offers an attractive way to understand these Principles. With the model theory in place, I shall now explain the model-theoretic results that Putnam brings to bear against external realism.

Putnam's model-theoretic arguments fall broadly into two camps: *indeterminacy* arguments and *infallibilism* arguments. Together these show that, for any ideal theory, there are guaranteed to be many different ways to make it true. This strikes at the very heart of the external realist's Credo.

2.1 Indeterminacy arguments

The indeterminacy arguments aim to show the following: *If there is any way to make a theory true, then there are many ways to do so.* This provides the external realist with an embarrassment of riches, since any one of many candidate correspondence relations would function perfectly well as *the* correspondence relation that she mentions in her Correspondence Principle. The most obvious threat is that it will be utterly *indeterminate* which of these relations *is* truth itself.[1]

The *permutation argument* is the easiest indeterminacy argument to explain.[2] Imagine that we were to lay out all the objects in the world, together with various labels (names) for them, and with other labels (predicates) for

---

[1] As Putnam (1981c: 33) notes, these relate to Quine's (1960: §§7–16; 1968; 1970; 1987) arguments for the indeterminacy of translation.

[2] See Putnam (1981c: 33–5, 217–18). Permutation arguments have a lengthy history, and are to be found in Frege (1893: §10), Carnap (1928a: §§153–5), and Newman (1928: 145–6). Closer to our present concerns, they occur in Jeffrey (1964: 82–4), Winnie (1967: 226), Field (1975: 376–7), Wallace (1979: 307), and Davidson (1979: 229–30).

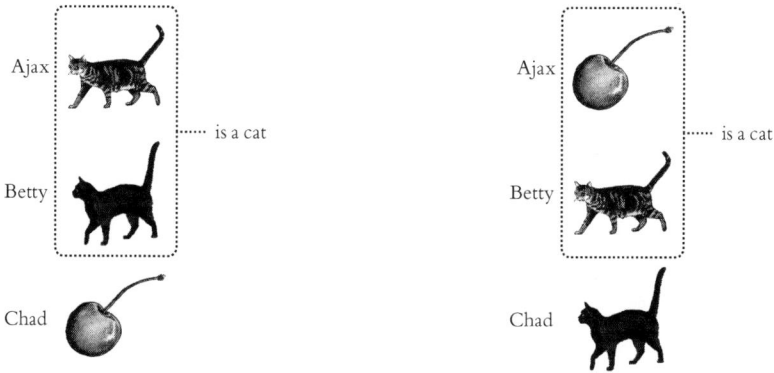

Figure 2.1 Two models of the theory whose sentences are just 'Ajax is a cat', 'Betty is a cat', and 'Chad is not a cat'. We begin with an assignment of names to objects and predicates to collections of objects (left). This model is transformed into the permuted model (right) by shuffling around all of the objects without altering the labels.

collections of them. Suppose we now shuffle the objects around. So long as we do not disturb the labels, exactly the same sentences will come out as true after the shuffling as were true before the shuffling. A very simple instance of this idea is illustrated in Figure 2.1,[3] but the idea is wholly general. If W models the external realist's favourite theory, then a *permutation* over the domain of W will systematically shuffle the objects around, yielding a distinct but *isomorphic* structure, P. Since W and P are isomorphic, they make exactly the same sentences true or false. Thus we obtain:

The Permutation Theorem. Any theory with a non-trivial model has many distinct isomorphic models with the same domain.

(I offer a formal proof in Appendix I, and a definition of a 'non-trivial model'.) Sticking with our models W and P, we can regard either of the following schemes as presenting us with the reference relation:

$$\text{'}t\text{' refers to } t^{W}$$
$$\text{'}t\text{' refers to } t^{P}$$

---

[3] Inspired by Putnam's (1977: 484, 490) diagrams, and by his use of cats and cherries (1981c: 33–5) in discussing permutations. Thanks to Helen Macdonald for these wonderful drawings.

Equally, we can treat either of these two schemes as presenting us with the correspondence relation (for atomic sentences):

$$\text{`}Rt_1 \ldots t_n\text{'} \text{ is true iff } \left\langle t_1^{\mathcal{W}}, \ldots, t_n^{\mathcal{W}} \right\rangle \in R^{\mathcal{W}}$$
$$\text{`}Rt_1 \ldots t_n\text{'} \text{ is true iff } \left\langle t_1^{\mathcal{P}}, \ldots, t_n^{\mathcal{P}} \right\rangle \in R^{\mathcal{P}}$$

In short, settling the truth values of every sentence in some language is insufficient to pin down the reference and correspondence relation that the external realist mentions in her Correspondence Principle.

A second indeterminacy argument is only marginally less intuitive. If the external realist's theory has a model, $\mathcal{W}$, then the theory must at least be consistent. But if it is consistent, it also has a *numerical* model. More precisely:[4]

The Completeness Theorem. Any consistent, countable set of sentences has a model whose domain only contains natural numbers.

The proof of this result is slightly more involved than that of the Permutation Theorem, and certainly harder to illustrate. But the overarching upshot is that the supposedly 'intended' model, $\mathcal{W}$, and the numerical model, $\mathcal{N}$, will likely be distinct. This will occur when $\mathcal{W}$ is uncountable, or if some of the objects in $\mathcal{W}$ are not numbers. Nevertheless, both $\mathcal{W}$ and $\mathcal{N}$ make exactly the same sentences true and false. So, as in the case of the Permutation Theorem, we have free choice concerning which model to think of as providing us with *the* correspondence relation.[5]

Further indeterminacy arguments can be offered by employing more sophisticated theorems from model theory (often some Löwenheim–Skolem result). If my focus were the philosophy of mathematics, I would need to discuss such theorems in detail. However, such a discussion would add very little to this book. (I elaborate on this remark in Appendix I.) Indeed, it could be rather harmful, since it might suggest that the model-theoretic arguments depend upon some sophisticated mathematics. Emphatically: *they do not.* They depend only on simple, elementary considerations. So the only indeterminacy arguments that I shall consider in this book are those from the Permutation and Completeness Theorems. (Indeed, in this regard I am largely following Putnam: in all his discussion

---

[4] I shall not distinguish between first-order and higher-order theories until Chapter 4.

[5] This obviously relates to Skolem's (1922) scepticism that there are any 'genuinely' uncountable sets. The Completeness Theorem also led Quine (1964) to realize that any theory could be given a model in the natural numbers, leading him to investigate (and reject) a kind of modern-day Pythagoreanism.

of the model-theoretic arguments, Putnam only once essentially invokes a result other than the Permutation and Completeness Theorems, and only there to raise problems for a certain kind of mathematical platonism.)[6]

In short, the indeterminacy arguments show that if there is any way to make a theory true, then there are guaranteed to be many ways to do so. This poses a challenging question to the external realist: *Which relation is the correspondence relation?*

2.2 Infallibilism arguments

There are many things that the external realist can say in response to this challenge. I shall consider some of these in Chapter 3. Before that, I shall outline the second kind of model-theoretic argument. Arguments of this kind aim to show the following: *If a theory is ideal, then there must be some way to make the theory true.* The immediate threat is that ideal theories will turn out to be infallible, thereby undermining the external realist's Cartesianism Principle, which requires that an ideal theory might be false. I shall therefore call such arguments *infallibilism* arguments.

Putnam's most famous direct attack on the Cartesianism Principle is his celebrated brain-in-vat argument. Though this is extremely important, it is not model-theoretic in nature, so I shall reserve discussion of it for Part C of this book.

The model-theoretic infallibilism argument runs as follows. If a theory is ideal, then it is presumably at the very least consistent. After all, if it is inconsistent, then it (classically) entails everything, and so it can hardly count as ideal. But if it is consistent, then, by the Completeness Theorem mentioned earlier, it has a model containing only natural numbers. If we like, we can substitute this for a model containing only concrete objects, by appealing to an idea like that used in the Permutation Theorem: we simply swap distinct natural numbers for distinct concrete objects. (I offer a formal explanation of this in Appendix I.) But the general problem is simply that, if the theory is ideal, then there is guaranteed to be some way to make the theory true. So, if the external realist thinks that an ideal theory might

---

[6] Putnam (1980b: 467–9) invokes the Downward Löwenheim–Skolem Theorem in discussing the Axiom of Constructibility in set theory; I discuss this in Button (2011). Putnam (1977: 485) invokes a General version of the Completeness Theorem which connects with the Upward Löwenheim–Skolem Theorem, but the vanilla Completeness Theorem will do the job (I explain this in Appendix I).

really be false, then she faces a second challenging question: *What prevents the model given by the Completeness Theorem from making the theory true?*[7]

2.3 Correspondence versus more generic truthmaking

Putnam's model-theoretic arguments apply pressure to the external realist's conception of truth (and falsity) in terms of correspondence between words and world. However, as noted in §1.2, truthmaker theory has recently gained support among realists. It is worth briefly explaining why abandoning correspondence in favour of a more generic truthmaker theory will not affect the model-theoretic arguments.

Recall from §1.2 that, in so far as truthmaker theory differs from correspondence theory, it is less prescriptive about the nature of the truthmakers and truthbearers. For a correspondence theorist, there must be some structural relationship between a sentence and the way the world is. By contrast, truthmaker theorists (who are not also correspondence theorists) are committed only to the view that a sentence is made true by some truthmaker. The sheer *lack* of structure demanded by such truthmaker theorists means that it is easier to run model-theoretic arguments against them than against correspondence theorists.

To offer a straightforward indeterminacy argument, we can simply permute over the truthmakers, so that each sentence is mapped to an 'unintended' truthmaker. The intuitive idea is depicted in Figure 2.2, and a general permutation result for truthmaker theorists is trivial to obtain.[8]

A completeness theorem is equally easy to obtain. Choose a single object, Top, which is to be the truthmaker for every true sentence and for no false sentence. (If the truthmaker theorist also believes in falsemakers, then choose a single object, Bottom, to be the falsemaker for every false sentence and for no true sentence.) If it is *possible* to make all of the sentences of a theory true, then the theory can obviously be given a 'model' using just Top (and Bottom). We can now use this completeness result to offer indeterminacy and infallibilism arguments, exactly as before.

---

[7] Putnam (1977: 485–6; 1980b: 472–4; 1989: 353); Taylor (2006: 58–9) also puts the argument this way. The history of this argument can be traced back to Newman (1928: 144–5) and Winnie (1967: 227); I return to Winnie's argument in §5.3.

[8] Let ι be the function that maps each true sentence to its 'intended' truthmaker. Let π be any bijection over the range of ι. Then $\iota \circ \pi$ is a new truthmaking function.

Ajax is a cat

Betty is a cat

Chad is not a cat

Ajax is a cat

Betty is a cat

Chad is not a cat

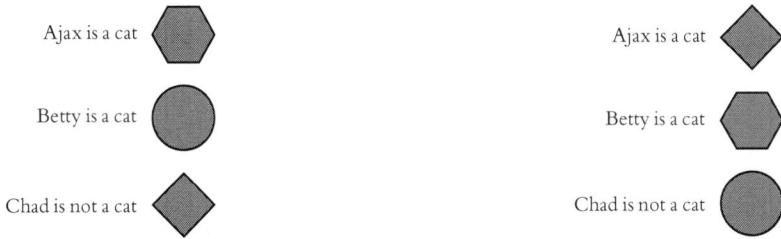

Figure 2.2 Two permuted models for truthmaker theorists. We begin with an initial assignment of true sentences to truthmakers (left). This is transformed into the permuted assignment (right) by a permutation which shuffles around the truthmakers without altering the sentences.

The truthmaker theorist may raise a *modal* objection against the models presented, on the grounds that a truthmaker should in some sense 'necessitate' its truth.[9] However, the correspondence theorist can raise the same objection. Moreover, since the correspondence theorist has access to the full structure of correspondence theory, her objection will be trickier to deal with. I shall return to all this in §3.4.

For now, the general point is straightforward. Truthmaker theorists (who are not also correspondence theorists) adopt a more permissive attitude towards truth than correspondence theorists do. It is therefore always strictly easier to raise problems for them, than for correspondence theorists. Accordingly, I shall not consider (generic) truthmaker theory in the remainder of this book, and shall instead stick with correspondence theory.

The moral of the chapter is easy to summarize. The external realist subscribes to a Credo that is susceptible to model-theoretic treatment. But model theory can then be used to show that every consistent theory (and so every ideal theory) can be made true in many different ways. The immediate challenge for the external realist is to explain what singles out (at most) one of these as capturing *the* correspondence relation. In other words, she must say what makes an interpretation *intended*.

---

[9] Thanks to Tim Williamson for suggesting this.

3

Attempts to constrain reference

In Chapter 2, we saw that the external realist cannot pin down a single correspondence relation just by producing her favourite theory. On these grounds, one might try to conclude that *nothing* can fix correspondence. But that would be too quick, as several commentators have noted in this connection and, indeed, as an earlier time slice of Putnam once argued against Quine.[1]

In this chapter, I shall sketch four attempts to constrain reference and correspondence. Each constraint presents a version of the worry, mentioned at the end of §1.4, that model theory is too mathematically permissive for metaphysical purposes. I should emphasize that I am merely sketching these constraints. The purpose of this chapter is not to determine what does fix reference and correspondence, but to pave the way for the discussion of Putnam's *just-more-theory manœuvre*.

3.1 The Causal Constraint

There are causal connections between language users and worldly objects. Cats sometimes cause us to exclaim 'cat!' More generally, our causal interaction with cats seems relevant to the question of how the word 'cat' came to refer to cats and not cherries (for example). Such thoughts might lead one to advance:

> **The Causal Constraint.** An intended interpretation must respect all appropriate causal connections between words and objects.

The models generated by model-theoretic arguments are built without any mention of causation. For example, when we advance a permuted interpretation according to which 'cat' refers to cats$^{\mathcal{P}}$, the latter might be a

---

[1] Putnam (1974: 30–1).

disparate jumble of molecules scattered throughout space and time.[2] Since
there is (presumably) no appropriate causal connection between tokens of
'cat' and these cats^P, the permuted interpretation would violate the Causal
Constraint. The general hope for the Causal Constraint is therefore that it
will seriously reduce the number of acceptable interpretations.

It is worth being aware of two intrinsic limitations on the Causal Constraint. First: if there are any entities which have no causal role, then the
Causal Constraint will not help the external realist to refer to them. For
example, if the external realist believes in an acausal realm of mathematical objects, then we can run a permutation argument which permutes
only among them. (Where π is our permutation, we would stipulate
that $\pi(x) = x$ iff x is causal, but allow $\pi(x)$ to vary otherwise.)[3] Second:
even where the entities in question are causal, there are many well-known
problems with any *purely* Causal Constraint on reference. In particular, it
is notoriously difficult to specify what counts as an appropriate causally
determined connection.[4]

These problems noted, I intend to set them to one side. If it is legitimate
to impose the Causal Constraint on interpretation, then it will substantially
draw the sting of the model-theoretic arguments.

3.2 The Eliteness Constraint

A related interpretative constraint arises from the idea that model theory
delivers lots of *pseudo-properties* and *pseudo-relations* for predicate letters to
pick out, but that *genuine* properties and relations are much sparser than
model theory might lead us to believe. To spell out this idea, the external
realist might invoke David Lewis:

Sharing of [genuine properties] makes for qualitative similarity, they carve at the
joints, they are intrinsic, they are highly specific, the sets of their instances are *ipso
facto* not entirely miscellaneous, there are only just enough of them to characterise
things completely and without redundancy.[5]

---

[2] Nothing hangs on my use of 'refers' rather than 'applies'; see §12.5.
[3] Taking a hint from Putnam (1981c: 218, Second Comment).
[4] Putnam (1980a: 101; 1981c: 51; 1984a: 85–90; 1987b: 37–40; 1992a: 50–6) moves from focusing on
the interest-relativity of appropriateness, to the interest-relativity of causation itself.
[5] D. Lewis (1986: 60).

The relevance of this is similar to the Causal Constraint: cats^P might be 'entirely miscellaneous', so that *being a cat^P* fails to qualify as a *genuine* property. If the external realist can insist that the interpretation of each predicate letter must be a genuine property or relation, rather than a mere pseudo-property, then she can ignore the permuted interpretation where 'cat' refers to cats^P.[6]

External realists who are tempted by this thought need not draw a sharp line between genuine properties and pseudo-properties. Indeed, Lewis himself suggests that we should think of properties as being *more* or *less* elite, where more elite properties and relations carve Nature *closer* to its joints.[7] This suggests:

> **The Eliteness Constraint.** An intended interpretation of each predicate is (typically) an *elite* (or, quite elite) property or relation.

In a slogan: more elite properties and relations are more *referentially magnetic* than their gerrymandered colleagues.

The main problem with the Eliteness Constraint is that it sounds so strongly like an article of faith. Lewis tells us that 'there are only just enough [elite properties] to characterise things completely and without redundancy'. It is unclear what warrants Lewis's confidence here, since surely there could be disjoint sets of properties, both of which are individually sufficient to characterize the world completely, but such that taken together there are redundancies. Of equal importance, it is something of a mystery what determines (and how we are to determine) just how elite any given property is. In short, nothing guarantees that there is one and only one maximally eligible interpretation of our very best theory.[8]

As with the discussion of the Causal Constraint, I raise such worries only in order to set them aside. As things stand, it seems that Putnam's model-theoretic arguments require a thorough assessment of the merits and defects of the idea of the Eliteness Constraint.

3.3 The Fullness Constraint

The next interpretative constraint I have to offer is rather more specific and technical (I elaborate on the technicalities in Appendix I). Suppose that the

---

[6] Merrill (1980: 80) makes this point, though he was no external realist.

[7] Lewis (1984: 227–8; 1986: 61).

[8] For problems in this area, see Williams (2007; 2015).

external realist has advanced a *second-order* theory. In Chapter 2, I used the Completeness Theorem to offer both an indeterminacy and an infallibilism argument. Certainly this result holds for second-order logic (just as it holds for first-order logic).[9] But the (Henkin) models of second-order theories yielded by the Completeness Theorem need not be *full* models. In particular, when the domain is infinite, the second-order variables do not range over all of the uncountably many combinatorial aggregates of objects in the domain, but only over a countable handful of those aggregates. This suggests:[10]

The Fullness Constraint. An intended interpretation of a second-order theory must be a *full* interpretation.

This Constraint would rule out any model-theoretic arguments which invoke the Completeness Theorem.[11] The obvious limitation of this Constraint is that it would not block the permutation argument, since nothing in the proof of the Permutation Theorem depends upon the use of first-order logic.[12]

3.4 The Modality Constraint

The final constraint that I wish to consider is modal. This is the most complicated constraint to explain, since it attacks the use of model theory from a rather different angle.

The models produced by the Permutation and Completeness Theorems assign a truth *value* to every sentence in the external realist's language. However, the external realist may demand more; she may demand an assignment of truth *conditions*. That is, she may insist that we have some grasp, not merely on the truth values that various sentences actually have, but on the truth values our sentences *would* have if things were different.

Putnam claims that this demand can be accommodated using model theory. A sentence's truth conditions comprise an exhaustive list of the

[9] Hence Putnam (1980b: 481; 1994c: 459n33; 1999: 16n33) is brisk on the distinction between first- and second-order theories.

[10] Shapiro (1991: 203–18) advocates this.

[11] Or any Löwenheim–Skolem theorem; see Appendix I.

[12] As observed by Hale and Wright (1997: 451).

situations in which that sentence would be true.[13] We can think of 'situations' here as *possible worlds*. And just as we have thought of the actual world as a particular model, so we can think of each possible world as a further model. Putnam now suggests that we can raise problems for the external realist by simply applying the model-theoretic arguments to *each* world.[14] For example, to run a permutation argument, we start with some given possible worlds. For each possible world, W_γ, we then define a permutation, π_γ, to obtain a permuted world isomorphic with W_γ. Each sentence will receive the same truth value in the permuted world as it received in the original world. And so, Putnam claims, the resulting system of permuted possible worlds will preserve the truth conditions of every sentence.

This thought, though, is a little bit too quick. Vann McGee has suggested:[15]

> **The Modality Constraint.** An interpretation must supply truth conditions rather than mere truth values, and must also respect the fact that certain designators are *rigid*. Such designators denote the same object in every world where that object exists, and are empty otherwise.

To illustrate the intended effect of this constraint, suppose the name 'Ajax' is to be a rigid designator. So on the standard interpretation, 'Ajax' denotes Ajax in every world where he exists. Given the way in which permuted interpretations are generated, the Modality Constraint would demand that $\pi_\gamma(\text{Ajax})$ is the same object in every world. This rules out many permuted interpretations immediately, since if we simply offer arbitrary permutations for each world, 'Ajax' will name different things in different worlds.

The obvious response would be to offer the same permutation for *every* world. But this will not be possible if some objects (including Ajax himself) only exist contingently, since different worlds will then have different domains. Moreover, the way we permuted the interpretation of 'Ajax' (in a world) was to take Ajax as the argument to a function defined over the

---

[13] There is a potential ambiguity here. A *truth clause* for a sentence φ is just a statement of the form: φ is true iff ____. As Wallace (1979: 316–18) and Taylor (2006: 56) note, the model-theoretic arguments supply each sentence with a truth *clause*. What concerns us here are truth *conditions*, as I have defined them in the main text.

[14] Putnam (1981c: 25–7, 32–5, 217–18); Hale and Wright (1997: 451–2) make the same suggestion.

[15] McGee (2005: 405–8).

world's domain. So, if 'Ajax' is to be rigid, then 'Ajax' must (always) denote an object which exists in exactly the same worlds in which Ajax exists. McGee thus claims that the Modality Constraint 'rules out flamboyant changes of reference, like making "Ajax" denote a cherry' (as in Figure 2.1), since Ajax could have existed without that cherry having existed.[16]

It gets worse. On a standard treatment of the semantics for quantifiers, bound variables are dealt with by temporarily adding new constants to the language. (This is the approach adopted in Appendix I.) Such 'dummy names' are rigid designators just as much as 'Ajax' is. So the preceding argument generalizes from Ajax to *every* object (named or otherwise). McGee therefore notes that the Modality Constraint entails the following: if we want to permute x with y in some world, then x and y must exist in exactly the same worlds.[17] Given the contingent existence of most objects, this will be a serious constraint.

That said, the Modality Constraint does face two serious limitations. First, we can still offer a non-trivial (universe-wide) permutation if we can find some $a \neq b$ such that a and b belong to exactly the same worlds. To this end, McGee offers a permutation which 'exchanges every individual that isn't a unit set with its unit set'; that is, McGee swaps Ajax with {Ajax}, since these two objects exist in exactly the same possible worlds.[18] More generally, we can simply restrict our permutation to objects that exist necessarily (and so exist in every world). In an obvious case: if the external realist believes in abstract mathematical objects, we can permute among them, so that '0' refers to 729, '1' refers to 0, and so forth. In a more exciting case: some philosophers have maintained that *all* objects exist necessarily,[19] in which case the Modality Constraint would offer no real obstacle to a permutation argument at all.

Second, even if the Modality Constraint hinders the use of the Permutation Theorem, it has no effect on the Completeness Theorem. If the external realist provides a theory that tells us which objects belong to each possible world, and specifies that certain terms are to be rigid, then that theory has a model in which each world and each world-member is a natural number. Taking these natural numbers as the referents of our terms will preserve their rigidity.

[16] McGee (2005: 406), though he discusses 'Peter Rabbit' rather than 'Ajax'.
[17] McGee (2005: 406).   [18] McGee (2005: 406).
[19] Williamson (2002) defends this.

Let me now set aside the specifics of the Modality Constraint, and sum up the chapter as a whole. The overarching moral is that the external realist has plenty of lines of response to the challenge laid down at the end of Chapter 2. Granted, each potential interpretative constraint has its limitations. But as things stand, it seems that we cannot deliver a verdict on Putnam's model-theoretic arguments without further investigation of these constraints, both individually and in various combinations.

4

The just-more-theory manœuvre

To deal in depth with the interpretative constraints of Chapter 3 would be boring, long-winded, and inevitably piecemeal. Crucially, we could not hope to vindicate Putnam's model-theoretic attack on external realism via such a piecemeal approach. Putnam wants to undercut the entire *picture* of external realism. A piecemeal attack on a variety of purported interpretative constraints will not demonstrate conclusively that the picture itself is at fault: even if we can show that the Causal, Eliteness, Fullness, and Modality Constraints fail to address Putnam's model-theoretic arguments, some *other* interpretative constraint may yet wait in the wings to save external realism. Thus, to vindicate his model-theoretic arguments, Putnam requires a completely general manœuvre for dismissing all interpretative constraints.[1]

Notoriously, he offers us one: his *just-more-theory manœuvre*.[2] The main purpose of this chapter is to understand how Putnam's just-more-theory manœuvre might be supposed to work, so that in Chapters 5–7 I shall be in a position to defend it as an attack on external realism.

4.1 Putnam's notorious manœuvre

The external realist has advanced a constraint which, in its simplest form, is something like:

Causation fixes reference.

This sentence had better be part of the external realist's ideal theory, or it will be dismissed on other grounds. But the model-theoretic arguments

---

[1] Bays (2008: 207–12) is therefore right that Putnam's just-more-theory manœuvre is completely general; I shall argue, though, that he should not be critical of this.

[2] Putnam (1977: 486–7, 494; 1980b: 477; 1981c: 45–8; 1982a: 38; 1983a: xi; 1984a: 84). The manœuvre has historical precedents in Winnie (1967: 228–9), Field (1975: 383–4), and Wallace (1979: 309–11).

in Chapter 2 were wholly general, and so apply to *any* ideal theory. Thus there are many possible interpretations of 'causation' (and 'fixes', and 'reference') all of which make it true to say 'causation fixes reference'. Thus, whatever the external realist says, she has not managed to *fix* reference or correspondence. This, in a nutshell, is Putnam's rebuttal to the Causal Constraint.

If this rebuttal is successful against 'causation', then it will clearly be equally successful against 'eliteness' or 'fullness'.[3] The latter case merits specific comment. When the external realist demands a 'full' interpretation, we take her to be saying the following:

> Where the domain of interpretation is the set M, n-place second-order predicate-variables range over the powerset of M^n, and n-place second-order function-variables range over the set of all functions $M^n \longrightarrow M$.

This is now regarded as just more theory; in particular, as a sentence of some *set theory*. Such a set theory can be given multiple deviant interpretations, in all the ways laid out in Chapter 2.

Similar comments apply to the Modality Constraint. We take the external realist who invokes it to be saying:

> Certain designators are rigid; that is, they denote the same object in each world where that object exists, and are empty otherwise.

We can simply give multiple interpretations to the word 'rigid'.[4] One way to do this is by providing multiple interpretations of the phrase 'the same object'.[5] Another is to offer multiple interpretations of the word 'exists'. (This is salient since, as I noted in §3.4, the Modality Constraint only imposes any obstacle if we think that different objects exist in different worlds.) Let us stipulate that every possible world has the same domain, whilst introducing a primitive monadic 'existence' predicate, 'E'.[6] We then interpret the external realist's sentences of the form 'x exists at $\mathcal{W}_\beta$', not as telling us that $x \in \mathcal{W}_\beta$, but simply as stating that x satisfies 'E' in $\mathcal{W}_\beta$; or

---

[3] This is ultimately how I understand Taylor's (2006: 109–24) lengthy discussion of the 'vegetarian alternative' to the Eliteness Constraint.

[4] So it is ironic that McGee (2005: 406–8) himself employs essentially this strategy to deal with the Causal Constraint, interpreting the external realist's word 'causation' as referring to *quasicausation*.

[5] First replace each object x in world β with the pair $\langle x, \beta \rangle$; think of this as replacing each object in a world with an indiscernible but distinct counterpart. Next, define permutation functions over these 'worlds of counterparts'. Finally, say that $\pi_\beta(\langle x, \beta \rangle)$ is identical* with $\pi_\gamma(\langle y, \gamma \rangle)$ iff x is identical with y.

[6] This follows Priest's (2008: ch. 15) 'free logic' approach to variable domain modal logic.

perhaps that $\pi_\beta(x)$ satisfies 'E' in $\mathcal{P}_\beta$, given that permutations are now in the offing.

The overall strategy should now be completely clear. Putnam treats any statement of an additional interpretative constraint as *just more theory*: more grist for his model-theoretic mill. This is his *just-more-theory manœuvre*, or *JMT manœuvre* for short.

4.2 Accusations of question-begging

As Putnam himself notes, external realists have tended to reject the JMT manœuvre vociferously, offering responses like the following:

'You are caricaturing our position. A realist does not claim that reference is fixed by the conceptual connection (i.e., the connection in our theory) between the *terms* "reference", "causation", "sense impression", etc.; the realist claims that reference is fixed by causation itself.'[7]

This is a fair summary of a swathe of responses to the JMT manœuvre.[8] However, Putnam has never been fazed by them, replying as follows:

Here the philosopher is ignoring his own epistemological position.... What *he* calls 'causation' really is causation, and *of course* there is a fixed, somehow singled-out, correspondence between the word and one definite relation in *his* case. Or so he assumes. But how this can be so was just the question at issue.[9]

If this reply were all we had to go on, then we would have no option but to side with the external realist against Putnam. The JMT manœuvre has not, for example, discussed *causation* at all, but has only discussed the *word* 'causation'. The external realist's complaint is therefore reasonable. Moreover, on one way of reading his reply, Putnam is *assuming* that nothing can fix correspondence for the external realist, so that the external realist fails to achieve anything when she claims 'causation fixes reference'. But this is just to *assume* at the outset what Putnam's argument was supposed to *establish*.

There is consequently a fairly broad consensus that Putnam has utterly begged the question against the external realist. For this reason, many

---

[7] Putnam (1983a: xi; see also 1986b: 113).
[8] See: Glymour (1982: 177–8), Pearce and Rantala (1982: 42–4), Devitt (1983: 298–9; 1984a: 189–91; 1984b: 276), D. Lewis (1984: 225), Brueckner (1984: 137), Resnik (1987: 154–5), Heller (1988: 123–6), Van Cleve (1992: 349), Hale and Wright (1997: 440–1), Bays (2001: 342–348; 2008: 197–207).
[9] Putnam (1983a: xi; 1986b: 113).

philosophers abandon the model-theoretic arguments at this point. This is unfortunate, for this is the point at which the arguments become truly philosophically interesting. The JMT manœuvre is not hopelessly question-begging, but is instead a gateway to our investigation of the realism debate through the lens of various forms of scepticism.

4.3 Metaphysics and magic

Showing this will occupy the remainder of Part A. But to hint that there is more to the model-theoretic arguments and the JMT manœuvre than is usually understood, let me start by raising an interpretative puzzle for those who think that Putnam has simply begged the question against his external realist opponents.[10]

Putnam admits that the external realist might avoid the model-theoretic arguments by postulating 'magical theories of reference',[11] or a 'direct (and mysterious) grasp of Forms'.[12] He likewise allows that the external realist could avoid the model-theoretic arguments by reverting 'to medieval essentialism',[13] or by invoking 'noetic rays',[14] 'divine intervention',[15] or some other 'occult'[16] or 'spooky'[17] reference-fixing device. But this may be somewhat confusing since, as we saw in §4.1, Putnam's JMT manœuvre is utterly general: if it works, it does not depend upon any particular features of the interpretative constraint in question. So it may initially seem odd that Putnam believes that the external realist could avoid the model-theoretic arguments *even* by resorting to magic. After all, suppose the external realist presents:

> **The Magical Constraint.** An intended interpretation must respect all appropriate magical connections between words and objects.

This has the same form as the Causal Constraint, and we can apply the JMT manœuvre to 'magic' just as we applied it to 'causation'.

To understand why Putnam allows that magic (and only magic) might fix reference, let us imagine running the JMT manœuvre against a magically-inclined external realist. As in §4.2, the magically-inclined external realist

---

[10] This puzzles D. Lewis (1984: 233) and Hale and Wright (1997: 440*n*23).
[11] Putnam (1980a: 101; 1981c: 3–5, 46–8, 51; 2000: 138).
[12] Putnam (1977: 487); see also his criticisms of certain kinds of platonism (1980b: 466; 1982c: 228).
[13] Putnam (1983a: xii).   [14] Putnam (1980a: 101; 1981c: 51; 1984a: 85).
[15] Putnam (1984a: 85).   [16] Putnam (1982c: 207).   [17] Putnam (1982a: 38).

may tell Putnam that he has begged the question. 'I am not claiming that magic-*talk* fixes reference', she might complain, 'but *magic itself*'. So let us (temporarily) grant the magically-inclined external realist her complaint. What do we do next? How do we assess her claim that magic fixes correspondence and reference? The Causal Constraint and the Magical Constraint are apparently rivals; but how would we decide between them? How would either of them fare against the view that reference is not fixed at all, but is instead radically indeterminate? Putnam answers that 'these different metaphysical views are *empirically indistinguishable*':[18] they all equally lack empirical content.

Putnam is consequently raising a dilemma against the external realist's attempts to constrain reference. On the one hand, if they have empirical content, then they are indeed just more theory. In that case, they cannot constrain reference. On the other hand, if they are supposed to constrain reference, then they will be bereft of empirical content. In that case, the external realist might as well come clean and admit that she is invoking *magic*, rather than continuing to employ the respectable veneer of empirically contentful causation-talk.

This resolves the interpretative puzzle.[19] It does not, of course, show that Putnam is *correct*. To vindicate Putnam's attack on external realism, I first need to defend Putnam's claim that (by the external realist's own lights) any attempt to constrain reference must be without empirical content. I undertake this task in Chapters 5 and 6. I then need to explain why the external realist cannot simply *accept* that her statements about reference are without empirical content. I do this in Chapter 7, thereby completing the attack on external realism.

---

[18] Putnam (2000: 140, Putnam's italics; see also 1982a: 38; 1984a: 83).
[19] Douven (1999: 485–90) suggests a similar resolution of the puzzle, and Putnam (2000: 138–40) largely endorses it. I discuss Douven's explanation of why interpretative constraints should be regarded as contentless in §7.1.

5

Empiricism and empirical content

Chapters 1–4 have brought us briskly over some heavily traversed terrain. The remainder of Part A proceeds more slowly, as we enter into territory that is less well mapped.

We have seen how Putnam's model-theoretic attack on external realism depends upon his JMT manœuvre, and we have some idea of how the latter might avoid being hopelessly question-begging. In this chapter, I shall start to defend Putnam's JMT manœuvre. In particular, I want to show that certain versions of external realism must accept that *any statement with empirical content is just more theory and so fails to constrain reference.* In Chapter 6, I shall show that *all* versions of external realism are committed to this claim.

I shall focus on the external realist's Cartesianism Principle, which states that even an ideal theory might be radically false. We think we know what external realists mean by a theory's being *false*—it involves a certain failure of correspondence—but we have not yet explored what she means by a theory's being *ideal*. In this chapter, I shall explore three empiricist approaches to this idea, all of which can usefully be related to certain readings of Rudolf Carnap's logical positivism and logical empiricism.[1]

5.1 Ideal theories and empirical content

The model-theoretic arguments showed that any ideal theory can be made true in many different ways. In §1.3, I offered a rough gloss on what it might mean for a theory to be ideal, but Putnam is much more explicit. On behalf of the external realist, Putnam defines an (epistemically) ideal theory as one

---

[1] In April 2009, I gave an introductory lecture on Putnam's model-theoretic arguments at Harvard, at which I briefly presented an early version of some material from this chapter and Chapter 8. Putnam replied, joking that he had perhaps 'been reading too much Carnap'. This remark set me thinking, and the result is this chapter.

'which violates no operational constraint and no theoretical constraint'.[2] So to understand what an ideal theory is, we simply need to understand what 'theoretical' and 'operational' constraints are. This terminology is Putnam's, and I shall connect it to a more standard vocabulary.

Theoretical constraints are essentially *super-empirical* virtues: virtues that a theory has, less as a result of *what* it says, and more because of *how* it says it. The list of super-empirical virtues is somewhat open-ended, and what we (as a community) count as a super-empirical virtue may well change over time.[3] However, it will likely include such notions as 'optimizing simplicity, elegance, coherence with past doctrine, plausibility, etc'.[4] As Putnam notes, these are not especially relevant to the model-theoretic arguments.[5] They essentially tell us what kinds of theories to favour: simple ones over complex ones, deterministic ones over indeterministic ones, computationally tractable theories over intractable ones, and so forth. Since the Permutation and Completeness Theorems apply to any consistent theory whatsoever— simple or complex, tractable or otherwise—we can largely afford to ignore super-empirical virtues when considering the model-theoretic arguments.

Operational constraints are trickier. Putnam stipulates that a theory meets all *operational constraints* if it 'impl[ies] predictions which seem to be true'.[6] I shall say much more about what this amounts to during the course of this chapter. But taking this as understood, it will help to introduce some standard nomenclature. The empirical *content* of a theory is the aggregate of all the theory's observable predictions. Two theories that make exactly the same observable predictions are called empirically *equivalent*. A theory which gets everything (or enough) right at this level is described as empirically *adequate*. And, when Putnam talks of a theory's meeting all operational constraints, he is essentially considering a theory that is empirically adequate.

This explication of empirical adequacy (or operational constraints) blurs the boundary between formal theories and their interpretations. During the course of the model-theoretic arguments, we treated theories as collections of utterly uninterpreted symbols to which we could supply interpretations using model theory. Now, for a theory to be empirically adequate, it must

---

[2] Putnam (2000: 136).   [3] As Putnam (1981c: 31–2) explores.   [4] Putnam (2000: 130).
[5] Putnam (1981c: 30–1) calls them 'formal properties of the theory.'   [6] Putnam (2000: 136).

'imply predictions which seem to be true'. But an utterly uninterpreted theory is *just* a bunch of strings of symbols. Whilst these can deductively entail another bunch of strings of symbols, they cannot imply anything that 'seems to be true'. Thus, for a theory to be empirically adequate, we must have linked the sentences of our theory up to our experiences.

There is now a balancing act to be performed. Suppose we think of experiences in a very wide sense. For example: suppose that when I see Betty the cat, we hold that my visual experience involves Betty herself, so that I would have had a different experience if I had seen a different cat, even if I would not have noticed any difference. With experience construed so widely, any connection between experiences and sentences that suffices for a theory to count as empirically adequate may end up supplying a complete interpretation of the theory's vocabulary. A reinterpretation of that vocabulary would then destroy the connection between our sentences and our experiences, leaving us with a theory that is not empirically adequate. The model-theoretic arguments would then fail, for an ideal theory would have a *unique* interpretation.

Actually, this line of thought is a bit too quick. After all, one might plausibly think that my visual experience of Betty involves Betty herself, but that it does not involve the very *molecules* that comprise Betty. In that case, stipulating that a theory is ideal will fix the referent of 'Betty', but it might stop short of supplying us with the interpretation of words like 'molecule'. I shall explore this point more fully in §6.4 and §10.5. For now, it suffices to note that a wide view of experience will certainly block any interpretation according to which 'cat' picks out anything other than the cats, and so it will block the *canonical* statements of the model-theoretic arguments. Those canonical statements require that we think of experiences more *narrowly*, so that experiences as of seeing a cat do not involve cats. We can therefore understand why Putnam has said that the model-theoretic arguments require the assumption

that each mental state has what Jaegwon Kim has called an 'internal core'. . . . In the case of perceptions, the internal core is supposed to be the sense data of having that perception. (What these must be, if a theory is to be 'epistemically ideal' is what the 'operational constraints' determine.)[7]

---

[7] Putnam (2000: 133; see also 1993b: 183; 1994c: 458–60, 464–5, 475, 488–90, 494; 1999: 15–16, 19, 30, 43–5, 48, 58, 101; 2000: 142) criticisms of 'Cartesianism *cum* materialism'.

For the remainder of this chapter, I shall set aside the main task of attacking external realism. Instead, I shall trace the idea of *narrow* experience—the 'internal core' just mentioned—through various versions of empiricism. This will achieve two things. First, it will highlight Carnap's influence on Putnam. Second, it will show that certain empiricist versions of external realism cannot really complain that the JMT manœuvre is question-begging.

5.2 A constructed world

I want to start by considering the methodological solipsism of Carnap's *Aufbau* (Carnap 1928a).[8] The principal idea in the *Aufbau* is the notion of a *constitution-system*. A constitution-system begins with a *basis* of primitive objects, and at least one primitive relation which holds among the basic objects. Carnap's ultimate ambition in the *Aufbau* is to provide a constitution-system within which any predicate in any scientific vocabulary can be explicitly defined in terms of the primitive relations holding among basic elements, using type theory. It will then follow that any scientific statement can be transformed, by digging down through a chain of finitely many definitions, into a statement which mentions only primitive relations holding between basic objects.[9]

Carnap investigates one particular choice of basis in great detail: the autopsychological basis. This basis is otherwise known as the *Given*, or the *stream of experience*, and the general idea is that the autopsychological basis consists of *elementary experiences*. But it is important that we understand this claim correctly. Suppose that some elementary experience in Carnap's autopsychological basis is apparently one of seeing a cat.[10] This might tempt us to ask several questions. Is the experience veridical or hallucinatory? If it is veridical, does that mean that cats are in the basis? And if so, does that mean that cats are (auto)psychological objects, rather than physical objects? Carnap's reaction to all such questions is clear:

---

[8] Much has been written on the extent of Carnap's 'empiricism' in the *Aufbau*. My aim here is not to give an accurate reading of Carnap, but to explain Putnam's argument. With that in mind, it is worth noting that Putnam (1991b: 86–90; 1994a: 281) favours an 'empiricist' reading of Carnap.

[9] Carnap (1928a: §§2, 41, 47).

[10] The example is for illustrative purposes only; the detailed system discussed in the *Aufbau* has only one primitive relation, namely *recollected similarity*.

The distinction between real and unreal objects does not exist at the beginning of the constitution-system. In the basis, no distinction is made between the experiences which are distinguished by later constitution as perception, hallucination, dream, etc.... At the beginning of the system, the experiences are simply to be taken as they are given; their presence in the real or unreal is not to be affirmed, but 'bracketed'; phenomenological 'abstention' (ἐποχή), in Husserl's sense, is exercised.[11]

The idea is that we must consider the experiences without considering what is going on behind them, what they designate, what they signify, or anything else of this sort; they 'are simply to be taken as they are given'. And since we do not (initially) entertain any objects lying behind the sensations, or indeed any other minds, even a solipsist would be happy with our starting point. Thus:

Since the choice of an autopsychological basis amounts to the application of the form and method of solipsism, but not the acceptance of its main thesis, we could speak here of '*methodological solipsism*'.[12]

Carnap hoped that such methodological solipsism would allow us to abandon certain metaphysical disputes.[13]

There is much more that we could say about methodological solipsism. But all that matters for present purposes is that the methodological solipsist's notion of a bracketed experience provides us with a way to consider experiences *narrowly*, in the sense required to get the model-theoretic arguments off the ground.

Let us imagine a philosopher, Anne, who follows the form and method of solipsism, starting with bracketed experiences and using type theory to build a constitution-system. Anne therefore believes that every scientific statement can be transformed into a statement about primitive relations holding between elementary experiences in the basis. Indeed, she thinks that this process of transformation supplies us with the empirical content of any claim that she might make. Let us also imagine that Anne is lucky enough to have an *ideal* theory; that is, her theory is empirically adequate and possesses various super-empirical virtues. But let us now imagine that Anne wants to ask a *metaphysical* question of the sort that would make Carnap wonder why he even bothered to write the *Aufbau*. In addition

[11] Carnap (1928a: §64).   [12] Carnap (1928a: §64, Carnap's italics; see also 1931: 461).
[13] See e.g. Carnap (1928a: §§52, 175–8).

to considering whether or not her theory is ideal, Anne wants to ask a question that carries her outside the constitution-system: *Is my theory true?*

In asking this, Anne flags that she believes in an 'unconstructed' world, made up of objects that are largely mind-, language-, and theory-*independent*. Moreover, she hopes that her theory *corresponds* with this unconstructed world. Admittedly, within the constitution-system, the words of her scientific theory—'molecule' and 'cherry', for example—are all eliminable, in favour of claims concerning elementary experiences. So Anne is hoping that the words of her theory can be pressed into a secondary service: she hopes that the unconstructed world contains *real* molecules and cherries for her words 'molecule' and 'cherry' to designate.

If Anne's question can even be asked, it faces a serious epistemological problem. Nothing would allow her to determine whether her constructions correspond with the unconstructed world, for the empirical content of any claim is exhaustively accounted for *within* the constitution-system itself. Accordingly, her question is likely to lead to a certain kind of Cartesian angst: no matter how wonderful her constructions are, they need not correspond with the unconstructed world. This is just the external realist's Cartesianism Principle again. And indeed it is obvious on a moment's reflection that Anne has signed up to the entire Credo of external realism. She is an external realist, cut from vintage cloth.

Since Anne is an external realist, we can run model-theoretic arguments against her, as in Chapter 2. These show that there are guaranteed to be *many ways* to make her constructions correspond with the unconstructed world. Anne may well want to respond by claiming, as in Chapter 3, that causation fixes reference. As in Chapter 4, Putnam will treat this claim as just more theory, and so will claim that Anne has failed to fix reference and correspondence. Anne is likely to complain that Putnam has begged the question against her. But the dialectical context of Anne's complaint has moved on from §4.2. Anne has some very specific epistemological-cum-methodological commitments and, in insisting that causation itself constrains reference, she 'is ignoring [her] own epistemological position.'[14]

Let us grant Anne that 'causation fixes reference' is a perfectly ideal claim. This is to say that it is part of an empirically adequate theory that satisfies plenty of super-empirical virtues; which is to say that, on digging down

---

[14] Putnam (1983a: xi).

through the type-theoretic definitions of the constitution-system, the claim says something right about the primitive relations that hold between the elementary experiences. But *that* way of understanding the claim is literally *just more theory*. It just says more about what happens *within* Anne's constructed world. It cannot possibly help to pin down a correspondence *between* Anne's constructions and the unconstructed world. Conversely, if 'causation fixes reference' is meant to pin down a correspondence relation between Anne's constructions and the unconstructed world, it must be a claim made outside of Anne's constitution-system. But given Anne's epistemological-cum-methodological commitments, she must accept that such a claim is without empirical content, for all empirical content is exhaustively accounted for within her constitution-system.

In short, Anne faces a dilemma. Either 'causation fixes reference' is simply meant as a claim within the constructed universe, in which case it has empirical content but is *mere* theory; or it is indeed meant to bridge between constructed and unconstructed worlds, in which case the claim is without empirical content. The JMT manoeuvre, as explained especially in §4.3, begs no questions against Anne's version of external realism.

I have spent so long on Anne's position, and its connections with Carnap's *Aufbau*, because Putnam himself frequently alludes to methodological solipsism. At a shallow level, the pejorative label 'metaphysical realism' ('*metaphysischer Realismus*') comes directly from the *Aufbau*.[15] At a more substantial level, before one presentation of the model-theoretic arguments, Putnam writes:

Husserl introduced a device which is useful when we wish to talk of what goes on in someone's head without any assumptions about the existence or nature of actual things referred to by the thoughts: the device of *bracketing*. . . . In effect, the device of bracketing subtracts entailments from the ordinary belief locution (all the entailments that refer to the external world, or to what is external to the thinker's mind).[16]

This recalls Carnap's invocation of Husserl when introducing methodological solipsism (see the quotations earlier in this section). But the influence of Carnap's methodological solipsism is clearest in one of Putnam's summaries of his model-theoretic arguments:

---

[15] Carnap (1928a: §52); Friedman (1992: 24) emphasizes Carnap's criticisms of 'metaphysical realism'.
[16] Putnam (1981c: 28), Putnam's italics.

If we limit psychology, for the moment, to 'solipsistic' description, description of what happens in the individual considered in isolation from his environment, then no psychological facts in this narrow sense, no facts about introspectible mental phenomena (or even unconscious mental phenomena) and no facts about brain processing can fix any correspondence between a word and a 'representation' and anything external to the mind or brain.[17]

The scare quotes around 'solipsistic' indicate that we are (temporarily) to embrace, not the main thesis of solipsism, but only its 'form and method'. Essentially, then, this passage highlights Anne's predicament: that methodological solipsists can never recover the ability to pin down reference or correspondence to an 'unconstructed' world.

Having drawn this connection with the *Aufbau*, I should immediately add that Putnam is fully aware that the *Aufbau* was too austere. Putnam's scare-quoted 'solipsism' is more relaxed than the strict methodological solipsism of the *Aufbau*. To explain this, I shall consider two approaches to empirical content that are more relaxed than the *Aufbau*, but that are both broadly inspired by (post-*Aufbau*) logical empiricism.

5.3 A split vocabulary

Anne holds that every contentful sentence can be transformed, by explicit definition, into a claim about bracketed experiences. This is too restrictive. We might also want to be able to invoke 'theoretical posits', which generally help us to navigate our way around experiences, without being correlated with any particular (kind of) experiences.

There is a straightforward way to accommodate this, again inspired by Carnap.[18] Suppose that the vocabulary of our theory is divided into two halves. On the one hand, there are *sensation-words*, designed to discuss (bracketed) sensations directly. On the other hand there are *posit-words*, designed to discuss theoretical posits. An example of a sensation-word might be the barbarous neologism 'catish-visual-sensation'; whereas 'cat' itself is to be a posit-word, since cats are posited as the (or one) cause of catish-visual-sensations.

---

[17] Putnam (1983a: ix).

[18] Carnap (1937: 9–12; 1956: 41–2); I say 'inspired', because Carnap's split is not between sensation-words and posit-words, but between an *observation* and a *theoretical* vocabulary.

On this approach, sensation-words are given empirical content by being correlated directly with (bracketed) sensations. Indeed, we can think about empirical adequacy simply in terms of a *correspondence* between sensation-words and sensations. A theory is then empirically adequate if it corresponds with the sensations.[19]

Posit-words do not talk directly about sensations, but they nonetheless acquire empirical content thanks to the (structural) *role* they play within the entire theory. Spelling this idea out in any detail is extremely challenging,[20] but for present purposes all that matters is that we consider *only* the connection that the posit-words have to the wider theory, and thereby their derivative connection to the bracketed sensations. All empirical content will therefore remain *bracketed*.

If we are feeling really quite Carnapian, then we shall stop here, and maintain that this exhausts everything there is to say about the meanings of the words in our scientific theories. To be sure, we might offer an *interpretation* of the theory by assigning particular objects to the posit-words. Indeed, Carnap himself considered assigning mathematical objects to the posit-words.[21] But this is not because he thought that the posited objects are really mathematical in nature; rather, it is precisely because Carnap thought that 'there is no question of their nature'.[22] He presented the mathematical assignment only to give 'the psychological help of connecting these expressions with useful associations and images'.[23]

But let us now imagine an external realist, Bea, who holds that there are sensation-words and posit-words, and who holds that empirical adequacy is determined by correspondence between sensation-words and sensations, but who departs from Carnap precisely in wanting to ask about the nature of the posited objects. Bea wants to know whether her posit-words correspond with a world of 'outer' objects that lie behind her 'sensations'; whether, that is, her posited objects *really* exist.

As with Anne before her: if Bea's question can even be asked, it faces a serious epistemic problem. Nothing would allow her to determine whether this correspondence obtains, for the empirical content of any claim is exhausted by the correspondence between her sensation-words and her

---

[19] Putnam (1980b: 472; 2000: 132, 141) discusses a similar idea.
[20] Carnap (1956: 47–52) offers a valiant effort.
[21] Though bear in mind the caveat in footnote 18.   [22] Carnap (1956: 46).
[23] Carnap (1956: 46).

sensations. The world 'behind' her sensations never gets a look in. Indeed, we might helpfully think of Bea's sensations as forming a *veil* between her and the objective world. (I shall return to this image in §5.5.)

Since Bea is an external realist, we shall of course want to run a model-theoretic argument against her. This will require some modification, for Bea thinks that an ideal theory must correspond with (bracketed) sensations. Consequently, Bea will be able to rule out some of Putnam's 'unintended' interpretations because they get things wrong at the level of her sensations. For example, they might interpret 'catish-visual-sensation' as picking out *cherryish*-visual-sensations, which Bea knows is a crude mistake.

Fortunately, as Putnam himself notes, both the Permutation and Completeness Theorems can be adjusted to accommodate Bea's idiosyncrasies. (The relevant model-theoretic background for these results is covered in Appendix I.)[24]

> **Permutation behind the veil.** Given W, shuffle around all the ordinary objects, but hold the sensations fixed. More formally: generate a permuted model from any non-trivial bijection, $\pi : W \longrightarrow W$, subject to the constraint that $\pi(x) = x$ for any x which is a sensation.[25]

> **Completeness behind the veil.** By the Completeness Theorem, any consistent theory has a model, $\mathcal{N}$, whose domain contains only natural numbers. Now just swap the appropriate sensations into $\mathcal{N}$. More formally, generate a permuted model from a bijection π defined thus: if Bea says that the referent of some term 't' ought to be some sensation e, whereas $\mathcal{N}$ interprets 't' as some natural number n, then $\pi(n) = e$; otherwise $\pi(n) = n$.[26]

Armed with these techniques, we can run both indeterminacy and infallibilism arguments against Bea. (An infallibilism argument, using Completeness behind the veil, is depicted in Figure 5.1.) Indeed, Completeness behind the veil shows that the mathematical assignment, which Carnap found to be of 'psychological' help, is a real threat for Bea.

---

[24] If we wanted to use Löwenheim–Skolem Theorems (see Appendix I) in our indeterminacy arguments, we could generate a Skolem Hull which contains all of Bea's sensations but only countably many posited objects behind the veil; this would follow Putnam (1980b: 467–9).

[25] See Winnie (1967: 226) and Putnam (1981c: 218).

[26] Winnie (1967: 227) presents this argument as a problem for scientific realists; Putnam (1980b: 473, 477) offers a similar argument.

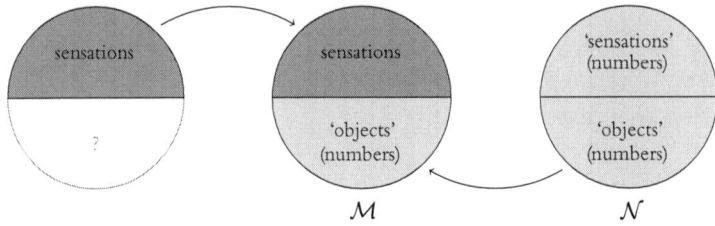

Figure 5.1 An infallibilism argument invoking Completeness behind the veil. Since the theory is ideal, we are sure to have some assignment to the sensation-terms, but the external realist worries that there may be no true assignment for posit-terms (left). However, the Completeness Theorem guarantees the existence of a numerical model, $\mathcal{N}$. Now $\mathcal{M}$ combines the intended assignments for sensation-terms with the numerical assignments for posit-terms.

The dialectic will now unfold exactly as it did with Anne. Bea will maintain that *causation* (for example) fixes reference, but Bea's methodological-cum-epistemological commitments leave her vulnerable to the JMT manœuvre. Bea believes that the empirical content of a sentence is given either by being directly correlated with sensations (as in the case of 'catish visual sense-data') or by its role within her wider theory. Since causation is not itself a sensation, if the word 'causation' is to have empirical content, it must be because it is an excellent theoretical posit that enables her to navigate her way around her sensations. But any claim about 'causation', in this sense, is literally *just more theory*. Conversely, if Bea hopes that causation will enable her to refer to the ordinary objects that lie behind the veil of sensations, then she must be using the word 'causation' in a way that is devoid of empirical content.

Bea, like Anne, faces a dilemma. Either 'causation fixes reference' is meant to have empirical content, in which case it is *mere* theory; or it is meant to burst through the veil of sensations, in which case the claim is without empirical content. The JMT manœuvre, as explained in Chapter 4, consequently begs no questions against Bea's variety of external realism.

5.4 A notional world

Anne held that any meaningful sentence can be transformed into a statement which mentions only primitive relations holding between entities in the basis. Bea held that the sensation-words are simply correlated directly with sensations. Both approaches were inspired by Carnap. But Carnap himself recognized that both approaches were too restrictive. He suggested instead that we might offer *probabilistic* connections between sentences and experiences.[27] The rough form we should expect is something like the following: if our theory entails such-and-such a sentence, then a certain experience is (un)likely.

There are various ways to offer probabilistic connections between sentences and experiences. On the one hand, we might (probabilistically) connect every sentence with certain experiences. This would give us a probabilistic version of Anne's attitude to empirical content. On the other hand, we might hold that some sentences (which mention 'theoretical posits') are not correlated with experiences directly, but are given empirical content by their role in the wider theory. This would give us a probabilistic version of Bea's attitude to empirical content. But, unsurprisingly, all we care about is that the empirical content of any claim should ultimately remain *bracketed*.

Where the *Aufbau* supplied us with the idea of a 'constructed world', here we might generically (following Putnam) speak of a *notional world*. This is just 'the totality of a thinker's bracketed beliefs', where a bracketed belief is just the bracketed content assigned to the sentences that someone believes.[28] Otherwise put: a notional world is just the totality of the (bracketed) empirical content of the theory that someone believes.

Since we considered the cases of Anne and Bea in such detail, we can be brisk in showing that this conception of bracketing is sufficient to run Putnam's model-theoretic arguments, accompanied by the JMT manœuvre. Imagine Cath, an external realist who subscribes to this extremely relaxed notion of bracketing. As an external realist, she wants to believe in a 'real' world lying behind her notional world. We will run model-theoretic arguments against her, exactly as we did against Anne or Bea. These will lead directly into the JMT manœuvre. And, as before, if Cath claims 'causation fixes reference', this can be taken in one of two ways. If it is simply meant as a claim 'about' the notional world, then it has empirical content, but it is indeed just more theory. If it is meant to constrain reference to the 'real' world lying behind the notional world, then it will be without empirical content, for all empirical content has been subsumed into Cath's notional

---

[27] Carnap (1956: 49).   [28] Putnam (1981c: 28).

world.[29] The JMT manœuvre, as explained in Chapter 4, consequently begs no questions against Cath's variety of external realism.

5.5 Early modern empiricism

Anne, Bea, and Cath represent three versions of *logical* empiricism. Or, perhaps more accurately, they represent three ways in which someone might (misguidedly) try to be both a logical empiricist and an external realist. To close this chapter, however, it is worth drawing some connection with *early modern* empiricism, and certain readings of John Locke. (This builds on suggestions by both Carsten Hansen and by Putnam.)[30]

On a reading of Locke made famous by Jonathan Bennett,

Locke puts the objective world, the world of 'real things', beyond our reach on the other side of the veil of perception; so I call this aspect of his thought his 'veil-of-perception doctrine'.[31]

Bennett goes on to criticize Locke, characterizing Locke's 'essential error' as

setting the entire range of facts about sensory states over against the entire range of facts about the objective realm and then looking for empirical links between them.[32]

Whether this is right or wrong as a historical reading of Locke, it is essentially the error that Bea has committed. When Bea draws her dichotomy between an 'inner' realm of sensations and an 'outer' objective realm, she automatically renders any links between the two realms *un*empirical. What I have emphasized is that this is as true for *semantic* links as for any other kind of link.

Anne and Cath are essentially guilty of the same mistake. Their *constructed* or *notional* worlds were (in principle) utterly transparent to their cognition, but they screened off what Anne and Cath took to be the *real* world. Any links between the constructed or notional world and the real world would have to be unempirical, and this includes *semantic* links. In short, *all three*

---

[29] See Putnam (1981c: 40).

[30] Hansen (1987: 90–5) and Putnam (1983a: viii; 1980a: 105; 1981c: 58–9; 1985: 47–8). I say more about Hansen in §6.1.

[31] Bennett (1971: 69).   [32] Bennett (1971: 69).

empiricist versions of external realism are tacitly employing some veil of sensations. This is why their attempts to constrain reference are all without empirical content: they are attempts to puncture through a veil of sensations.

The 'veil of sensations' locution is appropriately suggestive. But it is important to realize that it does not depend upon there being objects of a special sort—bracketed sensations—which have been woven into an impregnable curtain. If an external realist were to think of (bracketed) experience *adverbially*, essentially the same problems would arise.[33] In the limit, we can imagine an external realist who refuses even to dignify her (bracketed) experiences with any particular words. She might simply claim that, by some inscrutable act of ineffable introspection, she can ascertain whether or not a sentence is empirically adequate: she just knows that, sometimes, 'a cat is in front of me' is the ideal thing to say. If she provides us with no clue as to how she does this, we might well worry that her assessment of empirical adequacy is something of a black box. However, that is a further problem for her to deal with, and not my present concern. So long as empirical adequacy concerns only *bracketed* content—and so does not involve ordinary objects—then no (re)assignment of objects to her words will affect their empirical adequacy. Since she has no special words for sensations, we can present the plain vanilla versions of the model-theoretic arguments against her, as in Chapter 2. But, crucially, the JMT manœuvre now begs no questions against her. A veil of sensations is no easier to puncture for never having been mentioned.

---

[33] As Putnam (1980b: 475) notes.

6

Sceptical veils of various fabrics

In Chapter 5, I established the following. If the external realist is a bracketed empiricist, and so thinks that empirical content is exhausted by bracketed experience, then she cannot object to the JMT manœuvre. Specifically, she has to accept that any attempt to constrain reference is without empirical content, by her own lights.

To show that this raises any issues for external realism *itself*, I might try to show that external realism is automatically committed to the bracketed empiricist view of empirical content. In this chapter, I shall show that many external realists *are* so committed. However, I also want to demonstrate that the model-theoretic arguments are extraordinarily general. It transpires that, no matter *how* the external realist distinguishes between a theory's being true and its being ideal, she is unable to object to the JMT manœuvre.

6.1 Empiricism and the Cartesianism Principle

In §5.5, I phrased the problem for bracketed empiricist versions of external realism in terms of a veil of sensations. It is precisely such an image which (often) gives rise to deep seated anxiety about various Cartesian sceptical hypotheses. Thus it should come as no surprise that there is a significant connection between the external realist's Cartesianism Principle, on the one hand, and bracketed empiricism, on the other.

The external realist generically worries about nightmarish Cartesian sceptical hypotheses. These essentially come down to the following worry: a theory could get everything right with regard to appearances and still be undetectably and radically false. In order to have this worry, the external realist must think that it is possible to consider appearances whilst somehow *bracketing* away their reference, designation, correspondence, and so forth. That is, she is happy to talk about bracketed appearances herself.

If the external realist goes on to characterize 'appearances' in terms of first-person sensations, then our task is complete. She will have become a bracketed empiricist, and the arguments of Chapter 5 will now kick in. She will be forced to accept that any attempt to constrain reference is empirically contentless.

This is, indeed, the paradigmatic version of external realism that Putnam is concerned to attack. If the external realist worries that we might all be brains in vats,[1] then the external realist has surely adopted bracketed empiricism herself.[2] It is worth mentioning a couple of early commentators who realized this, but who did not quite realize its import.

Michael Devitt correctly observes that Putnam's attack on external realism depends on the idea that 'causal relations to a mind-independent world are not' 'accessible to the mind'. However, Devitt claims that it is simply part of his 'naturalism' that 'epistemic and semantic relations are no more inaccessible than other relations'.[3] Certainly semantic relations are no *less* accessible than other relations between mind and world. The problem is precisely that, for a bracketed empiricist, *all* relations between mind and world (and, for that matter, between world and world) are empirically inaccessible. This is Bennett's criticism of Locke, and our criticism of Anne, Bea, and Cath (see §5.5). But Devitt himself is both an external realist and a bracketed empiricist, for he holds that radical Cartesian scepticism of the brain-in-vat form is 'unanswerable.'[4] He declares it to be 'uninteresting' because it is implausible.[5] In this context, its unanswerability should perhaps have made it hypnotizing.

Hansen also suggests a link between a bracketed empiricist theory of empirical content and the model-theoretic arguments.[6] Indeed, Hansen specifically claims that Putnam's JMT manœuvre depends for its success on assuming that external realists embrace a Lockean veil of sensations. But then Hansen (unlike Devitt) simply denies that realists do embrace this veil, and concludes that Putnam has not refuted realism.[7] Here, Hansen misunderstands Putnam's aims. Putnam does not want to refute realism *tout court*, but only one species of realism, namely, external realism. Moreover, this is

---

[1] Putnam (1977: 485, 487; 1981c: 5–17; 1986b: 110–13; 1989: 352).
[2] That said, I discuss in §10.6 whether disjunctivists might have difficulties with such worries.
[3] Devitt (1984a: 194; see also 1983: 300; 1984b: 276; 1991: 57).
[4] Devitt (1984a: 5, 52); despite his criticisms (1984a: 54–5) of Locke.
[5] Devitt (1984a: 62).   [6] Hansen (1987: 90–5).   [7] Hansen (1987: 96–7).

no mere quibble over the word 'realism'. The main theme of this book, from Part B onwards, is the central role of scepticism in making sense of the realism debate.

Neither Devitt nor Hansen, however, noted that there is a gap between the Cartesianism Principle and bracketed empiricism. The Cartesianism Principle shows that the external realist wants to consider 'appearances' whilst bracketing everything that is going on 'behind' them. Moreover, the paradigmatic external realist regards 'appearances' as (bracketed) first-person sensations. But nothing prevents an (unconventional) external realist from treating 'appearances' in a different way, and thereby avoiding any commitment to bracketed empiricism.

She will not, however, be able to avoid admitting that any attempt to constrain correspondence is without empirical content. Indeed, with the veil of sensations as our heuristic guide, I now want to demonstrate the full generality of the model-theoretic arguments, by considering a variety of different *sceptical veils*. The various veils are woven from diverse fabrics; each simply offers a different approach to what it means for a theory to have *empirical content*. Thus I shall consider in turn: a veil of public senses; a veil of phenomena; a veil of observables; and a veil of flux. In its own way, each is as problematic as the (Lockean) veil of sensations.

(In passing, allow me to flag an issue of interpretation. When Putnam was most vigorously advancing the model-theoretic arguments, he claimed that they were of a very general shape. Putnam has more recently come to maintain that *all* versions of the argument depended upon a kind of bracketed empiricism. Here, I am siding with the old Putnam against the new, but I postpone discussion of this point until §10.5.)

6.2 A veil of senses

In Chapter 5, I showed that problems arise if we think of empirical content solely in terms of first-person, private, bracketed experiences. However, nothing much depends upon these experiences being first-person or private. All that matters is that they are *bracketed*.

To illustrate this, suppose the external realist effects a somewhat Fregean distinction between ordinary objects (the first realm), private sensations (the second realm), and Fregean senses (the third realm). She may then claim that public Fregean senses present us with *public* empirical content. It is easy to run a model-theoretic argument against this externalist-Fregean.

If we think of empirical content in terms of sensations, and truth in terms of reference to ordinary objects (or posits), then when we run a model-theoretic argument we mangle the relation *x is a sensation of ordinary object y*. Now let us think of empirical content in terms of Fregean senses, and truth in terms of reference to ordinary objects. If Fregean senses are modes of presentation of objects, then there is some function from senses to objects. Using model theory, we can distort this mediating function at will. For instance, we can simply define a non-trivial bijection, π, over the first realm, leaving the third realm untouched. We will thus mangle the relation *x is a mode of presentation of object y*. And the JMT manœuvre will remain unanswerable except by invoking magic, for a veil of public senses is no easier to penetrate than a veil of private ideas.[8]

To avoid confusion: I am *not* claiming here that Gottlob Frege was an external realist himself. (In particular, the argument depends upon the idea that senses should be *bracketed*, and that does not sound like something Frege believed.)[9] Furthermore, this model-theoretic argument is *not* Putnam's preferred argument against Fregean theories of meaning.[10] My point is just that the external realist cannot avoid the model-theoretic arguments *simply* by moving from a veil of private sensations to a veil of public senses. Her account of what makes a theory ideal will have to be more ambitious than *that*.

6.3 A veil of phenomena

Equally, the problems for external realism do not depend essentially on treating empirical content in terms of *mental experience*.

To illustrate this, consider a philosopher who believes in intrinsically differentiated noumenal objects, *things-in-themselves*.[11] Suppose the philosopher also believes that noumena are *represented* by phenomena. She may

---

[8] Compare Potter's (2000: 120) discussion of Russell's exchanges with Frege in 1904.

[9] Indeed, see Dummett (2006: 10).

[10] Putnam (1975b: 218, 222; 1981c: 27; 2007: 163–4) instead argues that an individual's 'grasp' of a public mental object must be determined by some *private* mental act, so that the view collapses back to bracketed empiricism once again.

[11] As Putnam (1980a: 106–8; 1981c: 44–5, 61–4; 1983a: xiii) does.

regard the empirical content of a sentence as concerning only phenomena, whilst holding that its truth concerns only noumena. (To be very clear, I am not claiming that this was Immanuel Kant's own view.)

It is easy to run a model-theoretic argument against this externalist-Kantian view. All we need to do is replace 'sensation' with 'phenomenon', and 'causation' with 'representation', in the arguments given earlier. Any attempt to bridge the noumena/phenomena divide will end up invoking something without empirical content. Or, as Richard Rorty rather more elegantly put it, 'no phenomenal term can describe the phenomenon–noumenon relation, and we have no other terms.'[12] We might as well appeal to magic.

6.4 A veil of observables

The argument equally applies to those who postulate a *gulf* between entities that are observable and those that are unobservable. We simply replace the word 'phenomenal' with 'observable' and 'noumenal' with 'unobservable', and exactly the same argument goes through. Any bridge between the observable and unobservable realm would be a bridge whose end point in principle vanishes from sight. Indeed, such an end point is as magical as the end of a rainbow.

The external realist is likely to protest that I am being unfair. She may well grant that only magic can save our externalist incarnations of Locke, Frege, or Kant. But, she continues, causation bridges the gulf between observable and unobservable. And, she says, this causal bridge is *not* a magical bridge, for the *very same* causal relation that holds between observable objects also bridges between observable and unobservable objects.

This external realist owes us an explanation of what it means to say that the 'very same causal relation' holds between the observable objects, as holds between observable and unobservable objects. To see why this is a serious challenge, we can very slightly rephrase an argument pushed by Putnam himself.[13] The external realist thinks that she can 'lasso' certain *observable* instances of causation (perhaps the striking of a match causing

---

[12] Rorty (1979: 89).
[13] Thus the remainder of this paragraph closely follows Putnam's (1980a: 102; 1981c: 53) criticism of an external realist's attempt to explain how our ability to refer to observed horses allows us to refer to unobserved horses too.

a fire). Grant this. However, by the external realist's own admission, the instances of causation which bridge between observable and unobservable objects are *in principle unobservable*, for they fall on the wrong side of the external realist's own gulf between observable and unobservable. She cannot claim to observe *them*, so she instead claims that her word 'causation' *automatically* covers those in principle unobservable instances of causation, since they are instances of *the same relation* as the observable instances. But this is just to make the claim that Nature has noumenal joints behind the veil of observables. In particular, it is to claim that it has noumenal *causal* joints.

I should emphasize that the problem here has arisen because our imagined external realist draws a once-and-for-all *dichotomy* between unobservable and observable objects. She postulates that there is a profound epistemological gulf at which observation ceases and mere theoretical speculation begins. This dichotomy is akin to a Kantian gulf between noumenal and phenomenal objects, and every bit as problematic. But none of this shows that there is something wrong with a rough-and-ready distinction between unobservable and observable objects. Someone who draws a distinction between observables and unobservables for a purpose, in a given context of enquiry, is not committed to the idea that the 'veil of observables' forever screens off what is happening 'behind' them, and so does not need to worry about this version of the model-theoretic arguments.[14]

6.5 A veil of flux

We can generate a final version of the problem by entertaining an ancient doctrine. On the one hand, everything around us is flux: temporary, unstable, uncertain. There is no real *truth* to be had concerning flux; one simply *gets by*. On the other hand, there is the realm of the Forms: eternal, immutable, certain. Only here can we aim for real *truth*.

Though it has dressed in different clothes, we once again have a *gulf* between appearances (flux) and Reality (Forms). This places us in a position to run any model-theoretic argument we like. In such a situation, the very idea that there is a debate between an external realist who advocates

---

[14] This thought takes inspiration from Maxwell (1962: 7–8, 14–15) and Okasha (2002: 316–19). It also connects with Putnam (1987b: 1, 20–1, 26–40) on distinctions versus dichotomies.

universals and an external realist who advocates tropes, for example, will simply evaporate away.

I expect that I will be told that *inference to the best explanation* is what gives content to such rarefied debates. I will be instructed to look at all the different metaphysical theories, work out which of them is the *loveliest*, and decide on those grounds that it is therefore the *likeliest*.[15] But what held for 'causation', when we discussed sensations, holds for 'inference to the best explanation', when we discuss the Forms. Remember that, on this picture, all the evidence we *ever* have for anything is from this dirty fluxing world around us. Perhaps inference to the best explanation is a very useful principle to apply to the flux, in the sense that it allows us to *get by*. But why should it really and truly apply to the unsullied crystalline purity of Platonic Heaven?

The reply will come that it is obviously rational to infer to the best explanation, simply because it is the *best* explanation.[16] This merely pushes the problem back. I am happy to concede that we know what 'best' and 'explanation' mean, as we use those notions to muddle our way through the flux. But what is the content of these words, when applied to the crystalline realm of the Forms? We are taking our grubby little notions of likeliness and loveliness, and projecting them heavenwards. To put it theologically: we are assuming that the gods like what we like and have configured the Forms according to those likes. Nothing mandates that assumption. Indeed, the *content* of the assumption starts to drift away.

In this chapter, we have considered five sceptical veils, cut from five different fabrics. Perhaps there are other fabrics waiting for us. However, the moral of the chapter is straightforward. The external realist's problems depend only upon the dichotomy she draws between a theory's being true and its being ideal. There is no particular need, then, to regard the external realist as committed to some version of the bracketed empiricist theory of empirical content. The shape of external realism is essentially schematic, but however the external realist completes the schema—however she spells out what it means for a theory to be ideal, and so to have empirical content— the model-theoretic arguments arise against her, and she must accept that her attempts to constrain reference are without empirical content.

---

[15] This is the rough framework for inference to the best explanation inaugurated by Lipton (1991: 61–6), though Lipton's focus is *scientific* realism; for a more metaphysical gloss, see D. Lewis (1986: 3–4).

[16] This is Armstrong's line (1983: 59), though in a somewhat different context.

7

From Cartesian to Kantian angst

In Chapters 5 and 6, I established that the external realist must accept that her attempts to constrain reference are without empirical content. Whatever her view of empirical content, her Cartesianism Principle sets up a sceptical veil between herself and the world, and between her words and the world.

Putnam is typically content to leave the matter there, but this is something of a dialectical mistake. To see why, we can imagine our external realist making a speech along the following lines:[1]

You have used the model-theoretic arguments to describe crazy sceptical scenarios: scenarios in which my word 'cats' refers to cherries, or in which every word refers equally to every thing. Moreover, the discussion of Chapters 5 and 6 has convinced me that my attempts to constrain reference—really constrain it, mind—are without empirical content.

But this situation is not exactly new to me. I am an external realist, and I adhere to the Cartesianism Principle. I worry that I might be a brain in a vat—really a brain in a vat, mind—although I do not think that I actually am one. Now, being a brain in a vat is compatible with any possible experience. So whether or not I am a brain in a vat transcends all possible empirical discovery. So I freely admit that the claim that I am a brain in a vat—or that I am not one—is without empirical content.

What you have shown me is simply that my sceptical worries should extend to my semantics. I shall have to add a few more unanswerable sceptical worries to my list, and recognize that a few more of my claims are without empirical content. But I do not see why I should give up on external realism.

To be sure, this not to say that I think that 'cats' refers to cherries, or that reference is indeterminate, or that any other sceptical semantical possibility obtains; any more than it is

[1] Thanks to Elijah Chudnoff for discussion on this. In what follows, I use block-quote italics for sceptical speeches.

to say that I think that I am a brain in a vat, or that the universe sprang into existence five seconds ago, or that any other Cartesian sceptical possibility obtains. But you are quite right: I cannot rule these sorts of things out, and all of these worries are equally devoid of empirical content.

My aim, in this chapter, is to explain why this speech is absolutely disastrous. With this recognition, our faith in external realism should expire.

7.1 The Douven–Putnam argument

I shall start by considering Igor Douven's imaginative reconstruction of the model-theoretic arguments.[2] This reconstruction broadly carries Putnam's seal of approval, though he has offered good reasons for modifying Douven's argument very slightly,[3] and so I shall present the argument with Putnam's modifications.[4] The Douven–Putnam argument ultimately fails, but it points us in the right direction.

Suppose that the external realist accepts the following principle:

(a) Necessarily: if nothing naturalistic fixes reference, then any ideal theory is true.

Consider a possible world in which the claim 'something naturalistic fixes reference' is part of an ideal theory. Either something naturalistic actually does fix reference in that world, or not. If something naturalistic does fix reference, then the external realist assures us that 'something naturalistic fixes references' is true in that world. But if nothing naturalistic fixes reference, then, by (a), 'something naturalistic fixes reference' will be true in that world too. So the external realist can conclude that:

(b) Necessarily: if 'something naturalistic fixes reference' is part of an ideal theory, then 'something naturalistic fixes reference' is true.

---

[2] Douven (1999: 487–90).
[3] Putnam (2000: 133–6); Putnam is explicit that it was not the argument he had in mind when he first outlined the model-theoretic arguments.
[4] And with a further modification: both Putnam and Douven discuss a principle which has as its antecedent roughly ' "something naturalistic fixes reference" is not true', but if we want to avoid running into the complaints of §4.2, we should distinguish a constraint from some sentence's being true.

This is strange, since it suggests that naturalistic approaches to reference enjoy a certain *immunity* from sceptical gerrymandering. After all, the external realist does not hold that:

(c) Necessarily: if 'I am not a brain in a vat' is part of an ideal theory, then 'I am not a brain in a vat' is true.

Rather, she thinks there is a world (maybe even this one) in which it seems that I am not in a vat, but where appearances deceive. This would suggest that the external realist's semantic hypotheses are *not* really on a par with the rest of her empirical hypotheses after all, contradicting the speech considered at the start of this chapter.

This is broadly the right strategy for arguing against external realism. Unfortunately, the Douven–Putnam argument is not effective. The essential problem is that we have been given no reason to think that an external realist must accept (a).[5] Here is a putative argument that she must. For any ideal theory, T, the infallibilism argument of §2.2 tells us that there is guaranteed to be a word–world relation which, if it were *the* correspondence relation, would make T true. If nothing 'intervenes', so to speak, then this relation will in fact make T true. Now, the argument continues, the external realist tells us that something (such as causation) ordinarily 'intervenes' to prevent this from happening. But in a world where nothing naturalistic fixes reference, nothing 'intervenes', therefore T is true in such a world.

This putative argument is a poor argument. The external realist has no reason to accept the metaphor of 'intervening'. She would do better to reason as follows: if nothing (naturalistically acceptable) fixed reference, then there would be no correspondence relation, so no theory would correspond with reality. Contra-(a), this would commit her to:

(d) Necessarily: if nothing naturalistic fixes reference, then no theory is true.

That commitment blocks the Douven–Putnam argument completely.

---

[5] In fairness to Douven (1999: 483), his argument is officially for the conditional: if the external realist accepts (a), then she will have problems.

7.2 Cartesian scepticism and Kantian scepticism

Although the Douven–Putnam argument fails to defeat external realism, it succeeds in highlighting the oddity of scepticism about semantical principles. To pursue this idea, I shall invoke a distinction between two kinds of scepticism: *Cartesian* scepticism and *Kantian* scepticism. This distinction has been particularly nicely expressed by James Conant.[6] Conant contrasts Cartesian and Kantian scepticism in a number of ways, but at a first pass we might consider the following table of differences:[7]

Cartesian scepticism	Kantian scepticism
[asks]: how can I know that things *are* as they seem?	[asks]: how can things so much as *seem* to be a certain way?
[asks:] which . . . thoughts are true, which . . . experiences are veridical[?]	asks: what does it take to have thoughts that are vulnerable to how things are?
takes the possibility of experience for granted; its question has to do with *actuality*.	[asks:] how is experience (so much as) *possible*?

In brief, Cartesian scepticism agonizes over whether our beliefs *are* true or false, whereas Kantian scepticism agonizes over how it is even *possible* for beliefs to be true or false.

It is worth pausing over what Kantian scepticism really amounts to. As Beatrice Longuenesse notes, a question of the form 'how is *x* possible?' can be posed in two rather different ways.[8] On the one hand, I might simply be asking for *information* on how to overcome a particular obstacle. Thus, to use Longuenesse's example, I might ask how it is possible to travel from London to Paris in under three hours, and you might tell me that train

---

[6] Conant's investigation is prompted by a comparison between Putnam and McDowell; I discuss this in Chapter 10.

[7] The table consists of quotation snippets from Conant (2004: 99–100).

[8] Longuenesse (2008: 511).

or plane will do very well. No sinister scepticism lurks in the background to that exchange. On the other hand, I might be asking the question in *desperation*, precisely because everything seems to indicate that the relevant x is simply impossible. This way of asking the question is sometimes brought out by phrasing the question as 'how is x *so much as* possible?' Kantian *angst* involves agonizing over such desperate questions, and Kantian *scepticism* involves embracing that impossibility.

7.3 Sliding from Cartesian to Kantian scepticism

Having distinguished Cartesian scepticism from Kantian scepticism, I shall now show that the model-theoretic arguments and the JMT manœuvre together act as a machine that converts Cartesian angst into Kantian angst.[9] To show this, I shall have to rehearse the dialectic of the book so far.

In Chapter 1, I presented the external realist's Credo. Note that the external realist began life with Cartesian angst, enshrined in her Cartesianism Principle. Having outlined the Credo, in Chapter 2 I presented some results from model theory to raise problems for her. I presented indeterminacy arguments, which seemed to threaten the external realist's Correspondence Principle, and an infallibilism argument, which seemed to threaten the external realist's Cartesianism Principle. All in all, these posed the following question:

How is it possible to refer to objects—how is it possible for there to be a correspondence between words and world—given that reference is not fixed by super-empirical virtues or a theory's empirical content?

Since this is a 'how is x possible?' question, it can broadly be read in one of two ways. If we treat it as a request for information, on a par with the question of how to get from London to Paris in under three hours, then it is not too troubling. We shall simply reply by noting that something *else* helps in fixing reference and correspondence. This was the gist of Chapter 3.

---

[9] Conant (2004: 118–19) criticizes Putnam (1994c) for 'hovering' between Cartesian and Kantian angst. I shall return to this in §10.3. For now, I shall say that these remarks are partly inspired by Putnam's reply to Conant, at the *Putnam at 80* conference at University College Dublin in March 2007, that the model-theoretic arguments were meant to raise both Cartesian and Kantian scepticism.

The JMT manœuvre is brought in at this point. Its purpose is to make it seem *impossible* that anything could fix reference. That is, the JMT manœuvre is supposed to show us that the question laid down by the model-theoretic arguments should be read, not as a simple request for information, but in sheer *desperation*.

Now, if we were only dealing with a simple request for information, then we would and should find the JMT manœuvre *bizarre* (see again §4.2). By analogy: when asked how to get to Paris in under three hours, we can simply point at the train and say 'that is how I might get to Paris'. If our questioner then asks 'but how is the existence of material objects such as trains *so much as possible?*' we are entitled to be a bit nonplussed. This, I hazard, is why most philosophers regard the JMT manœuvre as wholly question-begging.

But they are wrong to do so; or at least, they are wrong to do so when the JMT manœuvre is wielded against an external realist. To show this, I explored the external realist's theory of empirical content, which shines through from her Cartesianism Principle. After a lengthy discussion in Chapters 5 and 6 of various things that she might mean by empirical content, we concluded that her Cartesian angst forces her to take the JMT manœuvre seriously. The external realist cannot dismiss the JMT manœuvre as question-begging.

With this acknowledgement, she is forced to broaden the scope of her sceptical worries. She acknowledges this point in the speech at the start of this chapter. She began life with Cartesian angst, worrying that appearances might deceive. She now has additional worries: that she is hopelessly wrong about what her words refer to (indeterminacy arguments); that *every* (ideal) theory is true (infallibilism arguments); that there is no single correspondence relation, but a plethora of equally good candidates, so that no words refer to *any* object in particular (referential indeterminacy, prompted by indeterminacy arguments). Crucially, these are not worries that appearances deceive. They are worries about how our thoughts could even be 'vulnerable to' the world. In short, they are not expressions of Cartesian angst, but expressions of Kantian angst.

The moral deserves to be repeated, with emphasis. *The model-theoretic arguments and the JMT manœuvre form a machine that converts Cartesian angst into Kantian angst.*

7.4 The *reductio* of external realism

Whilst the model-theoretic arguments are not usually presented in this way, it is noteworthy that the model-theoretic arguments actually have served to generate Kantian angst. Lewis, for example, entertained reacting to the model-theoretic arguments by accepting that reference was radically indeterminate. He suggested that, in this case,

Something vital would be destroyed, but a lot would be left standing. There would still be a world, and it would not be a figment of our imagination.[10]

Similarly, J. J. C. Smart suggested:

I do not much mind the idea that reference slides freely over the surface of noumenal waters, except that I do not think of the noumenal waters as consisting of unknowable things in themselves: there are just the electrons, protons, stars, cats, cabbages and other perfectly knowable objects.[11]

As a response to the model-theoretic arguments, this is literally unintelligible. Smart wants to tell us something *about* cabbages and cats. Well, which things are the cabbages, and which are the cats? If referential indeterminacy is true, then Smart says of each thing 'it is a cabbage' and 'it is not a cabbage', to the same extent. In which case, when Smart says that the world is made up of 'electrons, protons, stars, cats and cabbages', if he makes any assertion at all, he asserts only *that there are some objects*.

Indeed, referential indeterminacy 'may retain the world, but at the price of giving up any intelligible notion of *how* the world is'.[12] The objects comprising the noumenal waters need have no particular 'intrinsic' features: all we require from them is that they form a domain, and model theory will do the rest.[13] Moreover, not only can they be *blank*, but they can also be rather *scarce*: by the Completeness Theorem, we shall only need countably many

---

[10] D. Lewis (1984: 231).

[11] Smart (1995: 309); 'noumenal waters' is a reference to Putnam (1989: 361–2). Devitt (1984a: 84–5) entertains radical referential indeterminacy; he is unimpressed with the charge of self-stultification (which I favour), but ultimately rejects referential indeterminacy on other grounds (1984a: 98–9). Taylor (2006: 57–8) sympathizes with Smart and Lewis, although Taylor is not an external realist.

[12] Putnam (1977: 491), Putnam's italic, though he writes 'the world' in small-caps. Almost the same passage occurs in Putnam (1978a: 44). Putnam makes such claims in defence of conceptual relativity against the 'hardcore realist'; I discuss this in Chapters 18 and 19.

[13] As Putnam (1983a: xiii; 1993b: 180) notes.

of them. Finally, referential indeterminacy leaves no way to make sense of the worry that an ideal theory might *really* be false:[14] any consistent theory is guaranteed to have many models (and many countermodels) in the noumenal waters. In short, there is not really any difference between claiming that every sentence is (equally) about every *thing*, and claiming that no sentence is about *anything*.[15] To embrace radical referential indeterminacy is simply to embrace Kantian scepticism.

The point of all this is not simply that the external realist has to contend with new sceptical scenarios. That was how the external realist attempted to present the situation, at the start of this chapter. But the problem is that Cartesian scepticism and Kantian scepticism are rather different beasts. Kantian scepticism is radically incoherent. How can I worry that my words express nothing about the world? Really: *How?* If the worry is right, nothing could express it. No worry could be more self-stultifying. To take a less dramatic—but equally incoherent—example, the canonical presentation of the permutation argument raises the sceptical scenario:

'Cats' does not refer to cats, but instead refers to cherries.

If the external realist is to entertain that this sceptical scenario might actually obtain—as she is happy to entertain that she might actually be a brain in a vat—then she needs to be able to think *about* cats, so that she can contemplate that the word 'cat' fails to pick them out. But if the sceptical scenario obtains, how can she do this? Certainly not by writing down the words '"cats" does not refer to cats', for if the scenario were in fact actual, then that last word would not pick out the cats. Once we try to think through what the permutation scenario involves, we realize that the (Kantian) angst it is supposed to engender is simply *incoherent*, in a way that Cartesian angst does not seem initially to be.[16]

At long last, we have a reason to reject external realism. *External realists entertain Cartesian angst. The model-theoretic arguments show that they must also entertain Kantian angst. But Kantian angst is incoherent. So external realism itself is incoherent.*

---

[14] As Hale and Wright (1997: 429) emphasize.

[15] Contrast defenders of Quinean ontological relativity, such as Hylton (2006: 143–5).

[16] I shall say more on this, however, in Part C.

7.5 The limits of argumentation

To retain one's faith in the Credo of external realism in the face of this argument, the only option for the external realist is to execute a complete *volte-face* from the speech she presented at the start of this chapter. Instead of allowing scepticism to infect her semantic principles, she might allow that the incoherence of Kantian angst simply provides her with an a priori (or conceptual, or what-have-you) proof that she should not entertain semantical sceptical scenarios. Indeed, she might regard herself as offering a transcendental argument, of the following form:

My thoughts express claims about the world.

In order for that to be possible, something must fix reference.

So: something fixes reference.

An initial concern with this sort of argument is that transcendental arguments can only ever supply extraordinarily weak conclusions.[17] Suppose we have a successful transcendental argument that hypothetical imperatives depend upon the existence of some categorical imperative. Then even at best, we know only that there *is* some categorical imperative, not *what* it is; all we have is a bare existential. Suppose we have a successful transcendental argument that shows the existence of an external world. Then even at best, we know only that there *is* such a world, not whether any particular objects (such as my hands) exist; all we have is a bare existential. Similarly in the present context: even at best, the external realist's transcendental argument establishes the bare existential that *something* fixes reference. Suppose, for example, that the external realist wanted to go beyond the transcendental argument, and maintain that causation fixes reference (as in §3.1), or that Nature's elite joints fix reference (as in §3.2).[18] Neither claim could possibly be justified, for the transcendental argument establishes that 'a *one-knows-not-what* . . . solves our problem *one-knows-not-how*.'[19]

The force of this point can be appreciated by recalling a beautiful passage from James's *Pragmatism*:

Metaphysics has usually followed a very primitive kind of quest. You know how men have always hankered after unlawful magic, and you know what a great part in

---

[17] Brueckner (1983: 551–2) puts this point very well.

[18] I was inclined to read Lewis (1984) as offering this transcendental argument for the Eliteness Constraint himself; thanks to Ross Cameron for making me realize that this is not straightforward.

[19] Putnam (1983a: xii), though I may have pushed Putnam's jibe beyond its intended target.

magic *words* have always played. If you have his name, or the formula of incantation that binds him, you can control the spirit, the genie, afrite, or whatever the power may be. Solomon knew the names of all the spirits, and having their names, he held them subject to his will. So the universe has always appeared to the natural mind as a kind of enigma, of which the key must be sought in the shape of some illuminating or power-bringing word or name. That word names the universe's *principle*, and to possess it is after a fashion to possess the universe itself. 'God,' 'Matter,' 'Reason,' 'the Absolute,' and 'Energy,' are so many solving names. You can rest when you have them. You are at the end of your metaphysical quest.[20]

The present point is that all attempts to constrain reference—'Causation', 'Eliteness', 'Fullness', 'Modality', or anything else—are simply so many *solving names*.[21] These magical words of power may bring us to the end of our metaphysical quest, but what can that possibly be worth?

My main concern, though, is not that the appeal to a transcendental argument leads the external realist into bankrupt metaphysical speculation. My main concern is that the transcendental argument is itself open to question. We have found that Kantian angst is incoherent. If Kantian angst is, indeed, a natural corollary of the external realist's initial picture, then it is a cheat for the external realist to say: *it might look as if Kantian angst arises inevitably on this picture, but in fact it does not, because something (utterly mysterious) blocks it from arising.* If the external realist's picture were right, then a transcendental argument might prove that there is such a thing. But if there is no such thing, then the very same argument establishes that the picture is hopelessly incoherent. Generically, then, the incomprehensibility of Kantian scepticism establishes only the following disjunction. *Either external realism is incoherent, or something (one knows not what) fixes reference.*

That is why the external realist can only save her position by appealing to magic. That is why we should have no faith in external realism. The model-theoretic arguments are vindicated.

---

[20] James (1907: 28).
[21] Compare Putnam's (1983a: xii; 1992b: 353–6; 1993c: 299–300; 2012a: 76) claim that external realism is without *content*.

Part B
The Tenacity of Cartesian Angst

8

How the serpent entered Eden

The model-theoretic arguments have destroyed our faith in external realism. That was the lesson of Part A. Two questions now emerge. First, how much of external realism must we abandon? Second, what should we adopt in its place?

In this chapter I shall explore the first question. Since external realism was committed to three principles, my task is simply to determine which of these three principles is responsible for the problems of Part A. I shall show that the Independence and Correspondence Principles are innocent bystanders. Indeed, it takes a perverse act of will to understand them as making *philosophical*—let alone *metaphysical*—claims. The guilty party must therefore be the Cartesianism Principle. This should come as no surprise. To repeat the moral of Chapter 7, the model-theoretic arguments and the JMT manœuvre form a machine that converts Cartesian angst into Kantian angst. To avoid being chewed up and spat out by this machine, we need to overcome Cartesian angst.

In the remaining chapters of Part B, I shall outline several ways in which we might try to do this, corresponding with three time slices of Putnam. These three positions are: nonrealism, natural realism, and justificationism. Each attempts to provide a philosophically satisfying account of why Cartesian angst does not arise. However, each is unsuccessful. The outlook at the end of Part B is consequently a little bleak.

8.1 Independence revisited

Recall that the external realist's Independence Principle states that some objects are in some relevant sense mind-, language-, and theory-independent. With this in mind, Clarence Irving Lewis once presented the following arch-'realistic hypothesis':

(a) 'If all minds should disappear from the universe, the stars would still go on in their courses.'[1]

This seems to capture the Independence Principle, at least with regard to the stars. And in its support, we might tell a short story.

> **The mass-extinction scenario.** At some point in the year 2312, a meteor strikes the Earth, destroying all life. Life never evolves again on Earth, nor on any other planet. So, in obliterating all human life, the meteor obliterates all minds, languages, and theories.

This scenario is surely physically possible. Nevertheless, in the mass-extinction scenario, the meteor has not obliterated the stars. The stars neither care that the Earth has become a dead planet, nor that their universe has become a dead place; they simply go on in their courses. So (a) is true, and the stars are indeed mind-, language-, and theory-independent. This seems to vindicate the Independence Principle. Some philosophers might think that this cheap vindication is immediately sufficient to establish realism (at least about stars). I shall call this the *Leninist argument* for realism, since it comes close to Lenin's 'paradoxes of positivism'.[2]

The Leninist argument raises an important point. Anyone who wants to deny (a) by denying that the mass-extinction scenario is physically possible is making a very strange empirical claim. Anyone who makes this empirical claim on a priori metaphysical grounds should be dismissed out of hand.

Whatever the realism debate amounts to, anyone who wants to occupy the 'anti-realist' camp should instead be both able and happy to make exactly the same empirical claims as her realist opponent. And (a) strikes us as true precisely because we *are* treating it as an empirical claim. We are led to say 'the stars are mind-independent' by a brief story describing an empirically possible situation, namely, the mass-extinction scenario. This is to read (a) as an *internal* sentence: it is simply an internal part of our favourite over-arching empirical theory, according to which we might all one day go the way of the dinosaurs. A decent anti-realist should be quite willing to assert (a) in this spirit. However, she will then give (a) an anti-realist *interpretation*, which—whatever it is—is not the same as the realist's *interpretation* of (a).[3]

---

[1] C. I. Lewis (1934: 143).   [2] Putnam (2007: 158) draws the connection.
[3] Feyerabend (1993: 258) makes a similar point.

There is, therefore, no direct path from the truth of (a), when read *internally*, to any *philosophical* attitude about the stars. More generally, if we treat the Independence Principle itself as an internal sentence, and so regard it simply as a sentence of our best overarching empirical theory, then we have not yet committed ourselves to any *philosophical* thesis at all. The Independence Principle is philosophically innocent.

The argument that I have just presented goes back at least to the Vienna Circle.[4] Reacting directly to Lewis, Moritz Schlick wrote:

We are as sure of (a) as of the best founded physical laws that science has discovered.... Experience shows no connection between the two kinds of events. We observe that the course of the stars is no more changed by the death of human beings than, say, by the eruption of a volcano, or by a change of government in China.[5]

Carnap was similarly dismissive of the Leninist argument, and for much the same reason.[6] And Putnam had exactly the same point in mind when he wrote, half a century later:

Human minds did not create the stars or the mountains, but this 'flat' remark is hardly enough to settle the philosophical question of realism versus antirealism.[7]

The general point is that Putnam, Carnap, and Schlick are all quite happy to accept (a) when it is read *internally* to one's best theory.

8.2 Correspondence revisited

Similar comments apply to the Correspondence Principle. To show this, we shall start by considering reference. Consider a claim like:

(b) English speakers refer to cats with the word 'cat'.

---

[4] And perhaps to James (1904: 463–4).

[5] Schlick (1936: 368); I have replaced 'it' with '(a)', for uniformity.

[6] Carnap (1937: 37–8); this is prefigured in Carnap (1928a: §§176–8; 1928b: §§9–10).

[7] Putnam (1982a: 30); Putnam was criticizing Field (1982: 554). Putnam (1991c: 411, 421–2; 1992a: 114–15; 1992b: 355; 1993c: 301–2; 1994a: 265; 1994b: 179; 2007: 158–9) makes similar remarks, often against Devitt. Devitt (2010: 51–6) has replied, stating that '*constitutive* independence' from human minds, languages, and theories is a 'philosophical doctrine *par excellence*'. Maybe we are only now quibbling over what counts as a 'philosophical doctrine'. For thoughts supporting Putnam, see LePore and Loewer (1988: 470) and Silva (2008: 12–14).

Once again, we could tell a relatively straightforward story to explain how this came about. Unfortunately, my knowledge of etymology is sufficient only to tell a 'just so' story. So I shall instead consider a simpler case:

> **The terrible-Muriel scenario.** My friends have a cat, whom they love very much. They decided to call her 'Muriel'. Everyone agreed that she looked like a Muriel—she was, after all, simply *terrible*—so everyone else called her 'Muriel' too. And that's how Muriel got her name.

This (true) story is surely even more banal than the mass-extinction scenario. But it discusses reference; indeed, it allows that reference is constrained by things like causation, intention, consensus, pop-cultural allusion, and wit. It tells me, in the most humdrum of ways, how a certain semantic relation came into being. It would be as much of a mistake to offer an a priori argument against the Correspondence Principle, as it would be to offer an a priori argument against the Independence Principle.

It is worth noting that what goes for causation, intention, and pop-cultural allusion holds for various other ways to constrain reference. To take one which has received particular focus: it would be crazy to deny that certain objects are more salient than others to humans in their environments. After all, there are limitations on human perceptual acuity (bee eyes can detect certain patterns on flowers that human eyes cannot) and practical matters affecting human interests (burying nuts is normally a greater priority for squirrels than for humans). It might almost be plausible to think that properties and objects might usefully be ordered according to how 'referentially magnetic' they are; not 'absolutely', of course, but to *humans*, in their *environments*, and given their *concerns*.[8] This ordering might be entrenched in some future empirical semantic theory. Or it might not be. But we had better not aim for an a priori argument against the very idea of a correspondence between words and more or less salient objects.

There is an important caveat to this defence of Correspondence. When I defended the Independence Principle, I did not want to establish that *every* object is mind-, language-, and theory-independent: as I cautioned

---

[8] This is how I read Putnam's (1993a: 67ff.) advocation of non-'transcendental', latter-day Aristotelian *forms* whilst attacking Lewis's 'totally magical' Eliteness Constraint. Compare Taylor's (2006: 109–24) discussion of vegetarianism.

in §1.1, we built cities, sculpted statues, started wars, and invented Esperanto. Similarly here, I am not trying to argue that every word refers. At its
most obvious, 'Muriel' names a cat, but 'Chimæra' fails to name anything.
More intriguingly, it might be possible to outline the functions and histories
of certain ways of speaking, without ever speaking in (anything approaching) those ways oneself. In that case, we may be able to say everything
that we want to say about those ways of speaking, *without* saying that they
involve either reference or correspondence. I freely concede all of this, but
note only that the (in principle) possibility of such local genealogies no
more threatens the Correspondence Principle than the mind-dependence
of some objects threatens the Independence Principle.

There are, then, relations of reference and correspondence between
words and the world. But, to repeat Putnam's sentiment from just a moment
ago, this 'flat' remark does not settle the philosophical question of realism
versus anti-realism, and for just the reason that the mind-independence of
the stars does not settle that question either. Our ability to refer to cats is
no more nor less mysterious than our ability to keep them as pets. Our
ability to refer to stars is significantly less mysterious than their twinkling.
The anti-realist should not in principle resist (b), or any other semantic
claim. Rather, she should simply provide these claims with an anti-realist
interpretation.[9]

During his 'internal realist period', Putnam often mentioned Michael
Dummett's view that a globally anti-realist view of truth is anti-realist 'all
the way up (or down)'.[10] The present point is that there is no philosophical
significance to employing a correspondence theory of truth *almost* all the
way up (or down), as it were. This is why Carnap was able to sketch a
theory of reference in the *Aufbau*.[11] Equally, it is why Putnam can think of
correspondence 'as part of an *explanatory model* of the speakers' collective
behavior', so that he can employ 'a similar picture' to the external realist,
but '*within* a theory', thereby avoiding external realism.[12] The point is that
discussions about reference and correspondence are to be taken as *internal*
claims. They must be presented as empirical theories—in the broadest sense

---

[9] Putnam (1977: 487–9; 1980b: 479), Shapiro (1997: 48), and Button (2011: 332) emphasize this; a
slightly different idea comes through in Putnam (1994c: 503; 1999: 58; 1995b: 21–2).

[10] Putnam (1977: 487–8; 1980a: 103; 1981c: 56–7; 1983b: 83–4; 2007: 158), drawing on Dummett (1963: 148–50; 1991: 322–37), for example.

[11] Compare Carnap (1928a: §141) on 'weight' with Evans (1973) on 'dominance'.

[12] Putnam (1977: 483–4; 1979c: 228); for clarification, see Putnam (1992b: 353–4; 2012b: 56).

of the word 'empirical'—about how signs produced by humans get hooked up to objects in the world. The terrible-Muriel scenario is just that.

8.3 Cartesianism revisited

The Independence and Correspondence Principles are innocent, when read internally. And, as yet, we have no conception of how *else* they might be read. Unless we can come up with something, we face the thought that anti-realism, when properly followed through, coincides with pure realism.[13]

At this point, there is a real danger that the realism debate will dissolve into bluster. Since we have accepted that there are objects, and that our words pick them out, what room for disagreement is left? We end up trying to be realists without being Realists. Or we try to discuss what there is without considering what there Really Is. A novice to the literature might be forgiven for believing that the realism debate reduces to a debate about proposed typographical conventions. And it does not help the novice to hear that metaphysicians want heavyweight objects when their opponents want only lightweight ones; or that metaphysicians want substantial properties rather than thin ones. That is just more metaphor. Nor is the novice brought to understanding by being told that realists adopt a distinctively 'philosophical' attitude, for (post-Quinean) metaphysicians immediately deny this and maintain that metaphysics is 'continuous with science'. The novice is forced to ask the ironic question: *Is the realism debate even a debate?*

The answer to that question comes from reconsidering the Cartesianism Principle. We saw in Part A that the Cartesianism Principle generates an unbridgeable gulf between mind and world. Belief in such a gulf shapes what the external realist means by her Independence and Correspondence Principles. When the external realist presents the Independence and Correspondence Principles, she does not intend to present them as 'flat', internal remarks. Rather, she presents them with this gulf in mind, as philosophically substantive, metaphysical theses.[14] The Cartesianism Principle moves them from 'internal' platitudes to 'external' theses.[15]

---

[13] I am deliberately alluding to Wittgenstein (1921: §5.64).

[14] Similar thoughts occur in Wright (2000: 349) and Putnam (2012a: 75–6).

[15] There are obvious strains here of Carnap's dichotomy between internal and external questions. As I shall make explicit in §16.8, I do not embrace that dichotomy.

It is unclear how we would even begin to assess such 'external' claims. Perhaps, however, we do not need to. Since the Cartesianism Principle turns them from 'internal' to 'external' claims, perhaps we can content ourselves with a war by proxy, directed against the Cartesianism Principle. That Principle is the obvious source of all the problems of Part A. It is what enables us to press the JMT manœuvre, overcoming the charge of question-begging and yielding a machine for turning Cartesian angst into incoherent Kantian angst. If we are to avoid our problems, and overcome external realism, we have no option but to jettison the Cartesianism Principle.

8.4 The God's Eye point of view and Moorean contradictions

For the remainder of Part B, I shall consider three different attempts to avoid Cartesian angst. Before I consider them, however, I wish to consider a response to Cartesian angst that is superficially tempting, but ultimately much too quick.

When philosophers claim that something is possible, they often tell a story that illustrates that possibility. In the course of presenting his 'internal realism', Putnam suggests that we should respond to such stories by asking:

The Perspective Question. 'From whose point of view is the story being told?'[16]

The worry is that some stories cannot reasonably be told by any *person*, but would have to be told from a *God's Eye* point of view. Since the God's Eye point of view is the *external* realist's favourite perspective, and since Part A has sent us fleeing from external realism, Putnam's suggestion is that we must reject such stories and the associated possibilities that they purport to describe.

I have told two stories in this chapter, and the Perspective Question raises no particular problems for either story. I narrated the terrible-Muriel scenario in my ordinary tone of voice, for that story is simply true. I did not say who narrated the mass-extinction scenario, but again it might easily have been me: perhaps I was prophesying our doom; perhaps I was lobbying my

---

[16] Putnam (1980a: 100; 1981c: 50); Putnam has this in italics.

government to build a giant anti-meteor defence system and send it into space to forestall such possibilities; whatever.

But suppose now that I try to tell a mundane empirical story according to which the Cartesianism Principle comes out as true. In particular, suppose that I try to tell a story in which our own theory, T, is ideal but false. In keeping with Putnam's suggestion, we should ask ourselves the Perspective Question: *'from whose point of view is the story being told?'* Since T is ideal, it is certainly consistent; so anyone who says that T is false is not working within T. Thus it would seem that the story cannot be told from *our* point of view, given that T is our own theory, but must instead be told from some *external* perspective. It would seem, then, that all that is necessary to overthrow the Cartesianism Principle is a shift in our philosophical picture. We simply replace the God's Eye point of view with our own human point of view, and reflect this shift in our Perspective Question.

Unfortunately, this thought is much too quick.[17] To see why, it will help to draw an analogy.[18] Consider the following sentence:

(M) I believe that it is raining, and it is not raining.

This is known as a *Moorean contradiction*.[19] It would be very strange—perhaps outright inconsistent—for me to *believe* (M). After all, if I believe it, then I believe the second conjunct, so I believe that it is not raining; so it would surely be very strange for me also to believe that I believe that it is raining. Nonetheless, it does not follow that any story containing (M) must be told from a perniciously God's Eye point of view. Rather, my favourite theory—indeed, very mundane commonsensical reasoning—has no great difficulty in representing a situation in which it is not raining but I believe that it is. Here is a very boring story which describes that possibility:

The errant-sprinkler scenario. I glance out of the window and see water falling. I thereby come to believe that it is raining. In fact the water is not rain, but the spray from a nearby errant sprinkler system. So I believe that it is raining, and it is not raining.

---

[17] I do not mean to suggest that it has ever been Putnam's thought.

[18] I am here deploying ideas connected with Brueckner's (1996: 277) argument against Stroud (1994: 246). I reconnect with this in §12.5.

[19] G. E. Moore (1942: 543).

Accordingly, we can tell a story containing (M), in the sense that our own theory—indeed, mundane common sense—allows that the Moorean contradiction *might* be true. The moral is that some *bona fide* possibilities cannot be captured by any story which could coherently be narrated as known fact.

With the analogy in hand, let us return to the attempt to use the Perspective Question to overthrow the Cartesianism Principle. A theory cannot reasonably say that it *is* false, just as I cannot reasonably assert (M). Nonetheless, a theory might well be able to *represent the possibility* of its own falsity, just as I can represent the situation described by a Moorean contradiction. And the Cartesianism Principle does not state that our theory *is* false (even though ideal) but that it *might* be. We cannot overthrow the Cartesianism Principle by trading in the God's Eye point of view for a myopically human point of view. If we are looking for an intuitively satisfying reason to reject the Cartesianism Principle, then we shall have to dig much deeper.

9

Nonrealism

Starting in the late 1970s, Putnam has outlined three positions that might hope to avoid the Cartesianism Principle. The first aim of this chapter is to provide an overview of the broad trajectory of Putnam's thought, and a rough characterization of those three positions. The second aim is to clarify and criticize Putnam's earliest positive response to the model-theoretic arguments, his *nonrealism*.

Putnam's nonrealism paints a philosophical picture that immediately leads to the rejection of the Cartesianism Principle. This is very welcome, given the discussion in Chapter 8. However, the picture is painted from a perspective which is every bit as external as that of the external realist. Nonrealism turns out to be external subjective idealism, and so must be rejected.

9.1 Three alternatives to external realism

Putnam first presented the model-theoretic arguments and the JMT manœuvre in 'Realism and Reason' (Putnam 1977). Even as he announced the demise of external realism, he announced 'internal realism' for the first time. Unfortunately, he used this expression somewhat ambiguously.[1] At the start of 'Realism and Reason', Putnam used the phrase 'internal realism' to draw attention to the fact that everyone can accept both the Independence and Correspondence Principles when read 'internally' (as noted in Chapter 8). He described his positive response to the model-theoretic arguments as 'nonrealism', the central plank of which was an explicit commitment to a verificationist 'theory of understanding'.[2] Truth would follow in the wake

---

[1] As Putnam (1992b: 352–3; 2012b: 54) himself explains.

[2] Putnam (1977: 487–9; 1980b: 478–82).

of understanding, so that the nonrealist would also be an 'internal realist', in the sense just mentioned. However, towards the end of 'Realism and Reason', Putnam simply conflated 'nonrealism' with 'internal realism'.[3] To avoid confusion, I shall describe the position that responds to the model-theoretic arguments by embracing a verificationist 'theory of understanding' as *nonrealism*.

From the early 1980s, Putnam adopted the label 'internal realism' to describe his positive position. During this time, he continued to use the model-theoretic arguments to attack external realism, and to defend those arguments with the JMT manœuvre.[4] But Putnam's emphasis became to articulate a particular '*conception of truth*'.[5] In the early 1980s, Putnam explicitly identified truth with idealized justified belief or idealized rational acceptability.[6] Later on, he distanced himself from an identification per se, but he continued to maintain that truth could not outstrip the possibility of justification.[7] I shall use the name *justificationism* for the position that subscribes to this conceptual connection between truth and idealized justification. To be clear, I am not suggesting that Putnam himself drew much distinction between nonrealism and justificationism; I am simply highlighting two different points of emphasis in Putnam's 'internal realist period'.

In the early 1990s, however, Putnam abandoned both nonrealism and justificationism entirely. Indeed, he explicitly rejected 'the view that a statement is true if and only if acceptance of the statement would be justified were epistemic conditions good enough'.[8] Putnam now maintained that the problems raised by the model-theoretic arguments were connected to a faulty theory of perception, and suggested that the correct reaction to the model-theoretic arguments would involve adopting a naïve realism about perception. He described the ensuing position as *natural realism*,[9] and I shall follow him in this.

---

[3] Putnam (1977: 494–6).

[4] Putnam (1981c: 22–48; 1982a: 38; 1982c: 206–7; 1983a: viii–xii; 1984a: 84).

[5] As Putnam (1990b: viii) explains.

[6] Putnam (1980a: 100–3; 1981c: 49–56, 122–3; 1981a: 200; 1982a: 41; 1983a: xvii; 1983b: 84–5; 1986b: 115).

[7] Putnam (1988: 115; 1990b: viii–ix; 1991c: 421; see also 1987b: 31–2).

[8] Putnam (1994d: v; see also 1991a: 268; 1992b: 366; 1994a: 242–3; 1994b: 179; 1995a: 299; 1995b: 11–12).

[9] Putnam (1994c: 454; 1999: 10; 2012b: 60).

One thing that remained constant across these three broad positions was Putnam's endorsement of 'conceptual relativity'. The simple fact that this was a constant suggests, correctly, that the discussion of conceptual relativity can be detached fairly cleanly from the project of responding to the model-theoretic arguments. Since the latter is my current focus, I shall set aside all discussion of conceptual relativity until Part D. (Indeed, we shall be better placed to deal with conceptual relativity, having first dealt with the problems of Part A.)

The main purpose of this extremely brief historical survey is simply to highlight that no single position called 'internal realism' sprang into being, fully formed, at exactly the moment that Putnam presented the model-theoretic arguments. Instead, we can usefully distinguish three broad attempts to overcome the problems associated with external realism: *nonrealism*, with its theory of understanding; *justificationism*, with its conceptual connection between truth and idealized justification; and *natural realism*, with its naïve philosophy of perception. I shall consider these three positions over the next three chapters.

In this chapter I shall focus solely on nonrealism; that is, Putnam's first positive response to the model-theoretic arguments. I shall show that the nonrealist sketches a position according to which the Cartesianism Principle is obviously mistaken. This is very welcome, given that the Cartesianism Principle is the source of all of the problems of Part A. However, I shall have to endorse Putnam's later criticism that nonrealism is objectionably close to solipsism.[10] Indeed, nonrealism is an external form of subjective idealism.

9.2 The theory of understanding

Putnam presents his model-theoretic arguments for the first time in 'Realism and Reason'. More specifically, he presents the infallibilism argument and defends its significance with the JMT manœuvre. Seeing that this undermines external realism, Putnam then casts around for a way to explain how we understand the words that we use—for a '*theory of understanding*'[11]—that is not vulnerable to this sort of argument.

A first thought would be to equate the theory of understanding with some theory of meaning. But Putnam immediately rejects this approach, since one component of meaning is reference, 'and reference is what the problem is all about!'[12] (This is a revealing error, to which I shall return in §9.4. For now, I shall play along with it.)

Instead, Putnam declares that our theory of understanding must be presented solely 'in terms of the notions of *verification* and *falsification*', where these notions do *not* themselves presuppose reference.[13] Now,

once [someone] has succeeded in understanding a rich enough language to serve as a metalanguage for some theory T..., he can define 'true in T' à la Tarski, he can talk about 'models' for T, etc. He can even define 'reference' (or 'satisfaction') exactly as Tarski did.[14]

So we can ultimately start to talk about reference and correspondence. But crucially, 'reference is given through sense, and sense is given through verification-procedures and not through truth-conditions'.[15]

This accords perfectly with the discussion of Chapter 8. Putnam's theory of understanding will not involve reference at all. But it will enable us to understand and employ a theory which itself makes claims about the mind-independence of objects and about word–world semantic relations. Indeed, our theory might well contain the mass-extinction scenario (of §8.1) and the terrible-Muriel scenario (of §8.2). Thus the nonrealist will advance the Independence and Correspondence Principles *internally*.

9.3 Nonrealism and a bracketed basis

This nonrealism obviously bears extremely close similarities with (certain readings of) Schlick and Carnap (see §5.2 and §8.1).[16] However, Putnam writes:

What makes this different from the old phenomenalism is that there is no 'basis' of hard facts (e.g. sense data) with respect to which one ultimately uses the truth conditional semantics, classical logic, and the *realist* notions of truth and falsity.... Understanding a sentence, in this semantics, is knowing what constitutes a proof (verification) of it. And this is true *even of the sentences that describe verifications*.[17]

---

[12] Putnam (1977: 489).

[13] Putnam (1977: 487, Putnam's italics; see also 1980b: 480n8). Putnam notes the influence of Dummett's William James lectures, which were published as Dummett 1991; Putnam's (1977: 487–8; 1979c: 228) discussion of 'soft facts' draws from Dummett (1979: 222–3).

[14] Putnam (1980b: 479).   [15] Putnam (1980b: 479), Putnam italicizes this entire clause.

[16] On the question of how one should read Carnap, I repeat my caution from footnote 8 in Chapter 5.

Mention of a 'basis' is, of course, a nod towards Carnap's *Aufbau* (see §5.2). But, despite appearances, Putnam is not asking us here to abandon the idea that there *is* a basis. Putnam immediately continues by offering three examples of potential 'primitive sentences', namely, 'I have a red sense datum', 'I see a cow', and 'such and such neurons fired'.[18] There are still primitives, and they are still to be understood in terms of bracketed, first-person experience (or in terms of a neuroscientific surrogate thereof). The only difference is that we are to approach these primitives in terms of *understanding*, rather than in terms of correspondence.

Putnam insists upon this difference because he thinks that the model-theoretic arguments make it unintelligible that thoughts could correspond with sensations.[19] In more detail, Putnam thinks that anyone who maintains that their thoughts correspond with their bracketed experiences will inevitably confront an unanswerable radical Cartesian sceptical worry, concerning whether they could be radically mistaken about all of their past sensations. This will enable us to press the JMT manœuvre against such a person, as in Chapters 5 and 6—substituting 'true' with 'corresponding with all sensations' and 'ideal' with 'corresponding with present sensations'—and disaster will ensue exactly as before. (In passing, this suggests that we may have been too generous when we granted, in §5.3, that Bea could easily determine whether or not her words correspond with her sensations.)

Approaching sensations via correspondence-free understanding may help us to avoid a replay of the model-theoretic arguments. However, the distance between Putnam's nonrealism and 'the old phenomenalism' is hardly vast. Putnam occasionally shows some discomfort with this fact. In particular, Putnam sympathizes with Nelson Goodman's idea that we 'write many versions' of the world,[20] and explicitly defends Goodman's pluralism about what to treat as basic or primitive.[21] Putnam therefore asks us to consider, not a single static basis, but 'an evolving network of verification procedures'.[22] All of this might make us hope that 'understanding' encompasses

[17] Putnam (1977: 487).   [18] Putnam (1977: 487; see also 1980b: 475).
[19] Putnam (1977: 488; see also 1980b: 475–6; 1980a: 106–8; 1981c: 62–72).
[20] Putnam (1977: 496).   [21] Putnam (1979b).
[22] Putnam (1980b: 480). He has never abandoned this idea, but has since been able to take it seriously; see Putnam (1990b: ix; 2005: 577; 2008: 29–30).

rather more than bracketed experience. Such hopes, however, are dashed by Putnam's later commentary:

> I could, and in fact did, grant that the notion of 'observation' could be extended to include observation with the aid of instruments (in 'Models and Reality'), but I could not grant any significance to this concession . . . , since I could not grant any significance to even the fact that we normally speak of perception as being of things that we perceive without the aid of instruments.[23]

In short, during his nonrealist period, Putnam thought that the idea of verification and falsification could not be extended beyond the mind. Putnam's natural realism, to be discussed in Chapter 10, embraced a much wider notion of understanding. So rather than waste time asking whether the nonrealist could adopt a wider notion of understanding than Putnam himself did, I shall leave such matters until Chapter 10, and shall simply stipulate (if needs be) that the nonrealist regards *understanding* as an essentially private, first-person psychological phenomenon.

9.4 Nonrealism is external subjective idealism

Given this general theory of understanding, the nonrealist will understand all talk 'about mind-independent objects' purely in terms of her first-person bracketed experience. There is therefore no possibility that her bracketed experiences might *deceive* her concerning outer objects—that is, objects that are not bracketed experiences—since the outer objects themselves, and reference to them, come into view only via bracketed experience. Nonrealism consequently has no truck whatsoever with Cartesian scepticism. And this is good, since Cartesian angst is responsible for all of external realism's woes. (In particular, it allows the JMT manœuvre to get a grip, and for Cartesian angst to slide into Kantian angst: see Chapters 7 and 8.)

However, this method for avoiding Cartesian scepticism is deeply suspicious. Given her focus on first-person bracketed experience, the nonrealist is embracing a 'veil of sensations', just as described in Chapter 5. Of course the nonrealist, unlike the external realist, does not think that there is anything 'behind' the veil of sensations. Her 'outer' objects sit on her side of the veil of sensations. But this simply means that the nonrealist is an *extreme*

---

[23] Putnam (1994c: 465*n*46; 1999: 20*n*46).

Cartesian sceptic, who does not *really* believe that there are any *outer* objects. Or so the external realist complains.

The nonrealist will, of course, protest loudly against this. After all, 'there are outer objects' is a claim that her best theory makes; and she understands that theory; and she uses it. So, she says, utterly sincerely: 'there are outer objects'. What more does the external realist want?

The problem is that, having said 'there are outer objects', the nonrealist adds, in a stage whisper, 'as I understand that claim'. This stage whisper utterly undermines her protest. In order to articulate *that* she is a nonrealist, she has to insist that all of her claims (even 'claims about outer objects') are to be understood purely in terms of bracketed experience. And in the same spirit in which she insists on this, she must also say that none of her claims are understood in terms of outer objects. So, in the same spirit in which she articulates her own philosophical position, she must take the external realist's objection on the chin. Conversely, when she attempts to duck the external realist's objection by insisting that she *does* speak about outer objects ('all the time, in fact'), she is speaking from a position which leaves her unable even to articulate *that* she is a nonrealist.

What this shows is that the nonrealist still hankers after an external perspective.[24] She does not present her 'theory of understanding' as an attempt to supply the best possible empirical theory (in the broadest sense of the word 'empirical') of how humans get about in the world and make sense of it. (If she were to do that, then she would surely *have* to mention outer objects.) Rather, her 'theory of understanding' is every bit as much of an a priori, metaphysical imposition as anything advanced by the external realist. Indeed, in her theory of understanding, the nonrealist embraces the external realist's radically external perspective. She adopts the God's Eye point of view, and then declares that there is no God there, and no objects (other than bracketed sensations). Or perhaps, better: finding herself alone, she declares *herself* to be God, building the world from her experiences. Putnam's nonrealism is *external subjective idealism*.[25]

The source of the nonrealist's attachment to a God's Eye point of view can be traced back to Putnam's insistence that the theory of understanding must not mention reference, on the grounds that 'reference is what the

---

[24] See Putnam (1992b: 365) and Silva (2008: 13–14).

[25] So Putnam must partially endorse one of Devitt's (1984b: 277) criticisms of nonrealism. As I explain in §10.3, Putnam must also endorse another of Devitt's criticisms.

problem is all about!'[26] (see §9.2). In making this claim, Putnam sets himself the problem of addressing head-on the question of how reference could be *so much as possible* (see Chapter 7). He is deep in the grip of Kantian angst, and he is struggling to *answer* Kantian scepticism.[27] This is a mistake: once Kantian angst has arisen, it tends to deprive you of any adequate tools for dealing with it.

Here, then, is an alternative approach that Putnam might have followed. We saw in Chapter 7 that the model-theoretic arguments together with the JMT manœuvre form a machine for converting Cartesian angst into Kantian angst. So instead of trying to tackle Kantian angst first and foremost (as the nonrealist does with her theory of understanding), Putnam could instead start by tackling Cartesian angst first and foremost (rather than as afterthought, as the nonrealist does). Then the JMT manœuvre will get no purchase (see Chapters 5–8). And then, far from saying that 'reference is what the problem is all about!', there will be no problem with reference *in the first place*. This framework sets the scene for our discussion of Putnam's natural realism.

---

[26] Putnam (1977: 489).
[27] See also Putnam's (1983a: viii) autobiographical remarks on the origins of his 'internal realism'.

10

Natural realism

In Chapter 9, I rejected Putnam's nonrealism, and largely for the reasons that Putnam outlined whilst he was a natural realist. So in this chapter, I shall consider his *natural realism*, as announced most fully in 'Sense, Nonsense, and the Senses' (Putnam 1994c) and *The Threefold Cord* (1999).

Putnam's natural realism utterly rejects the bracketed empiricist approach to 'understanding' that is characteristic of nonrealism. Moreover, it attempts to avoid the problems raised in Part A by tackling Cartesian angst head-on. This is an excellent strategy. Unfortunately, natural realism attempts to tackle Cartesian angst by embracing naïve realism about perception. And this means that it fails to deal adequately with Cartesian scepticism. This is a crucial failing, since Cartesian angst is all that is needed to feed the machine of the model-theoretic arguments and the JMT manœuvre, and so it is Cartesian angst which needs to be overcome.

10.1 An outline of natural realism

During the 1990s, Putnam advanced a self-consciously naïve position that he called *natural realism*.[1] In the context of the model-theoretic arguments, the most important aspect of Putnam's natural realism is captured by the following passage:

How could the question 'How does language hook on to the world?' even appear to pose a difficulty, unless the retort 'How can there be a problem about talking about, say, houses and trees when we *see* them all the time?' had not already been rejected in advance as question begging or 'hopelessly naive'? The 'how does language hook on to the world' issue is, at bottom, a replay of the old 'how does perception hook

---

[1] Putnam (1994c: 454; 1999: 10; 2012b: 60).

on to the world' issue. . . . Is it any wonder that one cannot see how thought and language hook on to the world if one never mentions perception?[2]

Putnam's claim is that we can speak about trees, because we perceive them directly. Perception does not 'stop short' of the world—at sense data, qualia, bracketed first-person experiences, or anything similar—but reaches 'all the way out' to the world. This allows language to do the same, so that Putnam can endorse Ludwig Wittgenstein's claim:

When we say, and *mean*, that such-and-such is the case, then we do not stop anywhere short of the fact with what we mean; but mean that *such-and-such— is—thus-and-so*.[3]

The overarching thought is that once we have set our philosophy of perception in order, we shall not need to worry about the model-theoretic arguments. Indeed:

When we hear a sentence in a language we understand, we do not associate a sense with a sign-design; we perceive the sense *in* the sign-design. Sentences that I think, and even sentences that I hear or read, simply do refer to whatever they are about.[4]

We find Putnam talking here naïvely of 'understanding'. However, his notion of 'understanding' has widened dramatically since his nonrealism. For the natural realist, understanding is not a matter of narrow first-person psychology; understanding involves the world.

Given the problems discussed in Chapter 9, this is all to the good. However, in the context of the model-theoretic arguments, such claims are likely to raise as many questions as they answer. I can surely ask how to interpret a speaker of a language that I do not know. I can wonder about how I acquired a language in the first place. I can ask why 'cat' refers to cats. I can wonder what pins down reference and correspondence. Indeed, this was just the question posed by the model-theoretic arguments.

In his natural realist period, however, Putnam sometimes seems to *reject* all such questions. This is initially perplexing, and it brought Dummett to declare:

---

[2] Putnam (1994c: 456; 1999: 12; see also 2012b: 61).
[3] Wittgenstein (1953: §95), Wittgenstein's italics. Putnam (1994c: 492–3; 1999: 47–8) quotes this approvingly, with a slightly different translation.
[4] Putnam (1994c: 491; 1999: 46).

I do not understand what Putnam's [natural realism] amounts to. It looks like an admonition to give up philosophy of language and have nothing to do with anybody who speaks a language other than your own. It obviously cannot be this; but to divine what it is defeats me.[5]

My first task is to answer Dummett on Putnam's behalf.

10.2 McDowell and Kantian angst

As Putnam notes,[6] there is a large amount of convergence between his own natural realism and the position McDowell brings to fruition in *Mind and World* (McDowell 1994). Like Putnam, McDowell approvingly discusses the passage from Wittgenstein quoted in the previous section.[7] Moreover, like Putnam, he indicates that the questions posed by the model-theoretic arguments are not so much to be answered as rejected:

The need to construct a theoretical 'hook' to link thinking to the world does not arise, because if it is thinking that we have in view at all . . . then what we have in view is *already* hooked on to the world; it is already in view as possessing referential directedness at reality.[8]

To understand Putnam's natural realism, then, it will help to consider how McDowell would respond to Dummett's insistence that we must say something about someone who speaks a language which is not our own (see §10.1). Do we not have to 'hook' that person's utterances up to the world? Or are they hooked up to the world '*already*'? There is a real danger of becoming hopelessly lost in metaphors here, so I shall proceed slowly and with an eye to deflating metaphors.[9]

Suppose we come across someone who speaks a language other than our own. If we want to know what she is saying, we shall have to interpret her. In so doing, we shall employ some of our own concepts. We may also end up acquiring some of her concepts. All of this is comprehensible enough. But McDowell then insists that, in the course of this interpretation, we

---

[5] Dummett (2007b: 182).
[6] Putnam (1992b: 358; 1994c: 453–4, 462–3, 483; 1999: 10–11, 18, 37–8).
[7] McDowell (1994: 27–34).   [8] McDowell (1992: 45), McDowell's italics.
[9] I am here presenting a reading of McDowell (1994: 34–6).

never 'break out through a boundary that encloses the system of concepts.'[10] This is one of the dangerous metaphors that I just mentioned, and it needs to be deflated.

In fact, McDowell himself tells us how to deflate it.[11] In providing a Tarskian semantics, we might present claims like:

'Betty' refers to Betty.
'Betty is a cat' is true iff Betty is a cat.

McDowell's point is that we do not merely *mention* these sentences, nor merely *say of* them that they are true, but simply *assert* them. Now, 'Betty' is a word and Betty is a thing in the world, so we are committed here to the existence of semantic relations of reference and correspondence between words and the world (for what that is worth; recall the discussion from §8.2). 'But we affirm these relations without moving outside the conceptual order'.[12] Or, deflating the metaphor once again, we affirm these semantic relations *using* our language.

Ultimately, McDowell is simply drawing attention to a truism: in order to say how we (or anyone) thinks about the world, we must use words. This is an instance of the more general truism: *in order to talk about anything, I have to talk.* But this truism is to be put to a therapeutic role, in soothing away *Kantian angst.* To explain this, I want to return to McDowell's image that thought 'is *already* hooked up to the world',[13] and to imagine someone asking McDowell: *How did thought first come into being?* There are two very different things that this question might mean, one of which is unproblematic, the other of which must be spurned. (These track the two different ways that we can ask 'how is *x* possible?' discussed in §7.2.)

The question might be presented as a demand for *justification*: as a demand that we must proceed as if there are no thoughts until we can show that we are justified in recourse to thoughts. Such a demand is *literally* incoherent. In order to answer the question (indeed, even to regard it *as* a question) I shall have to assume that I am expressing thoughts, and I shall thereby assume as justified what supposedly stands in need of justification. Now, this might lead the philosopher who demanded a justification into the depths of wild

---

[10] McDowell (1994: 36). McDowell ultimately takes this claim much further than I will here, in claiming that all content is conceptual. I shall take absolutely no stance on this issue, nor on the issue of re-enchanting the world.

[11] McDowell (1998: 489).   [12] McDowell (1998: 489).   [13] McDowell (1992: 45).

Kantian angst. But it need not and should not. We simply need to keep our heads, and realize that the demand for justification is senseless, for it violates the blandest of truisms. It forgets that, in order to talk about something, I have to talk.

This is how I understand McDowell's claim that thought is '*already*' directed at the world. We must dismiss as nonsense the question of how thought 'first' comes into being, when such talk is treated as a demand for a justification. Equally, it is how I understand Putnam's similar claim:

> The right alternative to thinking of truth as a 'substantive property' à la the metaphysical realist … is to recognize that empirical statements already make claims about the world.[14]

For both Putnam and McDowell, the word 'already' is a bit of harmless nonsense, directed at helping us to overcome some terrible nonsense, namely, Kantian angst.

However, if we hear the word 'first' as indicating the *temporal* order, then there is nothing wrong with asking 'how did thought first come into being?' We can ask how creatures evolved who were (biologically) capable of thought. We can ask how a thoughtless embryo grew into a thoughtful adult. We can ask how a mere sign, 'cat', became attached to cats. But answers to these questions will involve human histories and life-stories and etymologies and cats. They are simple requests for information, rather than desperate expressions of Kantian angst, and they are treated as such. Metaphorically put: the answers do not picture reality 'as outside an outer boundary that encloses the conceptual sphere',[15] since the answers are given on the assumption that reality already falls within our conceptual order. More blandly put: in giving my answer, I presuppose that I am talking about things.

All told, we have an answer to Dummett's worry. I can certainly talk to people who do not speak my own language. I can engage in certain questions raised by philosophers of language. But I must give up on a certain 'justificatory' project as incomprehensible.

---

[14] Putnam (1994c: 501; 1999: 55).
[15] McDowell (1994: 26; see also 1994: 34–6, 41–2, 82; 1998: 445–6).

10.3 Curing Cartesian angst to cure Kantian angst

I have discussed some similarities between Putnam and McDowell. Conant, however, has noted a difference which is extremely relevant in this context. In *Mind and World*, McDowell aims first and foremost to lead us away from Kantian angst, in the way just described. McDowell has surprisingly little to say about Cartesian angst. As Conant explains, this is because

> McDowell thinks that it is only once we think through what is hopeless about the . . . Kantian bind . . . that we will be able fully to free ourselves from Cartesian worries about the character of our perceptual relatedness to houses and chairs.[16]

Conant goes on to note that Putnam's natural realism reverses the order of priorities. Putnam wants to make sure that we can *trust* our senses to tell us about the world. This is to tackle Cartesian angst first and foremost:[17] Putnam is not initially concerned with the question of the 'vulnerability' of our senses to the world, but with the question of whether things are as our senses suggest they are. As Conant points out, Putnam's natural realism therefore implicitly suggests 'that the various forms of Kantian scepticism that have come to seem so urgent in recent philosophy can be exorcised simply through the treatment of Cartesian scepticism'.[18]

Conant has drawn attention to an interesting difference between Putnam and McDowell. However, it is worth appreciating *why* this difference has arisen. In particular, we must recall the way in which the model-theoretic arguments raised problems for the external realist.

As Chapter 7 explained, the model-theoretic arguments and the JMT manœuvre form a machine for turning Cartesian angst into Kantian angst. The external realist starts with Cartesian angst. This leads her to postulate a gulf between a theory's being true and its being ideal. The model-theoretic arguments and the JMT manœuvre then lead her towards Kantian angst. If she is to appreciate her predicament, she must certainly think through the hopelessness of the 'Kantian bind'. But *merely* thinking it through will not get her out of her bind. She got into a bind because of her Cartesian angst. To get out of her bind, she needs to overcome her Cartesian angst. Thus Putnam's strategy is as follows: *cure the external realist of her Cartesian angst, and she need never experience Kantian angst.*

---

[16] Conant (2004: 121).   [17] Putnam (2012b: 60) himself describes it this way.
[18] Conant (2004: 121).

Putnam's strategy here is completely in keeping with the diagnosis that I have offered in previous chapters. Unfortunately, Putnam's natural realism goes on to offer a very *specific* analysis of the source of the external realist's Cartesian angst, by focusing on a naïve philosophy of perception. In the remainder of this chapter, I shall explain how this is supposed to work, and why it fails to help us respond to the model-theoretic arguments.

10.4 The natural realist's invocation of naïve perception

As I mentioned earlier, Putnam's natural realist maintains 'that empirical statements already make claims about the world.'[19] His point is that the empirical content of my sentence 'Betty is on a chair' is just *that* Betty is on a chair. This means that Putnam is rejecting the notion of empirical content adopted by the bracketed empiricist in Chapter 5, according to which the empirical content of the claim will concern *only* bracketed experience.

Putnam does not merely reject the bracketed empiricist notion of empirical content, but also rejects the empiricist's notion of perception, in favour of a naïve philosophy of perception, as characterized by one of Putnam's pragmatist heroes, John Dewey. Reflecting on experience, Dewey asks us to consider how an activity like *viewing a chair* is treated by self-styled empiricists. For them,

the chair disappears and is replaced by certain qualities of sense attending the act of vision. There is no longer any other object, much less the chair which was bought, that is placed in a room and that is used to sit in, etc. If we ever get back to this total chair, it will not be the chair of direct experience, of use and enjoyment, a thing with its own independent origin, history and career; it will be only a complex of directly 'given' sense qualities as a core, plus a surrounding cluster of other qualities revived imaginatively, as 'ideas'.[20]

One of Dewey's aims here is to wrest the word 'experience' from the hands of self-styled empiricists, and to return it to its normal, fulsome meaning, according to which we *see chairs*. Putnam embraces this idea. Moreover, he thinks that it will allow him to wrest the notion of empirical content from

---

[19] Putnam (1994c: 501; 1999: 55).   [20] Dewey (1929: 17). Compare Putnam (1999: 159).

the hands of (bracketed) empiricists, and return it to its normal, fulsome meaning. As Barry Taylor summarizes, 'what turns the trick in thus welding representational content onto the world is perception', and naïve perception at that.[21]

It is worth emphasizing the contrast with Putnam's nonrealism, discussed in Chapter 9. Determined to address Kantian angst head-on, the nonrealist retained an extremely narrow conception of experience. The natural realist rejects that conception of experience in favour of something much broader, and then denies that there is any need to engage with Kantian angst at all. Instead, and with self-conscious naïveté, she says simply that we refer to trees with the word 'tree'.[22] And when asked how this is possible, she replies that it is because we see trees—in the naïve sense—all the time.

It is also worth emphasizing the contrast with Devitt's response to the model-theoretic arguments (discussed in §6.1). The natural realist will entirely agree with Devitt's observation that 'we do not need to start from scratch in epistemology and semantics';[23] indeed, to try to start from scratch in semantics is to embrace Kantian scepticism. However, whereas Putnam's natural realism aims to reject the Cartesianism Principle by providing an appropriate philosophy of perception, Devitt's 'naturalism' embraces the Cartesianism Principle. This is absolutely crucial in the context of our discussion, given that our strategy is to avoid Kantian angst by avoiding Cartesian angst.

For all its merits, however, Putnam's natural realism fails to address the full generality of the model-theoretic arguments. Whilst the abstract strategy is right—cure Cartesian angst to cure Kantian angst—the natural realist's focus on philosophy of perception simply fails to address Cartesian angst in its many forms. This is what I shall now explain.

---

[21] Taylor (2006: 138).

[22] Baghramian (2008: 90) states that Putnam's natural realism rejects 'the correspondence theory of truth and an ontology of facts'. Certainly Putnam does not believe in correspondence in the way that the external realist does, but Putnam (1994c: 503; 1999: 58; 1995b: 21–2; 2012a: 85; 2012b: 68–9) undoubtedly countenances reference, and correspondence too, in the minimal sense that I have been discussing; see §§1.2 and 8.2.

[23] Devitt (1984b: 276; see also 1984a: 194).

10.5 The generality of the model-theoretic arguments

A central version of the model-theoretic arguments arises from the idea that the world sits behind a veil of sensations. It is initially plausible that we will be able to block that argument by setting our philosophy of perception aright (though I shall question this in the next section). But, as I explained in Chapter 6, sceptical veils can be woven from fabrics other than sensations—there are veils of public ideas, of observables, of phenomena, and of flux—and it is just implausible that the associated versions of the model-theoretic arguments can be resolved by focusing on philosophy of perception. Natural realism is therefore insufficiently general to handle the genuine generality of the model-theoretic arguments.

Naturally, Putnam suggests otherwise. He considers the case of (un)observables in some detail. A model-theoretic argument arises here when an external realist of a certain stripe draws a sharp line between observables and unobservables. Wherever she draws this line, we can characterize it as giving rise to a veil of observables behind which the unobservables mischievously lurk. Or so Putnam thought, as of 'Models and Reality' and for some while longer.[24] But having adopted natural realism, Putnam revisits this:

> The problem that really bothered me was not that 'the problem would arise anyway wherever one drew the line between observables and unobservables' (although that is the way I thought about it); the real source of the problem, although I failed to recognize it, was that one 'place to draw the line,' namely, at *qualia,* seemed to have absolute metaphysical priority.[25]

Putnam is telling us that, when he first formulated the model-theoretic arguments, he believed that all 'outer' objects—even canonically observable objects such as cats and cherries—are unobservable in principle. Thus the veil of observable objects just *was* the veil of sensations, so far as he was concerned.

This is interesting intellectual autobiography from Putnam. And certainly if an external realist likewise regards cats as unobservable in principle, then she too will have conflated the veil of sensations with the veil of observables. Her problems might then be resolved by a solid grounding in philosophy of perception. But other attitudes are available to the external realist. Imagine an external realist who has a wide but shallow view of perception (I mentioned such a character in §5.1). She thinks that a visual experience

---

[24] Putnam (1980b: 472; 1989: 353).   [25] Putnam (1994c: 465n46; 1999: 20n46).

of the cat Betty involves the world directly, rather than going via interme-
diary 'inner' objects. Or at least, she thinks that the experience involves
Betty directly, and allows us to refer to Betty because we see her all the
time. But our external realist also thinks that the experience of Betty does
not involve the very *molecules* that comprise Betty. Molecules themselves
are not directly perceived, she says, for they are (canonically) *unobservable*.
And our external realist now starts to entertain the following worry: even if
we knew absolutely everything there is to know about all the (in principle)
observables—which are given in experience—*still* we might be massively
and hopelessly mistaken about the (in principle) unobservables.

To run the model-theoretic arguments against this external realist, we
do not need to establish that she is *tacitly* endorsing a view according to
which all she ever 'really' observes is her sensations. Indeed, we can grant
her that there is *no* question concerning our access to cats, say. What we
need her to realize is that she has bought into a picture of empirical content
according to which a veil of observables screens off the unobservables (this
was the point in §6.4). Cartesian angst will now give way to Kantian angst,
concerning how we could even have *thoughts about* things that are too small
to see. To overcome this version of the model-theoretic arguments, then,
we need to do more than embrace a naïve view about *perception*. We need
to explain how to avoid postulating a veil of observables at all.

The same point is even clearer when we consider the version of the
model-theoretic arguments that concerns the 'veil of flux' (see §6.5). One
response to this problem is simply to maintain that there simply are no
eternal Forms lurking behind the veil. This has some undeniable appeal.
But the veil of flux can easily be recast as a veil of *concrete* objects that
screens off all *abstract* objects, and there are notorious difficulties in denying
that there are any abstract objects at all. So let us suppose that we do want
to talk about abstract objects. Then we need to avoid thinking in terms of a
sceptical veil of concrete objects. But we cannot hope to show that *this* was
the product of a faulty philosophy of perception. It would be nothing short
of desperation to maintain (for example) that naïve perception allows us
to enter into epistemological and semantic connections with mathematical
objects.[26] The veil of sensations has nothing to do with *this* problem.

---

[26] As once suggested by Maddy (1990: 58–67); compare MacFarlane's (2004: 264–5) worries about
'McDowell's Kantianism'.

This shows that a plausible natural realism needs to do more than wed itself to a naïve philosophy of perception. And, of course, Putnam does offer us more. For example, he tells us that both the use of instruments and the use of language are 'way[s] of extending our natural powers of observation' to canonically unobservable objects like individual molecules.[27] Concerning instruments, canonically observable objects function as intermediaries for investigating canonically unobservable objects: we look at the computer display to find out about the happenings in the particle accelerator. Concerning language: we begin to individuate the molecules as objects that are 'too small to see' but which comprise Betty.

This strikes me as exactly right. However, the crucial point of this claim is that we are able to extend our powers of *observation* to canonically unobservable objects, in part because we can *refer* to unobservable objects. So, perhaps we can respond to the question 'how can we talk about cats?' by saying 'because we see them all the time' (see §10.1). But we cannot respond to the question 'how can we talk about molecules?' by saying 'because we see them all the time'. It would be better to say that we can observe molecules because we can talk about them *and* that we can talk about them because we can observe them. And it would be best of all to drop the idea of a directional 'because', and simply say: *our referential and observational capacities cannot be sharply separated.*

10.6 Renewed Cartesian angst about ordinary objects

We have just seen that philosophy of perception cannot be all of our response to the model-theoretic arguments. In fact, I now want to suggest that philosophy of perception is simply a red herring. Naïveté about perception does not even help us to deal with Cartesian scepticism about observable objects.

Natural realism is certainly not committed to the view that even an ideal theory might be radically false, where 'ideal' means 'getting everything right at the level of experiences'. After all, natural realists think that I have genuinely different *experiences* when I see a cat and when I hallucinate a cat (if the latter is even an experience). This naturally leads to a *disjunctivist* theory

---

[27] Putnam (1994c: 502; 1999: 56; see also 1994b: 186; 2005: 577). McDowell (1998: 464–5) says similar things, though see Putnam (2012a: 86n41).

of perception, so called because (simplifying a little) when it seems to me as if I am seeing a cat, I am in one of two subjectively indiscernible states: I am *either* seeing a cat, *or* I am hallucinating one.

To formulate her central thesis, the disjunctivist evidently needs to help herself to the idea that two distinct states can be subjectively indiscernible. But as Crispin Wright has noted, this is enough to generate Cartesian angst.[28] Let us say that a theory is *subjectively ideal* just in case it seems to me as if I have all the experiences that the theory says I have. More precisely, whenever a subjectively-ideal theory says that I have an experience, *either* I am actually having that experience *or* some subjectively indiscernible bad disjunct obtains. Cartesian angst now returns in the form:

Even a subjectively-ideal theory might be radically false.

Now, this might be thought to violate a second key thesis of disjunctivism, that the good disjunct and the bad disjunct have *no highest common factor*. However, this locution is apt to mislead, since the disjuncts have in common precisely that they are *subjectively indiscernible*. In fact, there are two ways to understand the rejection of a 'highest common factor',[29] but neither helps to deal with the renewed Cartesian challenge.

The disjunctivist might be making a *metaphysical* claim. In particular, she might be denying that there is a special *object* common to the good and the bad disjunct, in virtue of which they are subjectively indiscernible.[30] This is all very well, but it is irrelevant here. The renewed Cartesian challenge does not foist bracketed sensations (or any other *objects*) upon the disjunctivist. To repeat a point from §5.5, the 'veil of sensations' locution does not specifically indicate that certain objects can be stitched together into a curtain. Rather, it draws attention to the fact that there is a level of abstraction at which we can hold things fixed, whilst making changes elsewhere, in order to generate sceptical anxieties. Whether or not it is associated with special objects, the level of subjective indiscernibility—which the disjunctivist herself countenances—is just such a level of abstraction.

At one time, Putnam's natural realism explicitly denied that there is any special *object* common to the good and the bad disjunct.[31] However, for

---

[28] Wright (2002: 340–7; 2008: 397–400) pushes this worry against disjunctivists.

[29] I am drawing here upon Byrne and Logue's (2008: 65ff.) excellent discussion of metaphysical versus epistemological disjunctivism.

[30] This is Hinton's (1967: 226) point.

[31] Putnam (1999: 129–32, 152–4); for discussion, see Byrne and Logue (2008: 68*n*21).

reasons unrelated to the present discussion, Putnam has become dissatisfied with this.[32] Putnam now favours a position which emphasizes that 'what we perceive depends on a *transaction* between ourselves and the environment'.[33] Whatever its merits as a philosophy of perception, such *transactionalism* shares with disjunctivism the idea that there is a good state of perception—which Putnam characterizes in terms of a transaction with our environment—and a bad state of hallucination—which Putnam regards as something like engagement with a *fiction*—and the preceding worry can simply be reformulated in these terms.

So much for the metaphysical reading of the disjunctivist's claim that the good and the bad disjunct have no highest common factor. However, there is also an *epistemological* reading of that claim. The point here would be that there is no state of *evidence* (or *justification*, or *warrant*, or whatever) shared by the good and the bad disjunct. Crudely put: hallucinating a cat provides scant evidence that there is a cat in the vicinity, whereas seeing a cat provides rather better evidence.[34] An immediate corollary of this thought is that the disjunctivist cannot subjectively discern what evidence she has. Of course, the disjunctivist is welcome to think of evidence this way. However, it simply deepens the renewed Cartesian challenge. Holding everything fixed at the level of what is subjectively indiscernible will now *additionally* leave me without any evidence.

The disjunctivist, and naïve philosophy of perception more generally, provides us with no ammunition against the renewed Cartesian challenge. We can consequently imagine the natural realist making the following desperate speech:

I concede that I should feel some Cartesian angst. But the alleged problem with Cartesian angst is that it leads, via the model-theoretic arguments and the JMT manœuvre, to Kantian angst, and that the latter is incoherent. (At least, that was the argument against external realism in Chapter 7.) I agree with you that Kantian angst is incoherent. But I can resist the slide into Kantian angst. For my thoughts simply are *in contact with the world. To quote McDowell, they are 'already hooked on to the world'.[35] To quote Putnam, they 'simply do refer to whatever they are about'.[36]*

---

[32] See Putnam (2012c: 632–3).   [33] Putnam (2012c: 636).

[34] This is McDowell's (2008: 380–2) point; for discussion, see Byrne and Logue (2008: 65–8).

[35] McDowell (1992: 45).   [36] Putnam (1994c: 491; 1999: 46).

To see why this is so *desperate*, we must recall the dying words of the external realist, overheard in §7.5. We imagined an external realist who has recognized the incoherence of Kantian angst, and who responds to this incoherence by maintaining that this shows simply that *something* fixes reference. This external realist nevertheless clings tightly to her former theory of empirical content (perhaps adequacy to bracketed experience) and so continues to experience Cartesian angst. Indeed, she admits that her claim that *something* fixes reference is utterly without empirical content; it is, as it were, a *super*-empirical claim. The problem with the natural realist's speech is precisely that it will turn natural realism into a verbal variant of this desperate version of external realism. When that external realist talks of what is 'empirically adequate', our imagined natural realist will talk of what is 'subjectively ideal'; when that external realist uses the word 'super-empirical', our natural realist will talk of what is 'empirical'; but the outcome is exactly the same.

The natural realist must *not* fall into the trap of making the preceding speech. Nor will she, I hope. For nothing I have said shows that natural realists *must* entertain Cartesian angst. I have simply pointed out that natural realists have *yet* to explain how to avoid Cartesian angst. And more specifically, I have argued that the distinctive hallmarks of naïve philosophies of perception all fail to block Cartesian angst. (I shall offer the natural realist a way out of Cartesian angst in §13.2 but, as just suggested, it will not depend in any essential way upon her philosophy of perception.)

This indicates—with apologies to Putnam—that the entire issue of *direct* versus *mediated* perception is a red herring in the context of the model-theoretic arguments and our continued battle with scepticism. Perhaps a naïve philosophy of perception should be defended on other grounds; perhaps not. Either way, so long as our focus is on the model-theoretic arguments, we must set aside philosophy of perception and look elsewhere. The natural realist is right to aim for a position according to which Cartesian angst does not arise, but she has not given us one.

11

Justificationism

Throughout the 1980s, Putnam advanced *justificationism*, according to which there is a tight conceptual connection between truth and idealized justification. He ultimately dropped justificationism, in favour of natural realism. However, since his natural realism has failed to deal adequately with the problems of Part A, this might have been premature. Accordingly, we must investigate justificationism.

I make two claims in this chapter. First, the justificationist cannot present a plausible conceptual connection, sentence-by-sentence, between truth and (even idealized) justification. Second, even if the justificationist could connect truth with idealized justification, this would not provide us with a sufficiently broad response to Cartesian angst. The complicated literature that connects truth with idealized justification is—somewhat like the discussion of philosophy of perception—a red herring in the present context.

This chapter is a little technical, and it will help to introduce a few abbreviatory devices. I shall use '☆___' as a monadic sentential operator, which is to be read roughly as saying 'someone at some time has a justified belief that ___'. I shall say that φ is *justified* when $☆\varphi$, and I shall say that φ is *justifiable* when $\Diamond ☆\varphi$.

11.1 The gap between truth and actual justification

Here is a block-headed schematic attempt to connect truth with justification:

Simplistic Biconditionals. $\varphi \leftrightarrow ☆\varphi$

This scheme is utterly implausible. Truth is not sufficient for justification, as shown by the following example.[1] The number of hairs on my head is either even or odd. Suppose without loss of generality that it is even, and let '*e*' express this proposition. Clearly ¬☆*e*, since no one has ever counted the hairs on my head, and no one ever will. So *e* although ¬☆*e*.

Equally, justification is not sufficient for truth. If we were reading '☆___' as 'someone at some time *knows* that ___', then the factivity of knowledge would yield the right-to-left direction of the Simplistic Biconditionals scheme (so understood). But it is simply part of our own practices of giving and rescinding empirical justifications that *mere* justified belief is not factive.[2] Now, it might be countered that our practices need to be *reformed*, and there are in fact two possible positions according to which justifications are factive. However, neither is acceptable to the justificationist.

The first attempt to maintain that justification is factive begins by declaring that all empirical justification goes via 'inner' (bracketed) experiences. If justification, so obtained, is to be factive, then we must continue by declaring that certain 'inner' (bracketed) experiences are infallible guides to the presence of certain 'outer' objects. This approach obviously leads to a form of nonrealism inseparable from methodological solipsism.[3] For the reasons given in Chapter 9, the justificationist must reject this approach.

The second attempt to maintain that justification is factive embraces a kind of epistemological disjunctivism. The idea is as follows: if I am actually seeing a cat, then I am justified in my belief that there is a cat in front of me; but if I am merely hallucinating, then I have no justification at all.[4] Now, we could use the word 'justification' in this way if we liked, and this might well supply us with a factive '☆'-operator. However, the justificationist will find no solace in this notion of 'justification'. By the epistemological disjunctivist's own admission, I cannot subjectively discern which of the disjuncts obtains, and so I cannot subjectively discern whether I am 'justified'. So, exactly as in §10.6, Cartesian angst simply spills over into the question of whether I am *ever* 'justified'. This consequently provides no

---

[1] I take this example from Künne (2002: 160–3; 2007: 334–5), but similar examples abound in the literature.

[2] Compare Putnam (1977: 487–9; 1979c: 226–7; 1979b: 615; 1980b: 479–80; 1980a: 102–3; 1981b: 214n6; 1981c: 56–7; 1983a: xvi–xviii; 1983b: 84–6; 1986b: 114–15) on his affinities with, but ultimate distance from, Dummett.

[3] Indeed, the idea is strongly reminiscent of Carnap's (1928a: §49) notion of an indicator.

[4] Thanks to Rory Madden for discussion on this.

clue as to how to overcome Cartesian angst. Since the justificationist wants to link truth with justification precisely because she wants a satisfying way to avoid Cartesian angst, she must also reject this approach.

11.2 Idealized justification and counterfactuals

During the 1980s, Putnam attempted to avoid the difficulties just discussed by allowing himself some measure of *idealization*.[5] In particular, Putnam tells us that 'to claim of any statement that it is true ... is, roughly, to claim that *it could be justified were epistemic conditions good enough*'.[6] Putnam is suggesting that the very *concept* of truth is tied to the concept of (idealized) justification. If we ignore Putnam's caveat 'roughly', then his suggestion amounts to the following scheme:[7]

Idealized Biconditionals. $\varphi \leftrightarrow (c_\varphi \:\Box\!\!\rightarrow\: \star\varphi)$

where 'c_φ' describes appropriate epistemic conditions that would be good enough for obtaining a justified belief that φ, and where '$\Box\!\!\rightarrow$' indicates the standard subjunctive conditional.

The presence of a subjunctive conditional demands comment. On the standard Lewis–Stalnaker construal, we assess '$c_\varphi \:\Box\!\!\rightarrow\: \underline{\quad}$' by considering what holds at all arbitrarily close possible worlds at which c_φ. But which worlds are 'arbitrarily close' to the actual world depends upon what is actual. Thus our assessment of '$c_\varphi \:\Box\!\!\rightarrow\: \underline{\quad}$' *depends* upon whether or not φ. If the justificationist were trying to *define* truth, then this observation would prevent her from employing subjunctive conditionals. That, in turn, would bar her from invoking any measure of idealization.

The justificationist should reply by emphasizing that she is *not* aiming to define truth, or to reduce it to simpler notions. (Throughout the 1980s, this was always Putnam's line.)[8] Nor, for that matter, is she aiming to define justification.[9] Our justificationist holds simply that truth is *constrained* by the fact that it is *conceptually* connected with justification. She hopes that this

---

[5] Putnam (1980a: 100–3; 1981a: 200; 1981c: 49–56, 122–3; 1982a: 41; 1983a: xvii; 1983b: 84–5; 1986b: 115).

[6] Putnam (1990b: vii).

[7] Wright (2000: 343ff.) and Künne (2002: 153) read Putnam this way.

[8] Putnam (1978b: 108–9; 1980a: 103; 1981c: 56; 1988: 115; 1990b: viii; 1991c: 421); though Putnam (1992b: 373) confesses that he *had* held out hope of reduction after all.

[9] Putnam (1982a: 42; 1982b: 6, 10; 1983a: xvii).

conceptual connection will block Cartesian angst, and so will prevent her from sliding into incoherent Kantian angst.

The justificationist should make a similar response against the following objection, raised by the natural-realist Putnam:

> Let us suppose, as seems reasonable, that whatever makes it rational to believe that φ makes it rational to believe that φ would be justified were conditions good enough. If my understanding of the counterfactual 'φ would be justified if conditions were good enough' is *exhausted* by my capacity to tell to what degree it is justified to assert it, and that is always the same as the degree to which it is justified to assert φ itself, why did I bother to mention the counterfactual at all?[10]

This has the makings of an excellent objection against a *nonrealist* who wants to invoke counterfactuals. However, our justificationist simply denies that the understanding of a sentence is exhausted by an understanding of the degree to which it is *justified* to assert it. If it were to be exhausted by anything, it would be exhausted by an understanding of the degree to which it *would be justified* to assert it in sufficiently good circumstances.[11] But *exhaustion* is not really to the point in any case, since the justificationist is not aiming for anything *reductive*. She just thinks that there is a conceptual connection between truth and idealized justification.

In short, there is no reason in principle why a justificationist cannot invoke counterfactuals, as in the Idealized Biconditionals scheme. However, to give content to this scheme, we need to say more about what sufficiently good epistemic conditions might be like (i.e. what c_φ will look like, for each φ). Putnam proceeds by example:

> If I say 'There is a chair in my study,' an ideal epistemic situation would be to be in my study with the lights on or with daylight streaming through the window, with nothing wrong with my eyesight, with an unconfused mind, without having taken drugs or been subjected to hypnosis, and so forth, and to look and see if there is a chair there.[12]

It is worth emphasizing that these conditions are *not* narrowly first-person psychological. They involve chairs, sunlight, and drugs. There is no hint that we could explain (idealized) justification without mentioning what

---

[10] Putnam (2007: 162); I have replaced 'S' with 'φ', for uniformity. See also Folina (1995: 147–9) and Putnam (2012a: 79).

[11] The relevant idealized biconditional is just $(c_\varphi \; \Box\!\!\rightarrow \; \varphi) \leftrightarrow (c_{(c_\varphi \Box\rightarrow \varphi)} \; \Box\!\!\rightarrow \; \star(c_\varphi \; \Box\!\!\rightarrow \; \varphi))$.

[12] Putnam (1990b: viii; see also 1983a: xvii).

is happening in the world around us.[13] This is just to repeat that our justificationist is not a nonrealist.[14]

Now, sufficiently good epistemic conditions for forming a justified belief that there is a chair in my study might involve daylight streaming through the window. But bright sunlight is disastrous if we want to inspect very light-sensitive materials. More generally, we cannot expect that there is a single condition which is suitable for justifying *every* true proposition. Putnam notes this, offering two examples of pairs of 'statements which we can only verify by failing to verify other statements'.[15] Where φ and ψ are such statements, Putnam's point is that sufficiently good conditions for determining that φ are incompatible with sufficiently good conditions for determining that ψ. Now, Putnam does not mention it,[16] but an immediate consequence is that in such cases there are *no* sufficiently good epistemic conditions for determining that $\varphi \wedge \psi$. Consequently, $\varphi \wedge \psi$ might be an *unjustifiable truth*. Over the next two sections, I shall establish that there might be unjustifiable truths, and this will cause havoc for the justificationist's attempt to tie truth to (idealized) justification.

11.3 Fitch-like unjustifiable truths

I shall begin by looking for a purely *conceptual* source of unjustifiable truths. The search is inspired by Fitch's proof of a schematic source of *unknowable* truths.[17] Now, *knowability* and *justifiability* are obviously different notions, and our focus is on justifiability. However, both Wright and Wolfgang Künne have suggested that we can adapt Fitch's reasoning to provide us with a schematic source of unjustifiable propositions.[18] In this section, I shall explain why I hesitate to agree with them.

---

[13] Putnam (1991c: 421; 1988: 115–16) also emphasizes this.

[14] And if Putnam was only ever a nonrealist whilst he was a justificationist, then this is just to say that our justificationist is simply *inspired* by some of Putnam's work.

[15] Putnam (1990b: viii).

[16] Until Putnam (2001c), prompted by Wright (2000).

[17] See Fitch (1963: 138–9); this is a key step on the way to Fitch's knowability paradox.

[18] Wright (2000: 355–7) and Künne (2002: 157–65); see also Putnam (2001c: 596–7). Edgington (1985: 559) suggests that a slightly different version of Fitch-style reasoning will hamstring Putnam's 'internal realism' (I revisit this in footnote 30). Putnam (1990b: viii) comes tantalizingly close to discussing the problem himself; and as Künne (2002: 159–60) notes, Putnam (1969: 443) had considered such cases long before his internal realism.

In §11.1, we noted that it may well be true that I have an even number of hairs on my head even though no one ever has a justified belief to this effect; that is, $e \wedge \neg{\star}e$. Admittedly, no one *actually* has a justified belief in this conjunction, because no one has a justified belief in the left conjunct. But it would be easy (though tedious) for someone to obtain such a justification: all they would need to do is count the hairs on my head. Anyone who *did* count the number of hairs on my head would, though, no longer be justified in believing that nobody ever has a justified belief that e; for a moment's reflection would convince them that *they themselves* have a justified belief that e. More generally, it seems that it is impossible to be justified in simultaneously believing e and $\neg{\star}e$. That is, $\neg\Diamond{\star}(e \wedge \neg{\star}e)$.[19]

The foregoing informal argument is supposed to generalize, establishing all instances of the following scheme:

Fitchian Unjustifiables. $\neg\Diamond{\star}(\varphi \wedge \neg{\star}\varphi)$

The idea is that a little bit of logical-cum-conceptual reasoning will yield a wholly *schematic* source of unjustifiable truths. However, I want to contest this reasoning by offering two counterexamples to the scheme. (It is worth noting that both counterexamples depend upon the *non-factivity* of justification, which the justificationist defended in §11.1. This means that neither counterexample could be of any use in blocking Fitch's *knowability* paradox. In Appendix II, I discuss formal attempts to derive the Fitchian Unjustifiables scheme, and I explain where these two counterexamples would block that derivation.)

The first family of counterexamples is due to Christopher Kelp and Duncan Pritchard.[20] The counterexamples essentially involve 'Paderewski cases',[21] and here is an example in their style:

The bouffant-pianist scenario. Jo has counted the hairs on the head of Paderewski the pianist, and has come to a justified (true) belief that the number of hairs is even. Jo is also of the very sensible opinion that it is vanishingly unlikely that anyone should ever bother to determine the number of hairs on the head of Paderewski the statesman. Thus Jo has a justified (false) belief that nobody, herself included, will ever have a

[19] Künne (2002: 162) reasons in roughly this way; though I discuss this further in Appendix II.
[20] Kelp and Pritchard (2009: 335–8).
[21] As introduced by Kripke (1979: 265–6).

> justified belief that the number of hairs on Paderewski's (the statesman's) head is even. But, unbeknownst to Jo, there are not two Paderewskis: the pianist *is* the statesman. Jo therefore has inconsistent beliefs, but her beliefs are nevertheless justified.

Where 'p' expresses the proposition that Paderewski has an even number of hairs on his head, we have apparently described a possible scenario in which $\star(p \wedge \neg \star p)$, contradicting the Fitchian Unjustifiables scheme. However, this counterexample can itself be contested. Jo's beliefs only escape from being obviously contradictory (even to Jo) because she has not realized that Paderewski is Paderewski, as it were. For this reason, Jo would represent her conjunctive belief, not as being of the form '$\varphi \wedge \neg \star \varphi$', but as being of the form '$\varphi \wedge \neg \star \psi$'. Arguably, *we* should also represent her belief in this way, marking the difference between the two 'modes of presentation' of Paderewski in the beliefs we attribute to Jo. If so, then this fails to constitute a counterexample to Fitchian Unjustifiables.

I shall say more about the bouffant-pianist scenario in a moment. Before that, let me consider a second family of counterexamples. These play rather more freely with what it takes to have a justification.[22]

> **The opaque-justification scenario.** Kate has obtained a belief that φ, via an extremely reliable method. However, Kate does not believe that this method is extremely reliable. She thinks (mistakenly) that it is highly prone to mistakes, although she thinks that it is better than nothing. So Kate thinks (mistakenly) that her belief that φ falls short of *justification*. Thus Kate has a justified true belief that φ, though she (falsely) thinks that her belief is unjustified.
>
> In fact, Kate's caution is very sensible. All the evidence available to Kate suggests that she should *not* place much faith in the method by which she came to believe that φ. Now, Kate might also be aware that there are *other* methods for determining whether or not φ. However, Kate is basically certain that no one will ever implement them, and

---

[22] Thanks to Alex Grossman for suggesting examples in this direction.

rightly so: these other methods are extraordinarily arduous. So Kate comes to a justified (but false) belief that nobody will ever have a justified belief that φ.

Abstractly, we have described a possible situation in which $\star(\varphi \wedge \neg\star\varphi)$, again threatening the Fitchian Unjustifiables scheme. Perhaps this counter-example could be contested by questioning the notion of justification that it employs. Without getting drawn into that issue, this highlights an important point. The case for Fitchian Unjustifiables depends crucially on how we individuate beliefs (as in the bouffant-pianist scenario) and on what we think about justification (as in the opaque-justification scenario), and neither issue is philosophically uncontentious. We cannot look to *schematic* sources of unjustifiable truths without much more *philosophical* investigation.

11.4 Empirical unjustifiable truths

Let us suppose, which might be contested, that the bouffant-pianist scenario does indeed give us a situation in which $\star(p \wedge \neg\star p)$. This sort of scenario is very easy to reproduce. It requires only that we describe a scenario in which someone mistakenly (but with some justification) thinks that the same word is used for two different things, when in fact it is used for only one thing. Such mistakes can happen easily enough. Thus we may have found a machine for blocking wholesale the very idea that there are any *unjustifiable* truths of the form '$\varphi \wedge \neg\star\varphi$': if they are true, then someone in a Paderewski-esque scenario could be justified in believing them.

The opaque-justification scenario does not generalize so readily. It requires that there is, in fact, some method for coming to believe that φ which is good but not obviously so. Whether there is such a method will surely depend upon the φ in question, and is surely (at least in part) an empirical matter. This suggests that empirical issues bear upon the question of whether or not there are any unjustifiable truths. Once we have realized this, however, we do not need to immerse ourselves in Fitch-style skulduggery. We can just look directly to *empirical* sources for unjustifiable truths.

Künne has offered a lovely example of a straightforwardly empirical scenario that might yield an unjustifiable truth:[23]

Künne's fragile-fresco scenario. In a newly discovered catacomb workers are suddenly struck by the sight of a centuries-old fresco-painting. But, alas, it is so sensitive to light that it is bound to disappear very soon. Let us suppose that it would disappear within seconds if one were to throw so much light on it that one could recognize what it depicts, but that it would stay just long enough for carefully measuring its size if the lighting were to remain as dim as it is now. Then one can either verify a statement to the effect that on that wall there is now a fresco-painting which depicts such-and-such, or one can verify a statement to the effect that on that wall there is now a fresco-painting which measures so-and-so many square centimetres, but one cannot verify both.

In this scenario, we are supposed to conclude that there will be an unjustifiable truth of the following form: the fresco depicts such-and-such and it is so-and-so many square feet. However, the example falls slightly short of showing this. It may *now* be impossible for the workers who find the fresco to determine both the representational features and the size of the fresco. But there *was* a time at which both *were* easy to determine, for the frescoist herself *was* able to do exactly that. It is doubtful that the justificationist's notion of justification is limited to considering only what actual people would *now* be able to do, rather than what past (or future) people would have been (or would later be) able to do.[24] And indeed, our '☆'-operator is to be read in terms of some person at some time having a justified belief. Thus, in the permissive 'someone, somewhen' notion of justification that we have adopted, Künne's purportedly unjustifiable truth is justifiable after all.

---

[23] Künne (2002: 151); the scenario is a verbatim quote from Künne, which I have displayed in keeping with the other scenarios.

[24] As Wright (2000: 351–2) notes.

Here is a scenario designed precisely to avoid such temporal issues:[25]

The truth-and-beauty-bombs scenario. A conceptual artist creates a sculpture comprised of two identical lead boxes, A and B. Both boxes contain a small bomb and a radioactive source attached to a drawing mechanism. Both sources have a 50 per cent chance of decaying within a designated time period. If the source does decay within that period, the drawing mechanism will produce a beautiful picture within the box; otherwise, nothing will happen. Either box can be opened and inspected. However, the boxes are cunningly configured so that opening one box will detonate the bomb within the other box, thereby utterly obliterating its contents and making it impossible to know anything about whether or not a picture was ever drawn inside. As it happens, a picture is drawn in both boxes.

The truth-and-beauty-bombs scenario evidently overcomes one issue associated with Künne's fragile-fresco scenario. However, neither example is quite perfect. It is not, after all, *only* possible to investigate a fresco by examining it with the naked eye under natural light: we might be able to investigate it under very low light conditions by using some clever technology.[26] Similarly, depending on the precise set-up of the truth-and-beauty-bombs scenario, it might be possible to inspect the contents of the boxes without opening them: we might drill a small hole in the side of the boxes, through which we insert a fibre-optic camera, always being careful to avoid the explosives.

Interesting though these thoughts are, they do not fundamentally change the landscape. To bring this point home, here is a final example of an empirical unjustifiable truth, this one supplied by Putnam:[27]

The lonely-universe scenario. The origins of life are always completely random. This, among other things, prevents us from being able to form any decently justified beliefs about whether or not there are any aliens

---

[25] The conceptual artist was inspired by Strip 26 of *A Softer World*.

[26] Moretti (2000: 102) suggests this sort of answer.

[27] Putnam (1991c: 410; 1992b: 364–5; 1994a: 242n5, 261; 1994c: 503–4; 1995a: 293–7; 1995b: 12; 1999: 58, 95) presents this as an objection against his 'internal realism'. Putnam (1975b: 238) had once offered similar reflections on the possibility that there are infinitely many binary stars.

outside of our lightcone. As it happens, there are no intelligent extrater-restrials anywhere in our universe.

The last sentence of this story now comes across as a very plausible candidate for being an empirical truth that cannot be justified.

The import of all of these examples is as follows: *for all we know* a pri-ori, *it might be physically impossible to determine the truth value of some logically complex claims.* In Chapter 8, I maintained that a good anti-realist must not attempt to deny the possibility of the mass-extinction scenario (of §8.1) on a priori grounds. Equally, I suggest, she should not attempt to deny the mere possibility of empirical sources of unjustifiable truths on a priori grounds.

11.5 A failed a priori argument against unjustifiable truths

In fact, there *is* an a priori argument against the very possibility of unjus-tifiable truths. Moreover, it is one that might be tempting to would-be justificationists. The argument therefore deserves our immediate atten-tion. If successful, it will apply to every putative source of unjustifiable truths, but it will be easiest to approach the argument by focusing on the truth-and-beauty-bombs scenario.

Recall the Perspective Question, introduced in §8.4. When presented with a story which purports to describe a possibility, it is in keeping with a rejection of the God's Eye point of view to ask ourselves from whose point of view that story is being told. In particular, we must ask ourselves: *from whose point of view is the story of the truth-and beauty bombs scenario told?* The story ends by claiming that a picture is drawn in both boxes. However, by hypothesis, no participant in the story is in a position to affirm the conjunction. So the worry is that the story can only be told from a *God's Eye* point of view. If so, we might be able to rule out the truth-and-beauty-bombs scenario a priori.

There is a straightforward reply to this objection. Let us alter the end-ing of the truth-and-beauty-bombs scenario so that, instead of saying that pictures are drawn in both boxes, we say:

> ... The conceptual artist opens box *A* and discovers that it contains a picture. But inevitably, as box *A* opens, box *B* explodes, leaving us forever wondering what it contained. 'That's *art!*' the artist says with a grin.

The amended story could now simply be narrated by an art critic, reviewing the piece. ('*That's* art?', the review ends, with lip curled in disgust.) By logic alone, though, exactly one of the following conjunctions will be true in this amended story:

(i) a picture was drawn in box *A* and a picture was drawn in box *B*
(ii) a picture was drawn in box *A* and a picture was not drawn in box *B*

Since both conjunctions are equally unjustifiable, and since one must be true, there is at least one unjustifiable truth. Thus the narrator of the story—indeed, the artist herself—can point out that there is at least one unjustifiable truth, without apparently invoking any God's Eye point of view.

This reply, though, essentially depends upon employing *classical* logic; it fails immediately if we instead adopt *intuitionistic* logic.[28] Moreover, since no participant in the story could ever know *which* of the unjustifiable conjunctions is true, we might wonder what sense there is in claiming that one of them *is* true. Thus, one might react to this by maintaining that classical logic itself enshrines a God's Eye point of view, and retreating to intuitionistic logic.

This line of thought is clearly related to Dummett's core line of argument in favour of intuitionistic logic.[29] To explain why it should be resisted, it will help to recall the discussion of Moorean contradictions in §8.4. Our example Moorean contradiction was:

(M) I believe that is raining, and it is not raining.

(Note, in passing, the similarity between a Moorean contradiction and an instance of the Fitchian Unjustifiables.) As I pointed out in §8.4, whilst no one can reasonably assert (M), much less assert it as known fact, there is

---

[28] The inference $\varphi \vdash (\varphi \wedge \psi) \vee (\varphi \wedge \neg \psi)$ is not intuitionistically valid. The argument also assumes that (determinate) truth distributes over the logical connectives, which Dummett (2007a: 349–50) queries in empirical cases.

[29] Indeed, Dummett (2007a: 348; 2009) advocates principles that yield the scheme: $\varphi \rightarrow \neg\neg\star\varphi$. This turns any claim of the form $\varphi \wedge \neg\star\varphi$ into an intuitionistic contradiction.

no great difficulty in recognizing that (M) *might* be true. Indeed, we were able to represent the possibility described by (M), by outlining the errant-sprinkler scenario, and this story clearly did not require a God's Eye point of view. My claim is that the same is true of the truth-and-beauty-bombs scenario. The scenario is told from *our* point of view, not in the sense that someone could have reported the story as known fact, but in the sense that *our* own theory allows that the story *might* be true.[30] The possibility of unjustifiable truths is 'not the product of some metaphysical' imposition.[31] On the contrary, our own best physical theory allows for the possibility described by the truth-and-beauty-bombs scenario, and we should not try to overturn that theory a priori.

11.6 The difficulties in tying truth to idealized justification

The Idealized Biconditionals scheme of §11.2 is an immediate casualty of the preceding discussion. Let it be an unjustifiable truth that p. Since p, the relevant biconditional tells us that $c_p \,\Box\!\!\rightarrow\, \star p$. But the consequent of this subjunctive conditional is impossible, for it is *unjustifiable* that p. It must also therefore be impossible that c_p. So there are *no* (possible) epistemic conditions that are good enough for deciding that p (when p). This is not exactly happy but, as Wright has pointed out, it immediately gets worse.[32] Since it is to be true that $c_p \,\Box\!\!\rightarrow\, \star p$ (when p), and since it is impossible that c_p, it is *necessarily* true that $c_p \,\Box\!\!\rightarrow\, \star p$. The Idealized Biconditionals schemes is surely also presented as a necessary (conceptual) truth. So we obtain that $\Box p$, which is absurd. After all, each of our unjustifiable truths could easily have been false.

With these sorts of considerations in mind, Wright has suggested that Putnam should replace the Idealized Biconditionals scheme with:[33]

Provisional Biconditionals. $c_\varphi \,\Box\!\!\rightarrow\, (\varphi \leftrightarrow \star\varphi)$

---

[30] This answers Edgington's (1985: 559) objection. Our theory should not contain 'p and no theory ever devised implies that p', and nor should I believe 'p and no one ever believes that p'; but our theory and our belief system should be able to *represent* both possibilities.

[31] Putnam (2001c: 598); compare Putnam's (1990a: 71) remarks on 'the distinction between what is and what is not physically possible'.

[32] Wright (2000: 356n25).   [33] Wright (2000: 350).

Again, this advanced as a *conceptual* constraint on truth.[34] Now, in the case when it is an unjustifiable truth that p, the relevant provisional biconditional tells us simply that $c_p \,\square\!\!\rightarrow\, \neg p$. This does not sink the Provisional Biconditionals scheme in the way that it sinks the Idealized Biconditionals scheme. However, since it is *true* that p, this highlights that the Provisional Biconditionals scheme fails to deliver any verdict on whether or not any unjustifiable truths are actually *true*. Putnam therefore claims that, so far as the justificationist is concerned, the Provisional Biconditionals scheme offers no real advance over the Idealized Biconditionals scheme, since it leaves us without a definition of truth.[35]

Now, if the justificationist's aim were to define truth, Putnam's objection would indeed be decisive. But the justificationist's aim is emphatically *not* to define truth, but merely to *constrain* it (see again §11.2). More specifically, since she wants to reject the Cartesianism Principle, her aim is to rule out the possibility of a justified belief, that is incapable of any better justification, but that is nevertheless false. The Provisional Biconditionals scheme blocks precisely that possibility.[36]

In fact, if this is all the justificationist requires, then the Provisional Biconditionals scheme is slight overkill. She could instead make do with:

Provisional Conditionals. $c_\varphi \,\square\!\!\rightarrow\, (\varphi \rightarrow \neg \star \neg \varphi)$

This says simply that in sufficiently good circumstances, you will not form a justified but false belief. But in fact, both the Provisional Biconditionals and the Provisional Conditionals schemes are too strong. To show this, we can consider a final scenario:[37]

> **The indeterministic-error scenario.** We are testing whether or not φ. The test we are using almost invariably delivers the correct verdict when it is administered perfectly. And, indeed, we do so administer it. We

---

[34] Wright (2000: 362–4) suggests that it is appropriate for the natural realist.

[35] Putnam (2001c: 599–600); Putnam talks of a 'reduction sentence', rather than definition.

[36] Wright (2000: 349–50) makes this observation; thanks to Rob Trueman for pointing this out to me.

[37] This is a slight variation on Putnam's (2001c: 598–9n8; 2012a: 75–6) more recent discussion of intelligent extraterrestrials, where he describes a situation in which we are justified (on probabilistic grounds) but mistaken in believing that they exist. Wright (2000: 362–3n30) raises worries about indeterminacy (attributing them to Williamson), but does not particularly explore them since his only aim is to show that the Provisional Biconditionals scheme is at least as good as the Idealized Biconditionals scheme.

have excellent evidence for believing all of the above. We wait for the result, and it comes back positive. Based upon all of this, we come to believe that φ. But ours is an indeterministic universe, so that any test—no matter how perfectly devised or administered—can sometimes deliver the wrong verdict. And, sad to say, this is one of those very rare occasions where the test has given a false positive.

The attempt to connect truth with idealized justification is rapidly degenerating into the search for a 'logic of confirmation'. Given the fate of that project, I shall not pursue it any further. However, it is worth emphasizing that all of the difficulties that the justificationist has encountered arose from within our *own* practices. They are forced upon us 'internally', just as surely as is the Independence Principle. And we must not be tempted to ascend to some *external* perspective, just to try to repair the supposedly conceptual connection between truth and justification.

11.7 Renewed Cartesian angst, again

The preceding discussion has been both mildly technical and rather depressing. I shall close this chapter with something less technical but, sadly, no less depressing.

The justificationist's aim was to block Cartesian angst by claiming that truth is conceptually tied to justification. The Cartesianism Principle, recall, tells us that even an ideal theory might be radically false. Reading 'ideal' as 'ideally justified' (that is, 'justified in sufficiently good circumstances'), all of our various schemes—Idealized Biconditionals, Provisional Biconditionals, and Provisional Conditionals—would block this possibility, thereby blocking this potential inlet for Cartesian angst. This would have been most welcome, if only the schemes had been any good.

But here is another way to raise Cartesian angst. The sceptic grants that all of your beliefs are, in fact, justified. The question that she raises is whether any of them are *ideally* justified (that is, whether your beliefs were obtained in sufficiently good epistemic conditions). Unless we have a guarantee of that, we have no guarantee that they are not all false. Of course, the Simplistic Biconditionals scheme would have supplied such a guarantee, since it connected truth directly with unidealized justification, but we were forced to abandon that scheme. And all of our other candidate schemes connect truth with *idealized* justification, so they do not even speak to the sceptical problem just raised. We therefore have the following renewed version of Cartesian angst:

All of your beliefs could be justified but false.

This point is worth spelling out a little. In §11.2, I pointed out that sufficiently good epistemic conditions are *world-involving*. To repeat Putnam's example:

If I say 'There is a chair in my study,' an ideal epistemic situation would be to be in my study with the lights on or with daylight streaming through the window, with nothing wrong with my eyesight, with an unconfused mind, without having taken drugs or been subjected to hypnosis, and so forth, and to look and see if there is a chair there.[38]

So, to determine whether or not I am in sufficiently good conditions for assessing whether or not there is a chair in my study, I need to determine whether or not I have taken perception-altering drugs. How do I know whether or not *that* obtains? Presumably there are sufficiently good conditions for assessing whether or not anything is wrong with my eyesight, which will again be world-involving. But how do I know whether or not *those* conditions obtain? And so it goes.[39] Either at some point in this regress I withdraw entirely to within my own head—thereby collapsing into nonrealism—or all of my conditions remain world-involving and so, for everything said so far, perhaps never realized. In terms of our various attempts to connect truth with idealized justification, the question is simply whether we are *ever* in sufficiently good epistemic conditions for forming beliefs.

The problem just raised for the justificationist is very similar to the problem raised in §10.6 for the natural realist. Even if the justificationist can answer Cartesian angst, in its original form, Cartesian angst simply reformulates itself and returns to haunt us. And, as usual, unless we can block *all* levels of Cartesian angst, we shall slide ignominiously into Kantian angst. Justificationism has provided us with no solution to the problems of Part A.

---

[38] Putnam (1990b: viii; see also 1983a: xvii).
[39] This regress is hinted at in Putnam (1988: 115; 1992b: 373).

Part C
Dissecting Brains in Vats

12

Putnam's brain-in-vat argument

The constant challenge of Part B was to provide a satisfying way to prevent Cartesian angst from arising. We failed to rise to that challenge. Nonrealism adopted the picture of reasoning from a God's Eye point of view, and so amounted to external subjective idealism. Natural realism's focus on philosophy of perception was a red herring. And so was justificationism's attempt to connect truth with idealized justification.

It is worth comparing the two red herrings just mentioned. In both cases, we attempted to provide a satisfying barrier to some form of Cartesian angst, only to watch Cartesian angst reformulate itself and burrow under our barrier. For this reason, I am going to change tack. Instead of trying to produce a philosophically satisfying account of why some particular form of Cartesian angst does not arise, I shall look for a wholly general response to Cartesian angst. Proceeding at such a level of generality is likely to leave us bereft of any satisfying philosophical picture, but perhaps that is our fate.

12.1 The internal and external poles of realism

As I shall use the name, *internal realism* is a philosophical position defined as follows. It accepts the Independence Principle, for reasons given in Chapter 8. It likewise accepts the Correspondence Principle. However, it utterly repudiates *all* versions of Cartesian angst.

This use of the name 'internal realism' is multiply appropriate. First, it is obviously closely connected with Putnam's own use. Whilst Putnam's 'internal realism' was not one position but several overlapping positions, it always embraced the Independence and Correspondence Principles (at least from 'within'), and it was always opposed to Cartesian scepticism.

Second, as I emphasized in Chapter 8 and have reiterated several times since, the only concrete element in the debate between external realists and their opponents concerns the correct attitude towards Cartesian scepticism. Internal realism is therefore defined precisely in opposition to external realism on the one and only point of philosophical substance.

By itself, of course, this definition tells us nothing about *how* the internal realist will prevent all Cartesian angst from arising. However, the third reason for using the name 'internal realism' is that my internal realist will seek to block all Cartesian angst by appealing to Putnam's famous brain-in-vat argument, a high point of Putnam's 'internal realist' writings. This argument uses semantic reasoning to refute the thought that everyone, everywhere and everywhen, might really be a brain in a vat. In this chapter, I shall defend this argument, and in subsequent chapters I shall show that this argument provides us with precisely the resilient response to Cartesian angst that we were unable to find during Part B.[1]

This does not, though, mean that we must become internal realists. For there is a large middle ground between external and internal realism, as I have defined them. Indeed, we have a continuum of philosophical positions, with internal and external realism representing opposite poles. External realism frets about almost every Cartesian sceptical scenario. Positions towards the externalist pole countenance many (but not all) Cartesian sceptical scenarios. Positions towards the internalist pole countenance very few (but some) of them. Internal realism brushes them all aside. Our question therefore becomes: *where should we place ourselves between these two poles?*

To answer that question, I must determine exactly how much scepticism we should countenance. With that aim in mind, in Chapter 15 I shall consider a panoply of sceptical challenges of various lesser grades, such as the hypothesis that I (and only I) was only recently envatted. Here Putnam's brain-in-vat argument breaks down. This suggests that we cannot be internal realists. But it also suggests a methodology for determining exactly where to locate ourselves between external and internal realism. We could lay down a plethora of putative sceptical scenarios, determine exactly which ones succumb to a brain-in-vat argument, and then draw a line in the sand *there*, to indicate precisely where we stand on the spectrum between internal and external realism.

---

[1] A fourth reason for calling it 'internal realism' is to link it with Carnap's distinction between internal and external questions; I return to this in §16.8.

That methodology would be completely bankrupt. As I show in Chapter 16, there is nothing much to say about *where* to stand between external and internal realism. We must therefore abandon—or perhaps overcome—the debate between external and internal realism.

12.2 Putnam's BIV argument

Putnam asks us to consider the putative sceptical scenario:[2]

> **The BIV scenario.** All sentient creatures, including me, are eternally envatted brains. That is, for the entire duration of their lives, they were, are, and will always be brains in vats. However, everyone is wired into an infernal machine, which subjects us all to electronic neural stimulations, so that everything appears normal.

In the first instance, Putnam's BIV argument aims to show that this scenario does not obtain. But note the extremity of the scenario: every sentient creature, anywhere and anywhen, is envatted. In Chapter 15, I investigate what happens when we relax these strictures. Until then, I focus exclusively on this extreme scenario. Thus, I shall write 'x is a BIV' as a shorthand for 'x is an eternally envatted brain, and so is everyone else'.

The scenario is *so* extreme that we must immediately ask why anyone should much care about it. After all, showing that I am not a BIV gives me scant comfort that I know very *much* about the world. But as Putnam explains, his aim is not to investigate epistemology.[3] Instead, his aim is to pursue the realism debate, along the lines just outlined.

Let us say that a scenario is a *nightmarish* Cartesian sceptical situation if it renders false all of my contingent beliefs about the 'external' world. It may leave intact my beliefs about my 'inner' mental states (that I am having a certain sensation as of seeing a cat, for example). And it may leave intact my beliefs about certain necessities (perhaps that $2 + 2 = 4$; perhaps various physical laws). But almost everything that I believe about the specifics of my situation is false.

---

[2] Putnam (1981c: 5–17; see also 1977: 487; 1986b: 110–12). Naturally, the word 'envatted' is implicitly defined in terms of brains and vats, *pace* Chalmers (2005: §9 note 1).

[3] Putnam (1981c: 6).

The dialectical situation seems to be the following. The BIV scenario exemplifies *nightmarish* Cartesian scepticism (or near enough). And it can just seem *obvious* that we cannot rule out the scenario; *obvious*, that is, that we might actually be BIVs. So it can just seem to be a philosophically neutral starting point, that a theory which gives every appearance of being true could really be hopelessly false. Nightmarish Cartesian angst (and so also external realism) therefore presents *itself* as a neutral starting point for any philosophical enquiry.[4]

Putnam's BIV argument overturns this line of thought. Various different reconstructions have been offered of Putnam's BIV argument.[5] However, the most straightforward version of the argument is:[6]

(1) A BIV's word 'brain' does not refer to brains.
(2) My word 'brain' refers to brains.
(3) So: I am not a BIV.

From the two premises, it follows that my language is not the language of BIVs, so that I am not a BIV. I therefore take it that the argument is obviously valid. It remains to justify the premises. In brief, (1) will be justified by rejecting all magical theories of reference, whereas (2) will be justified by disquotation in my home language.

12.3 The language of BIVs

Let Brian be a BIV. By a process of exclusion, I want to show that Brian's word 'brain' cannot refer to brains, thereby establishing premise (1).

The most obvious way for Brian's word 'brain' to refer to brains would be for Brian to interact directly with brains, whilst using the word 'brain'. This might happen if Brian were a neurosurgeon. But, of course, he is not. Even if he is being fed electronic signals that simulate his being a neurosurgeon, Brian is simply a brain in a vat and has never wielded a scalpel. More generally, Brian never actually interacts directly with brains whilst using the word 'brain'.

---

[4] This is why, as Putnam (1992b: 362) reports, Lewis claimed that internal realism *must* be false; see also Stephens and Russow (1985: 211–12).

[5] Alternative reconstructions pursue Putnam's (1981c: 15; 1986b: 111) considerations of the truth clause for a BIV's utterance 'I am a BIV'. I shall touch upon this approach in Chapter 14.

[6] Drawing from Tymoczko (1989: 282), Brueckner (1992: 127), Ebbs (1992b: 239), Wright (1992a: 74), Putnam (1992b: 369), Warfield (1998: 129), and DeRose (2000: 124).

An alternative way for Brian's word 'brain' to refer to brains would be by interacting with someone else who had interacted directly with brains. Suppose, for example, that Brian had talked to a neurosurgeon; the neurosurgeon's word 'brain' would refer to brains, for sure, and Brian could presumably start to use words in the same way as the neurosurgeon. But, of course, this also never happens. Since Brian is a BIV, everyone else is a BIV (by definition). So no one else has ever directly interacted with a brain.

Another way for Brian's word 'brain' to refer to brains would be if 'brain' abbreviated a long (rigidified) description which happened to apply to precisely those (possible) things which are brains. But Brian's causal relationship with the world is *so* skewed that this cannot happen either.[7] Just as Brian has not (appropriately) interacted with brains, so he has not (appropriately) interacted with: skulls; water; pinkish-beige squishy things; or anything else that one might plausibly use to refer to brains descriptively. And what holds for descriptions holds equally well for *intentions*: Brian has no way to form intentions that would allow him to refer to brains.

The sceptic might attempt to contest all this, by making the following suggestion:

Brian can refer to the sensation *as of looking at a brain. He can then intend for the word 'brain' to mean something like 'anything which would cause sensations as of looking at a brain, when interacted with in certain appropriate ways'. This will enable Brian to refer to brains after all.*

Even granting that Brian can refer to his sensations, there are two deep problems here. First, Brian cannot talk about *causation*. Putnam asks us to consider a 'paradigm case' of what Brian would call 'causation'. There might

be a counterfactual-supporting relation between 'fires' (in certain 'substances') and 'smoke' in Brian's world; a relation that may be relied on, used to justify inference licences, etc., just as the relation of causation is relied on, used to justify inference licenses, etc., among the unenvatted, but it is not the same relation. Brian can no more refer to what the unenvatted call 'causation' than he can refer to what the unenvatted call 'fire'.[8]

---

[7] Putnam (1981c: 16–17; 1992b: 369; 1993a: 73) and Sainsbury (1991: 418–19) emphasize this point.

[8] Putnam (1992b: 362; 1994a: 287); I have amended the quotation slightly, to talk about 'Brian' rather than generic 'Brains in a Vat'.

Putnam's point is that the envatted 'fire-to-smoke' sequence is not a cause-and-effect sequence, but (at best) a sequence of two effects which share a common cause (the infernal machine into which Brian is wired). So the 'paradigm cases' of apparent causal sequences are not genuine causal sequences. Indeed, the only apparent causal sequences which are genuine causal sequences are those when Brian himself is the cause and the effect is a sensation.[9] For example, Brian's decision 'to move his arm' causes a sensation as of moving his arm. Consequently, Brian may be able to 'lasso' a few genuine cause-and-effect sequences under the word 'causation'—namely, those cases where he is the cause and a sensation in him is the effect—but it is implausible that Brian's word 'causation' thereby covers those cases where something *external* causes his sensations.[10] And that is what Brian would need to do, to refer to brains.

But Brian would need to do more than refer to causation, and this leads to the second problem with the suggestion. Given Brian's situation, electronic signals, rather than brains, *in fact* cause Brian's sensations as of looking at a brain. This is why Brian has to intend for the word 'brain' to mean something like 'anything which *would* cause sensations as of looking at a brain, when interacted with in certain *appropriate* ways'. The problem now is that Brian has never actually seen, heard, smelled, touched, or tasted anything, nor witnessed others doing so (since he actually has no eyes, ears, nose, skin, or tongue). So, even if Brian can get some grip on causation, he cannot get any grip on the requisite notion of a *possible, appropriate interaction*. Once again, there is just no way for Brian to talk about brains.

The moral really is very simple. Brian has a thoroughly messed-up relationship with the world. We should not, then, be surprised that his semantic relationship with the world is equally messed-up.[11] This is ultimately what prevents his word 'brain' from referring to brains. But I should add that there is nothing particularly special about Brian's word 'brain' here: parallel problems affect Brian's words 'vat', 'tree', 'hole', 'water', 'book', 'kettle', and 'geodesic'. No direct interaction, indirect interaction, description, or intention will allow Brian to refer to vats, trees, holes, water, book, kettles, or geodesics.[12]

---

[9] Thanks to Rob Trueman and Christina Cameron for pushing this point.

[10] This recalls the argument of §6.4, which extends one of Putnam's (1981c: 53) arguments.

[11] I am invoking a very mild form of semantic externalism here; I say more about this in Chapter 17.

[12] So it is not especially important that 'brain' should be a natural kind term, *pace* Chalmers (2005: §9 note 1).

12.4 Internal scepticism and magic

The sceptic might contest (1) by making the following suggestion:

Perhaps there is an intrinsic connection between certain narrow mental contents and certain objects, such that anyone (anywhere, anywhen) with that mental content thereby automatically referred to those objects. Then the envatted and the embodied can refer to exactly the same things.

The sceptic's suggestion is obviously not logically inconsistent, in the narrow sense that we cannot force the sceptic to contradict herself. Moreover, if there is an intrinsic connection of the sort the sceptic suggests, then the BIV argument fails.

It is worth emphasizing that the suggested intrinsic connection is precisely a 'noetic ray' between narrow mental contents and external objects.[13] It demands that objects *cry out* to be named in certain ways. It is a magical theory of reference, *par excellence*. It is utterly without empirical content, which was the force of Putnam's contention, discussed in Chapters 4–7, that the external realist requires a magical theory of reference. But it is magical in a *stronger* sense. It demands that there is *no* connection—not even a wholly 'unempirical' connection—between what we do in our environment and what we refer to.

An analogy might help show why this is *so* disastrous.[14] An utterly naïve divine command theory of ethical value would tell us that there is a property, *magical-goodness*, of situations or events, whose possession is settled by the whim of a capricious deity. Now, is it really possible that goodness itself *might actually be magical-goodness*? The idea is obviously not logically inconsistent, in the narrowly syntactic sense. But, whilst I can perhaps make sense of the idea that there are good gods or bad gods, the idea that these gods might decide what goodness *is* just fails to engage with the practice of *ethics*. Similarly: a magical theory of reference, of the sort the sceptic suggests, fails to engage with the practice of *talking about things*. It is *inconceivable* that reference might be that way.

Inconceivable though it is, the sceptic can always keep the BIV scenario alive by appealing to the *bare formal possibility* of a magical connection

---

[13] Putnam (1980a: 101; 1981c: 51; 1984a: 85).
[14] The analogy echoes Putnam (1983a: ix–x). Compare also Malchowski (1986: 171–3).

between thoughts and things. There is little more that we can say to convince such a sceptic that she is wrong. Fortunately, we are now justified in simply *ignoring* her.

In part, this follows simply from the aims of the BIV argument, as outlined in §12.2. BIV scepticism naturally arises from supposedly neutral observations concerning brains. Nightmarish Cartesian angst (and hence external realism) consequently presents itself as falling out of such philosophically neutral observations. If BIV scepticism is to be defended by appealing to magic, then it can no longer claim to be philosophically *neutral*. We shall have established what we wanted. However, this illustrates a more general pattern concerning when we must respond to the sceptic and when we can simply ignore her, and this pattern merits comment.

Some sceptics aim to raise problems from *within* our own web of beliefs. They aim to show that, by our own lights, we cannot rule out a certain sceptical scenario. Since they use our own tools of reasoning against us, Putnam calls them *internal sceptics*. In these terms, BIV scepticism clearly begins as a version of internal scepticism. And it would be irresponsible to dismiss the internal sceptic as presenting an unanswerable but uninteresting challenge.[15] She commands our interest precisely because she has employed our own tools against us.[16]

The BIV argument is a response to (a form of) internal scepticism. But, whilst discussing the argument, the sceptic notices that there is a gap in the argument which cannot be plugged by logic alone. In particular, the sceptic realizes that she can keep her scepticism alive by endorsing a magical theory of reference. But if she does this, then she cannot continue to claim to be an *internal* sceptic. She is no longer employing our own tools against us. Instead, she has presented a bare formal possibility as if it were something we should take seriously.

Sceptics who are not internal sceptics do not command our interest. There is no shame in ignoring them. To illustrate this point, a further analogy will help (again, due to Putnam). Suppose we had (somehow) proved that the sceptic's challenge did involve a bare formal contradiction. The

---

[15] Devitt (1984a: 50) recognizes that BIV scepticism is a form of internal scepticism, but dismisses it as 'unanswerable' but '*uninteresting*' (1984a: 52) because it is implausible. Sprevak and McLeish (2004: 228) rightly contest claims about plausibility in this context.

[16] Ebbs (1992b: 241), Putnam (1994a: 284–5; 1998: 525–7), and Wright (2008: 401) all press this point.

sceptic might respond by questioning the laws of logic that we employed in our proof. If we answer her there, she might question the assumptions that we used in that answer. So it goes. But such a sceptic has moved from internal scepticism to *infinitely regressive scepticism*.[17] As Putnam points out, we should feel under no pressure to attempt to refute the infinitely regressive sceptic. Indeed, we should realize that the very idea of *refuting* her is empty. Since the infinitely regressive sceptic can query any premise in any argument, the only hope of silencing her is to find an argument so powerful that anyone who questions it *spontaneously dies*.[18] Even then, the sceptic's ghost would haunt us, claiming that we had not *won* the argument, any more than we would have won an argument if we had told a joke so funny that our opponent had died laughing. The infinitely regressive sceptic is not to be silenced, but ignored.

The moral is sufficiently important that it bears repeating. We should only ever care about defeating the internal sceptic. When BIV scepticism is presented as a version of internal scepticism, we can establish premise (1). When the sceptic tries to defend the possibility that we are all BIVs by invoking magical theories of reference, her challenge can be ignored, because it is no longer an instance of internal scepticism.

12.5 Disquotation in my language

With (1) established, I turn to premise (2). This is justified by disquotation in my home language.

When I offer a semantics for my language, I have no option but to speak *in my language*.[19] Accordingly, I am allowed to disquote meaningful expressions in my language. And it can hardly be doubted that 'brain' is a meaningful expression of my language. Thus, my word 'brain' refers to brains.

Inevitably, things are not quite that simple. Pedants will need me to emphasize that I am restricting the argument to sincere, literal utterances in

---

[17] Putnam (1994a: 284–5).

[18] I owe this observation to a newspaper clipping posted on a pinboard in Harvard's Emerson Hall; sadly, I cannot track the clipping down.

[19] Brueckner (1986: 164–7) questions whether or not I can accept disquotation in *English*. But as Hill (1990: 109–10), Wright (1992a: 76–7), Christensen (1993: 304–13), and Falvey and Owens (1994: 127–8) note, what matters is disquotation in *my* language, whatever that language is. (The fact that I might have many 'home' languages, noted in Chapter 19, is obviously not relevant here.)

my habitual language.[20] A slightly more interesting issue arises from apparent reference failure. Consider the expression 'black bile', from the theory of medical humours. There is no black bile. So, does 'black bile' refer to black bile? It depends how we understand the claim. If we regard 'black bile' as the name of a special sort of thing—a kind, or a universal, or whatever— then the name 'black bile' is as referentless as the name 'Bilbo Baggins'. But there is no difficulty in saying that 'black bile' applies to black bile and only to black bile.[21] This is how we should understand talk about reference and natural kinds in the context of the BIV argument. Thus the premises of the argument should be read as follows:[22]

> ($1^\dagger$) It is not the case that a BIV's word 'brain' applies to brains and only brains.
>
> ($2^\dagger$) My word 'brain' applies to brains and only to brains.

Of course, if there are no brains in the possible world described by the BIV scenario, and if we also think that a BIV's word 'brain' applies to nothing at all, then we will obtain (vacuously): for all x, a BIV's word 'brain' applies to $x \leftrightarrow x$ is a brain. But this is doubly irrelevant. First, by definition, a BIV's world contains at least one brain. Second, the application conditions are not merely extensional: my word 'brain', unlike a BIV's, *would* apply to x if x *were* a brain.

These pedantries out of the way, I turn to a more serious objection to premise (2). To understand the objection, it will first help to consider the following Moorean response to BIV scepticism:[23]

> (4) BIVs have no hands.
>
> (5) I have hands.
>
> (6) So: I am not a BIV.

---

[20] 'Sincere' and 'literal' for obvious reasons; 'habitual' to rule out *faux amis* cases, e.g. where I (without realizing it) find myself surrounded by Germans and say the word 'Gift', thereby (arguably) referring not to gifts but to poison.

[21] This addresses a concern raised by Warfield (1998: 134) in this context, and by Brueckner (1999: 242–5; 2001: 111–12) for a related argument. I realized that this is how the point should be expressed thanks to discussions with Mark Sainsbury, David Sosa, Michael Tye, and Rob Trueman.

[22] So I understand the BIV argument very much on the lines of the 'New Simple Argument' discussed by Brueckner (2006: 438).

[23] G. E. Moore (1939).

This simply inverts the sceptic's standard challenge:

(4) BIVs have no hands.

(¬6) I am a BIV.

(¬5) So: I have no hands.

In short, the sceptic agrees with (4). However, (5) is precisely what she *contests*, since if I am a BIV then it will merely *seem* to me that I have hands, when in fact I have none. The sceptic thus accuses the Moorean of flagrantly begging the question. In a similar way, the BIV sceptic might respond to Putnam as follows:

I applaud your rejection of all magical theories of reference. Consequently, I endorse premise (1). However, this just shows us that BIVs are not merely deceived into thinking that they have hands. They are also deceived into thinking that their language disquotes.

The BIV sceptic is therefore offering the following sceptical challenge:[24]

(1) A BIV's word 'brain' does not refer to brains.

(¬3) I am a BIV.

(¬2) So: My word 'brain' does not refer to brains.

Putnam's BIV argument now looks like nothing more than a *semantic* instance of a more general Moorean anti-sceptical strategy.

Several Moorean moves are of course available to Putnam. However, I want to focus on a non-Moorean response to the sceptic that trades upon the distinctively *semantic* aspect of Putnam's argument.

If I am to understand the sceptical argument that concludes with (¬2), then the argument must be presented in *my* language. In particular, if I am in fact a BIV, the sceptical argument must be presented in the language of BIVs. So, whenever I use the word 'brain' or 'brains' during the course of the argument, I fail to talk about brains (given the argument in §12.3). But then I cannot even mean, when I assert (¬3), *that* I am a BIV. More generally, even to understand or talk about the BIV scenario at all, we need to rely on disquotation. Otherwise, the BIV scenario does not confront us with the worry *that* we are brains in vats. In short, premise (2) is required by

---

[24] Brueckner (1994: 80; 1995: 81ff.) sees Putnam's BIV argument as generating 'content scepticism' in essentially this way.

the BIV sceptic herself.[25] 'The game played by [scepticism] has been turned against itself.'[26]

Turning the tables in this way feels rather glorious. But, even as the sceptic retreats into the shadows, we might start to worry that the table-turning tactic is a bit too cheap. To make this worry vivid, consider:[27]

(N) Either it is raining or I do not believe that it is raining.

(N) is just the negation of the Moorean contradiction mentioned in §8.4. So no one can coherently deny (N). But, it can easily be false. Here, once again, is a mundane story which illustrates that possibility:

The errant-sprinkler scenario. I glance out of the window and see water falling. I thereby come to believe that it is raining. In fact the water is not rain, but the spray from a nearby errant sprinkler system. So I believe that it is raining, and it is not raining.

The sceptic may now argue as follows:

In turning the tables on me, you have shown only that (2) is something like (N). No one can coherently deny it, but it can still be false.

Fortunately, there is a *deep* difference between (2) and (N). As emphasized in the discussion of the Perspective Question in §§8.4 and 11.5, we can *represent* that (N) is false, though we cannot believe it to be. By contrast, the falsity of (2) is genuinely *unrepresentable*.[28] To see why, suppose we try to tell a story which ends with the claim:

... So my word 'brain' (as I habitually use it) does not refer to brains.

If the story is told in my (habitual) language, then how am I to understand the last word ('brains') in the story? Not, I have been told, as referring to brains. But then how? Really: *How?* I am simply at sea. So the story must instead be told in some other language. But then the story does not make

---

[25] This argument closely follows Tymoczko (1989: 284–6).

[26] Kant (1787: B276). This feature of the BIV argument allows it to qualify as a *transcendental argument* in the sense made famous by Strawson (1959; 1966).

[27] Compare Stroud's (1994: 246) response to a certain transcendental argument; thanks also to Daniel Elstein for prompting me to consider the relationship between the BIV argument and Moorean contradictions.

[28] So I am following Brueckner's (1996: 277) reply to Stroud (1994: 246).

(2) false, for (2) *is* a claim within my (habitual) language, and so if the story is true then (2) *itself* does not assert *that* my (habitual) word 'brain' refers to brains.

The moral here is that philosophers who think that (2) could be false have the following thought in mind. Ordinarily, I speak a *benighted* language. This means, for example, that the last word in the sentence 'that thing is a brain' fails to refer to brains. However, when I present the semantics for my language, I magically start to speak some *other* (more correct) language. This means that the last word in the sentence 'my word "brain" does not refer to brains' does refer to brains. But to think that I suddenly change my language when I present semantics is just to cling to a magical theory of reference for semantic claims.[29] This can be dismissed, for just the reason that we dismissed magical theories of reference in general.

12.6 The nature of brains

We have established (2). However, it is important to appreciate the limits of what can be established by appealing to disquotation in a home language. To illustrate them, it will help to shift the example.

We cannot know the chemical structure of (pure) gold without some empirical investigation. Consequently, we can sketch outré sceptical situations in which we are *mistaken* about the hidden structure of gold. These can generate a sceptical worry that

(7) It is not the case that my word 'gold' applies to exactly those things whose atoms (on the whole) contain 79 protons.

I have nothing very special to say about that worry. My point is only that entertaining it could not possibly give me any reason to doubt that

(8) My word 'gold' applies to gold and only to gold.

To rephrase the moral of the previous section: whatever fixes the meanings of the words we use in ordinary utterances (e.g. the meaning of the last word of my sentence 'that thing is gold') *also* fixes the meanings of the words we use in semantic claims (e.g. the meaning of the last word of my sentence

---

[29] Ebbs (1996: 514–18) similarly argues that content scepticism vacillates between a 'subjective' and an 'objective' point of view.

'my word "gold" refers to gold').[30] Both words are the *same* word, and so apply to exactly the same things. Probably these are things whose atoms (on the whole) contain 79 protons; but then again, given my sceptical worries, perhaps they are not.

Setting sceptical worries aside, it is physically necessary that x is gold iff x's atoms (on the whole) contain 79 protons. But this does not undercut the preceding comments either. All it shows is that my sceptical worry, expressed by (7), involves a physical impossibility. That is hardly news. Plenty of things that are (or were) epistemically possible are physically impossible. The moral is simple: disquotation in my home language is easy to come by, whereas knowledge of the structure of gold requires serious empirical investigation.[31]

This moral might, however, be thought to give us a fresh reason to reject (1) *without* embracing a magical theory of reference. The thought runs as follows:[32]

The BIV scenario should be read as presenting us with a hypothesis about the (utterly) hidden structure of the world. In particular, it presents us with the thought that every manifest object—be it a bar of gold bullion or a brain—is, at a more fundamental level, just an electronic signal generated by an infernal machine that causes certain sensations in the BIVs.

Having rejected all magical theories of reference, we might well wonder what a BIV's word 'brains' refers to. A natural thought is that it will refer to some electronic signal or other, since that is all that a BIV ever experiences. But since brains simply are electronic signals generated by an infernal machine (by my hypothesis), this means that a BIV's word 'brains' might refer to brains after all. So the justification of (1) assumes what was to be established: that we are not BIVs.

This sceptical thought is simply incompatible with the BIV scenario. The BIV scenario requires that brains are *not* themselves electronic signals. Rather, the scenario demands that brains are the pinkish-beige, squishy things which are wired into an infernal machine and *receiving* electronic signals. Equally well, the scenario demands that the infernal machine that generates the

---

[30] This point is due to Davidson (1987; 1988: 664) and Burge (1988: 659–61). Wright (1992a: 74–6) and Falvey and Owens (1994: 117–23) invoke it in (partial) defence of the BIV argument.

[31] So I am unmoved by Brueckner's (1995; 1999: 238–47; 2001) worries concerning content scepticism.

[32] This is inspired by Falvey and Owens (1994: 133–6) and Chalmers (2005: §§3–4); however, Chalmers's position is probably closer to *metaphysical scepticism* (see §14.4, especially footnote 16).

electronic signals is not *itself* an electronic signal. In short, the BIV scenario does not and cannot present us with a hypothesis about the (utterly) hidden structure of brains, vats, machines, or anything else involved in outlining the very set-up of the scenario. Unsurprisingly, these are precisely the things to which a BIV cannot refer unless reference is magical.

Time and again, we end up repeating the same point: the BIV argument defeats BIV scepticism, provided that we prohibit a magical theory of reference. This simple point has three immediate consequences. First, BIV scepticism cannot present itself as a version of internal scepticism. Second, nightmarish Cartesian angst has not yet been given any neutral motivation. And third, external realists cannot lend their philosophical picture an air of neutrality by leaning upon the 'obvious unanswerability' of BIV scepticism. But the BIV argument can provide us with still deeper consequences. The task for the remainder of Part C is to plumb its depths.

13

The resilience of the brain-in-vat argument

In Chapter 12, we saw the BIV argument defeat BIV scepticism. In this chapter, I shall show that the BIV argument provides us with a deeply *resilient* response to the Cartesian sceptic.

The Cartesian sceptic will likely contest this point. Although BIV scepticism fails, she will claim that a little reflection gives rise to worries of the form: *maybe our predicament is not so very different from Brian's.* In this way, Cartesian angst attempts to renew itself, as it has successfully renewed itself so many times throughout Part B. However, I shall show that we cannot resurrect a nightmarish Cartesian sceptical scenario—not even an ineffable one—by reflecting on Brian's situation.

Throughout this chapter, I shall continue to assume that Brian's situation exemplifies a kind of nightmarish Cartesian scepticism. In fact, it is far from clear that it does. Brian does not speak my language, so it is unclear that he thinks something false when he thinks (for example) 'I am looking at a zebra', or 'that cloud looks like a chimney stack', or 'the weather is unusually clement for August', or whatever. In Chapter 14, I shall investigate what happens when we stop regarding Brian as a victim of a Cartesian nightmare.

13.1 Rejecting a picture without creating a new one

In the first instance, the BIV argument simply undercuts a strut of support for external realism. Nevertheless, when Putnam first presented the BIV argument, he thought that it neatly highlighted 'the difference between [the] philosophical perspectives' of internalism and externalism.[1] In particular:

---

[1] Putnam (1981c: 49).

Internalist philosophers dismiss the 'BIV' hypothesis. For us, the 'BIV world' is only a *story*, a mere linguistic construction, and not a possible world at all. The idea that this story might be true in some universe, some Parallel Reality, assumes a God's Eye point of view from the start, as is easily seen. For *from whose point of view is the story being told?* Evidently *not* from the point of view of any of the sentient creatures *in* the world.[2]

This passage is the origin of the Perspective Question, '*from whose point of view is the story being told?*', as discussed in §§8.4 and 11.5. And this passage might give us hope that we can replace the 'externalist' picture—of reasoning from a God's Eye point of view—with some glorious new 'internalist' picture.

Certainly we should toss aside the picture employed by external realists. But for reasons that we have already seen, the Perspective Question needs to be handled with great care. In particular, it would be a disaster—akin to accepting that no Moorean contradiction could be true—to suppose that a story is incoherent unless it can be narrated as known fact. When a story is told in an effort to describe some putative possibility, we must ask ourselves only whether or not our best theories allow us to *represent* the possibility in question (see again §§8.4, 11.5, and 12.5). The Perspective Question, when handled appropriately, does not provide us with any new philosophical picture. It simply reminds us not to adopt the picture of the external realist.[3]

So: do our best theories allow us to represent the possibility described by the BIV scenario? Yes and no. Our best all-things-considered theory—an amalgam of physics, semantics, politics, poetry, and everything else—allows us to represent a physically possible world, all of whose sentient inhabitants are BIVs. Brian is a physically possible creature and his world is physically possible. But I cannot represent his world as *my* world. The BIV argument shows that I am not Brian, and that his world is not my own.

Is it then incoherent, or unintelligible, to suppose that I am a BIV?[4] This question is not straightforward. I know very well what it is for something

---

[2] Putnam (1980a: 100; 1981c: 50), Putnam's italics, though I have replaced 'Brain in a Vat' with 'BIV', for uniformity.

[3] Sprevak and McLeish (2004: 236) suggest that the 'internal realist' would present a different version of the BIV argument, and theirs is a plausible reconstruction of how a nonrealist would gloss the BIV argument. However, both Putnam (1992b: 368–9) and Ben-Menahem (2005: 139) note that the BIV argument is acceptable to internal realists exactly as it is.

[4] Both Doguoglu (2008: 119–20) and Ebbs (2012: §4.3) think so.

to be a BIV, and I know that I am no such thing. In that sense, it is simply coherent but false to think that I am a BIV. On the other hand, if the sceptic continues to insist that the BIV scenario has not been answered—that it continues to present us with a source of Cartesian angst—then she *is* using the words 'I might be a BIV' unintelligibly. This point will recur frequently throughout the remainder of Part C.

13.2 Dissolving Cartesian angst without philosophical pictures

The BIV argument does not yield a new philosophical picture. But it does yield a much more resilient response to Cartesian angst than anything we considered in Chapters 10 and 11. The natural realist and the justificationist were looking for neat accounts of how to avoid some specific version of Cartesian angst, but Cartesian angst found a way to sneak back into their lives. The BIV argument allows them to block Cartesian angst once and for all, but it also supersedes their attempts at blocking Cartesian angst. This is what I shall now show.

Disjunctivists distinguish genuine perception from apparent perception. In the *good* case, we see a cat; in the *bad* case, we hallucinate one. In §10.6, I imagined a sceptic asking the disjunctivist how she can rule out that the bad disjuncts *alway* obtain. Putnam hints at an intriguing answer to this sceptical question. He tells us that a hallucination 'is not *directly* a world involving state', but that its 'characterization refers to such a state'.[5] The idea is that there is no way to characterize what it means for two things to be subjectively indiscernible without reference to the good case in which one actually has the experience one hopes one has.[6] But this suggests that we cannot even understand the sceptic's challenge, unless we have sufficient semantic contact with the world to understand what the good case amounts to. This contains the seed of a response to scepticism.

The BIV argument allows this seed to sprout. The sceptic might hope to make her challenge more concrete, by asking us to consider Brian as a

---

[5] Putnam (2001c: 637; see also 1997: 616; 1999: 122; 2001b). I am not distinguishing Putnam's transactionalism from disjunctivism, for reasons given in §10.6.

[6] Compare McDowell's (2008: 380) suggestion that disjunctivists might attempt to run a 'transcendental argument' from the fact that 'experience purports to be of objective reality'. However, Wright (2008: 393) offers decisive criticisms of McDowell's own attempt to complete that argument.

paradigm of someone who only ever deals with the bad disjunct. But, just as Brian cannot talk about the BIV scenario, so Brian cannot talk about the scenario in which he only ever deals with the bad disjuncts. Indeed, he cannot even make sense of the distinction between good and bad disjuncts. Brian might come out with the following words:

The state I am now in is subjectively indiscernible from one in which I am seeing a cat. So either I am seeing a cat (the good disjunct); or I am hallucinating (the bad disjunct), perhaps because I am just a brain in a vat.

But Brian's word 'cat' no more refers to cats than his word 'brain' refers to brains. Brian's attempt to draw a contrast between 'the good disjunct' and 'the bad disjunct' therefore fails to draw the contrast between good and bad disjuncts. Accordingly, if I can even make sense of the sceptical possibility that I am always dealing with the bad disjunct, I know that I am not in that predicament. This is just the BIV argument, recast in disjunctivist terminology.

Such reflections acquire a poetic quality when applied to Putnam's more recent attempt to outline a version of naïve realism about perception. As mentioned in §10.6, Putnam's *transactionalism* maintains that hallucinated objects are something like fictional objects, and that the bad state of perception is something like engagement with a fiction.[7] In these terms, Brian only *ever* engages with fictions. When the BIV argument is recast in transactionalist terms, it amounts to the observation that one cannot engage with fiction unless one has at some point engaged with reality.

Naïve realists about perception can, then, offer their own version of the BIV argument in reply to the Cartesian angst that renewed itself in §10.6. However, this does not particularly speak in favour of naïve realism about perception, since exactly the same response can be offered by advocates of indirect theories of perception. The sense-datum theorist can equally well maintain that we cannot characterize sense data except by reference to what they are typically *of*. When the sense-datum theorist talks about having a catish sense datum, the barbarous neologism 'catish' is not something that I can understand, unless I understand that it is the kind of sense datum that one typically has when seeing a cat. So the sense-datum theorist should maintain that Brian's expression 'catish sense datum' no more refers

---

[7] Putnam (2012c: 637).

to catish sense data, than his word 'cat' refers to cats. In short: neither the problems that have arisen in this book, nor the BIV argument wielded as a general response to those problems, mandates any particular philosophy of perception.

Similar comments apply to the justificationist's attempt to avoid Cartesian angst by drawing a conceptual connection between truth and justification. At the end of Chapter 11, Cartesian scepticism renewed itself, by threatening that we might be entirely justified but never *ideally* justified, so that all of our beliefs were false. Brian is supposedly a paradigm of someone whose beliefs are all justified (or at least, as justified as they can be) but never ideally so (since his conditions are far from ideal). But, just as Brian cannot talk about the BIV scenario, so Brian cannot talk about sufficiently good conditions for justifying a claim. Suppose Brian were to come out with the following justificationist claim:

If I say 'There is a chair in my study,' an ideal epistemic situation would be to be in my study with the lights on or with daylight streaming through the window, with nothing wrong with my eyesight, with an unconfused mind, without having taken drugs or been subjected to hypnosis, and so forth, and to look and see if there is a chair there.[8]

Brian's words 'chair', 'study', 'lights', and 'window' would simply fail to refer to chairs, studies, lights, and windows. Brian therefore cannot even *characterize* the sceptical scenario that led us to declare that justificationism was a red herring. But this is just the BIV argument, recast in justificationist terminology.

The broad point is as follows. Whenever and however the sceptic attempts to reignite Cartesian angst by formulating some 'really bad scenario', her attempt succumbs to a BIV-style argument. We learn to avoid Cartesian angst, not because we can find some nice philosophical picture, or some nice philosophy of perception, or some nice theory of justification, or whatever. Perhaps we could cast around for a satisfying metaphor to illustrate the insight that we have obtained, but I think it will be best to put the point plainly. *We learn to avoid nightmarish Cartesian angst, just because our ability to make sense of nightmarish Cartesian sceptical possibilities shows us that we are not caught up in them.*

---

[8] This was Putnam's (1990b: viii) justificationist suggestion, discussed in §§11.2 and 11.7.

13.3 Sober scepticism and generic delusion

I have got ahead of myself a little. All I have really shown so far is that the BIV argument defeats *BIV scepticism*. This is a far cry from showing that the BIV argument defeats *all* attempts to formulate nightmarish Cartesian scepticism. Unless I can do that, I cannot claim that the BIV argument provides us with a completely general response to nightmarish Cartesian angst. For the remainder of the chapter, then, I shall explain just how general the BIV argument is.

A dedicated sceptic might accept that the BIV scenario fails, as a vehicle for Cartesian scepticism. However, she might keep her scepticism alive by maintaining that the BIV scenario is a *mere* vehicle for a much more sombre thought:

Just as fictional characters in a novel can exemplify the possibility of a certain kind of relationship, so, within the image, BIVs and the rest of the world can exemplify the possibility of a certain kind of person/world relation which we might call the delusive relation.[9]

The *sober sceptic* contends, then, that the BIV scenario is a fancy but ultimately faulty way to get at what we might blandly call:

The sober scenario. We stand in the delusive relation to the world.

Moreover, she can reasonably claim that her sober scepticism is a variety of internal scepticism (in the sense of §12.4), since it arises from reflection on a story that we think is physically possible (see §13.1).

To discuss this thought, let us imagine Delboy, standing in the delusive relation to the world. Straightforward application of BIV-style reasoning will show that I am not in Delboy's situation.

To begin, we must question the sober sceptic's appeal to fictional exemplification. Hector, of the *Iliad*, exemplifies many ancient Greek virtues. Now, it may seem to Delboy as if he is reading the *Iliad*, and thinking about ancient Greeks and their virtues. But, by hypothesis, this is all delusive. Just as Brian has never thought *about* brains, so Delboy has never *read* a book, nor thought *about* ancient Greeks, let alone their virtues (I shall return to virtues in §16.6). In exactly the same way: Delboy has never thought about

---

[9] Smith (1984: 121–2); this passage is a quote from Smith, but since it is a sceptical speech, I have reformatted it (and replaced 'brains in a vat' with 'BIV') for uniformity.

a fictional brain in a vat, since Delboy has never thought *about* brains or vats (given the ban on magical theories of reference). Thus: if my relation to the world is (*per impossibile*) the delusive one exemplified by the fiction of the BIV scenario, then in contemplating 'the BIV scenario' I am not thinking *about* a fiction which exemplifies anything.

The sober sceptic is likely to reply that the notion of fictional exemplification was only a *further* faulty vehicle for explicating the delusive relation. But my response continues in the same vein. Delboy is unable to talk about the delusive relation for three related reasons.

First: to be in the delusive relation to the world is, among other things, to stand in inappropriate causal relations with objects. So in order for Delboy to be able to talk *about* the delusive relation to the world (as such), he will need to be able to talk *about* inappropriate causal relations with objects. This is precisely what someone in a delusive relation will be unable to do. As in §12.3, Delboy will have great difficulty in talking about genuine cause-and-effect sequences; but even if he can talk about them, he will have absolutely no ability to distinguish appropriate from inappropriate ones.

Second: to be in a delusive relation to the world is to fail to respond appropriately to objects in your environment. But precisely because Delboy stands in a delusive relation to the world, he cannot talk *about* the objects in his environment, any more than Brian can talk about the walls of his vat.

Third: to be in a delusive relation to the world is, among other things, to be out of touch with the world's natural kinds. But someone in a delusive relation to the world cannot talk *about* the world's kinds.[10] To suppose otherwise is to suppose that when Delboy utters the words 'underlying natural kinds', he just *happens* to pick out the natural kinds, even though the kinds are (by hypothesis) completely screened off from Delboy by the delusive relation in which he stands to the world. Again, that would require a magical theory of reference.

In short, Delboy can no more talk about the delusive relation (as such) than Brian can talk about brains. But in that case, if I understand Delboy's situation, it cannot be my own. The BIV argument therefore defeats sober scepticism. And since sober scepticism was an attempt to articulate the most generic possible version of a nightmarish Cartesian sceptical scenario, we have discovered that nightmarish Cartesian scepticism cannot coherently

---

[10] As Putnam (1994a: 286–8) explains.

be articulated. We have found a resilient way to deal with nightmarish Cartesian angst.

13.4 Dead-sober scepticism and ineffable delusion

The Cartesian sceptic may claim that she has not yet been *defeated*. Although she cannot articulate it, she might claim that nightmarish Cartesian scepticism remains an ineffable but open possibility. Wright puts the worry thus:

The real spectre to be exorcised concerns the idea of a thought standing behind *our thought that we are not BIVs, in just the way that our thought that they are mere BIVs would stand behind the thought . . . of actual BIVs that 'We are not BIVs'.*[11]

The resulting form of scepticism is a close cousin of the sober scepticism just discussed. Like sober scepticism, it can paint itself as a version of internal scepticism, since it purports to arise from straightforward reflection on Brian's predicament, and we believe that Brian is a physically possible thinker (see §13.1). But where the sober sceptic falsely believed that someone who stands in the deluded relation to the world can *talk about* the deluded relation, our present sceptic agrees that this is impossible. She elaborates on this as follows:

Brian cannot talk about brains, trees, lampshades, holes, or tablecloths. He therefore cannot describe my possible world at all, and so cannot grasp the thought—that is, my thought—that stands behind his thought. I worry that my predicament is relevantly like Brian's (though I accept that my predicament is not actually Brian's, since I accept that I am not a BIV). My worry is that there is a thought standing behind my thought, and that this is a thought I cannot grasp.

This sceptic is simply gripped by the worry that we are ineffably deluded. Since Wright tells us that this worry needs to be exorcized, I shall call this ghostly cousin of sober scepticism, *dead-sober scepticism.*

Trying to say the unsayable inevitably involves a treacherous balancing act. In this particular case, our dead-sober sceptic has accepted that we are not BIVs, and that we are not nightmarishly deluded. Indeed, she has accepted

---

[11] Wright (1992a: 93); this passage is a quote from Wright, but since it is a sceptical speech, I have reformatted it (whilst retaining Wright's emphasis) for uniformity. Similarly, I have replaced 'brains-in-a-vat' with 'BIVs'. Nagel (1986: 73), Van Inwagen (1988: 106), and Forbes (1995: 220) express similar sentiments.

our earlier argument that those situations are epistemically impossible. For all that, she wants to say that there is an inexpressible sense in which we may yet be nightmarishly deluded. But this amounts to saying:

We cannot be nightmarishly deluded, but we might be nightmarishly deluded (in some sense).

She saves herself from explicit contradiction only by tacking on the words 'in some sense'. My immediate concern is that the sense in which the dead-sober sceptic worries that we 'might be' deluded is precisely the same as the sense in which reference 'might be' magical.[12] In one direction: it is because reference is not magical that Brian cannot fully grasp the thought that stands behind his thought. And conversely: if reference 'might' be magical, then we 'might' (in that sense) be nightmarishly deluded, for the BIV argument then fails completely. So the 'possibility' that we are deluded seems to be equivalent to the 'possibility' that reference is magical. If so, it can simply be ignored (see §12.4).

For argument's sake, however, I shall grant that we have some grip on the required attempt to say the unsayable. Nonetheless, I shall pull the rug out from under dead-sober scepticism by showing the following: if (in some ineffable sense) a thought stands behind ours like ours stands behind Brian's, then Brian has no thoughts after all.

My argument for this conclusion turns on the fact that there are only two kinds of thinker in the BIV scenario. There are ordinary, undeluded thinkers; there are 'deluded', eternally envatted brains; but there are *no other thinkers*.[13] To establish this point, it will help to violate (temporarily) the strictures of the BIV scenario, and imagine a world which contains some embodied people, and also some eternally envatted brains. The embodied people are undeluded thinkers. These happy souls might look at a vat, and pity the deluded state of the brains it contains. These deluded brains are a second kind of thinker. Now, it may seem to the deluded thinkers—the envatted brains—*as if* they are ordinary thinkers. Indeed, they may even believe they are 'looking at a vat, and pitying the deluded state of the brains it contains'. But in fact, they are not looking *at* a vat. They are not looking *at* any brains. Indeed, there are no *thinkers* there for them to pity. There are

---

[12] I am deeply in sympathy with A. W. Moore (1997: 147–8): 'The inexpressible, whatever else it is, is not that which carves up logical space awkwardly.'

[13] A. W. Moore (1994: 226–7) makes this observation.

only *mere delusions*, generated by the infernal machinery into which they are wired.[14]

So here is the problem. The dead-sober sceptic worries that, in some ineffable sense, there is a thought standing behind my thought, as my thought stands behind Brian's. Let us play along with the worry. Then in that same ineffable sense: when I point to Brian, I do not point to a deluded thinker, but only to a *mere delusion*. (After all, the BIV scenario allows only two kinds of thinkers.) But mere delusions cannot have thoughts. So Brian has no thoughts behind which mine might stand. Otherwise put: I cannot simultaneously worry that I am in a predicament like Brian's *and* regard Brian as a thinker who is so much as capable of being in a predicament.

The dead-sober sceptic had hoped to point to a thinker beneath her, and thereby come to understand what might stand above her. But if there is something above her, then there is nothing beneath her after all. This obliterates the purported motivations for dead-sober scepticism. And if the dead-sober sceptic responds by giving up the attempt to *motivate* her position, then she has ceased to be an internal sceptic. We can simply ignore her, for the reasons given in §12.4.

13.5 Exorcism and philosophical therapy

To say that we are ignoring the dead-sober sceptic, in this case, might give the mistaken impression that she is still *speaking*. To be sure, she is making noises at us and placing ink marks on paper, such as 'maybe we are ineffably but nightmarishly deluded'. But these noises and ink marks emphatically are not supposed to mean *that* we might be nightmarishly deluded. Moreover, whatever they are supposed ineffably to convey, it cannot have been motivated by anything that we *believe*. All they do convey, then, is the dead-sober sceptic's visceral *feeling of anxiety*. There is no reason to think that she gives a better voice to this anxiety, by an exclamation like 'maybe we are nightmarishly deluded!', than she would do by mournfully howling at the moon.

I have tried not to ignore such howls. I have done my best to diagnose the source of the dead-sober sceptic's angst: it stems from a lingering attachment to magic. This amounts to the beginnings of an error theory (and in §16.6

---

[14] In §16.6 I explain why an interpretationist cannot contest this point. In any case, interpretationists are likely to embrace Davidson's Cogito; see Chapter 14.

I shall suggest that the error might have noble origins). But Wright asks for an *exorcism*, rather than for an error theory. This turn of phrase deserves comment, for it is profoundly fitting.

The dead-sober sceptic has a visceral fear of ghosts. She probably realizes that she should not have this fear. But rather than asking how she might overcome her fear, she asks for an exorcism. She wants light magic, to ward away the dark. Performing an exorcism ceremony might give her some short-term comfort. But dousing everything with holy water will not help much in the long term. Exorcisms are impossible, given that there are no ghosts. The right strategy for overcoming fear of ghosts requires that we remember this.

A serious point is at stake here. A Wittgensteinian tradition holds that certain philosophical perplexities are the byproducts of a 'pathological' mindset. If this is right, then we should not attempt to provide answers to the perplexing questions. Instead, we should aim to treat the pathological mindset. (The aim of philosophy becomes 'to show the fly the way out of the fly-bottle'.)[15] A demand is therefore issued for philosophical *therapy*. In certain cases, this demand is surely reasonable. Indeed, if anything requires philosophical therapy rather than answers, then dead-sober scepticism does.

But the demand for philosophical therapy can often carry with it a very particular and wholly misguided conception of what therapy must look like. Useful therapy, in the psychological sense, rarely amounts to lying on a couch, awaiting the single perfect insight from your therapist, the master-key that will unlock all your problems. Equally, useful philosophical therapy will not amount to waiting for the single perfect aphorism-wrapped-in-a-picture, the sword that will slice through all Gordian philosophical knots.

I am not sure exactly what therapy will consist in. My tentative prescription for the dead-sober sceptic, though, would be something a little like the following. Whenever feelings of Cartesian angst occur, you should remind yourself that they are pathological. That is what the BIV argument shows, and shows resiliently. You should remind yourself that there is no content to your worries, beyond the mere fact *that* you are worried. If you can remind yourself of this, and resist the temptation to dwell in such episodes, then after a while the frequency and duration of episodes of angst might gradually diminish.

---

[15] Wittgenstein (1953: §309).

14

Davidson's Cogito

In Chapter 13, I showed that Cartesian scepticism can be neither articulated nor motivated. It amounts to nothing more than a feeling. In seeing this, we obtain the most satisfying general response to Cartesian angst for which we might reasonably hope. That said, it leaves us with no elegant philosophical picture to replace the picture employed by external realism. Moreover, it leaves open the question of just how internal our realism should be.

I shall return to the debate between internal and external realism in Chapter 15. In this chapter, I shall embark on a slight digression. I have been treating the BIV scenario as an attempt to generate nightmarish Cartesian angst. As Donald Davidson points out, however, it is very doubtful that Brian's beliefs are largely false. This forms the basis of what we might call *Davidson's Cogito*, which rebuts any attempt to formulate nightmarish Cartesian angst. In this chapter, I shall discuss that Cogito.

Davidson's Cogito is sometimes connected with a coherence theory of truth, and this can give rise to Kantian sceptical worries. Fortunately, we can easily avoid the coherence theory of truth. Indeed, any ineffable anxieties that might seem to arise from reflections on Davidson's Cogito are simply the result of a failure of nerve, rather than of any intelligible deep insight.[1]

14.1 Davidson's anti-sceptical argument

Davidson is an interpretationist about the mental. This leads him to claim that:

---

[1] Thanks to Christina Cameron for the fascinating discussion on Davidson and his Cogito; without her, I would have said many (more) false or superficial things.

a correct understanding of the speech, beliefs, desires, intentions, and other propositional attitudes of a person leads to the conclusion that most of a person's beliefs must be true.[2]

Consequently:

The question 'how do I know my beliefs are generally true?' thus answers itself, simply because beliefs are by nature generally true. Rephrased or expanded, the question becomes, 'How can I tell whether my beliefs, which are by their nature generally true, are generally true?'[3]

Applied to the case of Brian the BIV, Davidson's point is quite simple. If Brian is to qualify as a thinker at all, then most of Brian's beliefs must be true. (In what follows, I shall simply assume that Brian should be regarded as a thinker.)

Davidson's argument is evidently different from Putnam's. Putnam's argument concludes that I am not a BIV, and so that the BIV scenario fails to obtain. In the first instance, Davidson's argument concludes only that the truth values of my beliefs are (surprisingly) mostly unaffected by whether or not I am a BIV. That is, Davidson's argument does not (in the first instance) demonstrate that the BIV scenario fails to obtain, but that the scenario does not exemplify nightmarish Cartesian scepticism. More generally, Davidson holds that every scenario in which I remain a thinker fails to exemplify nightmarish Cartesian scepticism. Davidson's response to Descartes's first meditation is: *I think, therefore I am mostly right.* Call this *Davidson's Cogito.*

I shall not attempt to *defend* Davidson's Cogito here.[4] I only want to explore its relationship with Putnam's BIV argument, and with ineffable anxieties about the relationship between mind and world.

Despite the different primary conclusions of Davidson's Cogito and Putnam's BIV argument, the arguments are obviously compatible. In the first instance, neither argument provides us with referents for Brian's words. All that Putnam's BIV argument requires of Brian is that his word 'brain' does not refer to brains.[5] All that Davidson's Cogito requires is that, if we are to regard Brian as a thinker, then we must interpret him so as to make

---

[2] Davidson (1983: 146).   [3] Davidson (1983: 153).

[4] Perhaps the most interesting difficulty that it faces concerns the referent of Brian's word 'I'. Both Han (2010: 161–6) and Madden (2010: §§4–9) raise this as a problem for Putnam's BIV argument, but it is clearly not a problem for the BIV argument as I have reconstructed it, since my situation is not Brian's.

[5] At least, on the reconstruction that I have followed. Ebbs (1992b: 246), Davies (1995: 215–16), Brueckner (1999: 236–7), and DeRose (2000: 125–6) all make this point.

his beliefs mostly true. But Davidson also explicitly suggests that we should interpret beliefs as being *about* 'external events and objects'.[6] In Brian's case, this might be electronic signals, parts of the envatting machinery, features of the computer programme, or similar things that cause sensations in Brian. This is wholly compatible with premise (1) of Putnam's argument, and for just this reason, Putnam sometimes makes the same suggestion himself.[7]

14.2 Coherence versus correspondence

If we interpret Brian in this way, then we have obviously advanced a correspondence theory of truth for Brian's language (on the utterly minimal understanding of 'correspondence' that I have adopted throughout this book). However, a brief digression is necessary here, since in the same article that Davidson advanced his Cogito, he explicitly advanced a *coherence* theory of truth.

According to the coherence theory of truth, for our thoughts to be true is not for them to be about objects, but only for them to cohere with one another. This is rather terrifying. Even if my thoughts are mostly true—as Davidson claims—this is to say only that they mesh with one another. It is not to say that their teeth engage with the world.[8] Indeed, Davidson seems to suggest that the very idea of a 'confrontation between what we believe and reality ... is absurd'.[9] For the coherentist, our thoughts neither are nor could be about any *things*. But this is just to say that they neither are nor could be about *anything* (see Chapter 7). The coherence theory of truth amounts to Kantian scepticism.

Davidson came to realize that this was a disaster.[10] Indeed, he explicitly retracted the coherence theory of truth, and endorsed a simple correspondence theory of truth as plainly as he could:

the simple thesis that names and descriptions often refer to things, and that predicates often have an extension in the world of things, is obvious, and essential to the most elementary appreciation of the nature both of language and of the thoughts we express using language.[11]

---

[6] Davidson (1983: 151).   [7] Putnam (1992b: 362; 1994a: 287).
[8] This echoes McDowell's (1994: 18, 66) apt suggestion that the coherence theory of truth leaves us only with a 'frictionless spinning in a void'.
[9] Davidson (1983: 137).   [10] Davidson (2001: xv–xvi, 154–7).   [11] Davidson (1998: 107).

But this raises an interpretative puzzle. It is surely just *obvious* that a coherence theory of truth is incompatible with saying that Brian's words *refer* to their typical causes. However, Davidson wanted to say precisely that, even whilst he was advancing the coherence theory of truth. And to find out that he claimed that 'coherence yields correspondence' surely just *deepens* the interpretative puzzle.[12]

Allow me to offer a charitable interpretation of all this. Davidson had recognized the need to jettison a God's Eye point of view, for roughly the same reasons as Putnam.[13] He therefore presented an account of truth which, from the perspective of an external realist, could only be regarded as coherentist. Davidson embraced the label of 'coherentism' to flag his opposition to external realism. (However, he continued to advance a correspondence theory of truth 'internally', in the sense of Chapter 8.) But this was, at the very least, a dialectical mistake. The 'coherentist' label is only appropriate if one has accepted the intelligibility of adopting a God's Eye point of view. Once Davidson had fully appreciated the need to throw away the God's Eye point of view, he also (rightly) abandoned the 'coherentist' label.

14.3 Bubble scepticism

All of this discussion of coherence and Kantian scepticism might, however, lead the sceptic to prick up her ears. She might wonder whether we are *entitled* to a correspondence theory of truth. To press this objection, she might argue as follows:[14]

Although we say that Brian's sentences are 'true', none of the words that Brian uses really refer to any particular things. Really, Brian is only able to refer-in-his-vat-image to objects-in-his-vat-image. I worry that my predicament is relevantly like Brian's (though I accept that my predicament is not actually Brian's, since I accept that I am not a BIV). I worry that I can only refer-in-my-phenomenal-bubble to objects-in-my-phenomenal-bubble, and never

---

[12] Davidson (1983: 137).

[13] Davidson (1983: 140) discusses the connection with Putnam's 'internal realism'. Note, too, that Putnam (1980a: 100, 108; 1981c: 50, 64) flirted with a coherence theory of truth.

[14] This pursues A. W. Moore's (1997: 142–9; 2011: 47–53) suggestion that BIV-style scenarios can bring into focus 'one of the main impulses towards a radical version of transcendental idealism'. Note that Moore is neither a bubble sceptic, nor a transcendental idealist.

to things-in-themselves. I worry that all I have is correspondence-in-my-phenomenal-bubble, which is really only coherence. In short, I worry that I am really out of touch with the world.

The sceptic evidently wants to impress Kantian worries upon us. And we can easily imagine her employing Davidson's (erstwhile) coherentist rhetoric to back up these worries. She might tell us that to get outside our phenomenal bubble would require 'a confrontation between what we believe and reality; and the idea of such a confrontation is absurd'.[15] For obvious reasons, I shall call this *bubble scepticism*.

Like dead-sober scepticism, bubble scepticism is wholly ineffable. The notion of 'referring to things-in-themselves' or of '*really* referring' is supposed to be beyond my grasp. (It, too, is supposed to be 'absurd'.) As with dead-sober scepticism, then, the most I can aim to do is show that bubble scepticism is not internally motivated, and so that it can be ignored.

The bubble sceptic claims that Brian refers-in-his-image to things-in-his-image. This is the thought which prompts the angst that I merely refer-in-my-phenomenal-bubble to objects-in-my-phenomenal-bubble. But the thought needs unpacking. As I noted earlier, Davidson had suggested that Brian refers to the typical causes of his beliefs: electronic signals, or parts of the envatting machinery, or features of the computer programme, or something similar. We can *call* these things 'things-in-Brian's-image' if we like. However, if we do, then we must *not* be misled by the locution: these things are just ordinary empirical things, in the ordinary empirical world. On this line of thought, though, the bubble sceptic has simply been misled by the locution. To repeat, her worry is that I (merely) refer-in-my-phenomenal-bubble to objects-in-my-phenomenal-bubble. Once we remove the misleading locutions, her worry deflates to the following: that I (merely) refer to ordinary empirical things. And this is not worrying at all.

To keep bubble scepticism alive, the bubble sceptic will have to deny that the things-in-Brian's-image are just ordinary empirical things. The bubble sceptic must instead hold that things-in-Brian's-image are *objects that belong within Brian's conceptual scheme but not within ours* (or something similar). But if she does this, then the BIV scenario is no longer what drives us towards bubble scepticism. Rather, we are driven there by a prior commitment to

---

[15] Davidson (1983: 137).

conceptual relativism; to the view that objects and kinds (and not just our words for them) are scheme-relative.

In Chapter 18, I shall show that conceptual relativism is incoherent. For present purposes, it suffices to show that bubble scepticism faces the same problems as dead-sober scepticism. As I pointed out in §13.4, the BIV scenario allows for only two levels of thinker. Consequently, if I am nightmarishly deluded (as the dead-sober sceptic assumes Brian to be), then Brian is not even a thinker who is so much as capable of being in a predicament (sceptical or otherwise). A similar point applies here. The bubble sceptic worries that all thinkers are trapped inside their own phenomenal bubbles. Presumably this is the worry that all of the *noumenal* thinkers are trapped inside their phenomenal bubbles. But if I am trapped inside my phenomenal bubble, then surely what I call 'Brian' is a mere *phenomenon*, rather than a noumenal thinker. To worry that I am in his predicament is, again, to exclude him from being in a predicament. Conversely, to think that I somehow manage to refer to a *noumenal* Brian (who is phenomenally a brain in a vat) is to lean upon a *noumenal* magical theory of reference. As I worried in §13.4, the desire to say the unsayable here boils down to a desire for a magical theory of reference. It should be ignored, or perhaps treated (see §13.5).

14.4 Metaphysical scepticism

The sceptic might retreat from the preceding worry, to something a little less terrifying:

I grant that Brian's thoughts are mostly true. I grant, indeed, that Brian succeeds in talking about some particular objects in the world (perhaps certain electronic signals). So Brian's thoughts have content: he is in touch with the world. (I am not a bubble sceptic.) Nonetheless, Brian has scarcely any grasp on the nature of those objects. He is unaware that his thoughts are about electronic signals. He does not know what electronic signals are. I worry that my predicament is relevantly like Brian's (though I accept that my predicament is not actually Brian's, since I accept that I am not a BIV). I worry that the nature of (most) things is fundamentally beyond my ken.

To be clear, the sceptic who makes this speech does not suppose that the *physical* nature of things is beyond her ken. She may have great faith in the physical sciences to tell us about our world. Rather, the sceptic worries that there is a 'level' of reality, buried beneath the (mere) physical sciences, as the discoveries of the physical sciences are buried beneath the (mere) discoveries of the 'physical sciences' that are 'undertaken' in Brian's world. The sceptic worries, in short, that the *meta*physical nature of things is forever beyond her ken. I therefore call this *metaphysical scepticism.*

It is worth emphasizing that metaphysical scepticism is every bit as ineffable as dead-sober scepticism and bubble scepticism.[16] In order for Brian to attain our level of understanding concerning the (physical) nature of things, Brian would have to be transformed into one of us, by being removed from his envatting machinery and housed in a normal body. But if Brian can neither talk about brains nor talk about vats, then he certainly has no grasp of the physically possible process whereby he is removed from his vat and housed in a human body. So if my predicament is indeed analogous to Brian's, as the metaphysical sceptic claims, then I should equally have no grasp on the 'physically possible process' whereby I am given a 'proper' understanding of 'the nature of things'. I cannot simply imagine being given the ears of a bat, electron microscopes for eyes, and new sensory organs that allow me simply to *feel* the recession of distant galaxies. The point is that if I even try to talk of a 'physically possible process that would bring me to a full understanding of the nature of things', I will fall *hopelessly* short of the mark. Thus metaphysical scepticism is meant to be genuinely *ineffable.*

Gary Ebbs criticizes a position like metaphysical scepticism, by pointing out that

> our understanding of a representation of the world and our thoughts about what the world is like are essentially interconnected. So we don't really understand the idea of a representation of the world which is radically detached from and independent of our ability to express its content.[17]

I expect that the metaphysical sceptic will simply agree with this claim. She has already conceded that her position is ineffable, which is to say precisely that 'we don't really understand' what it is that we are missing. But once we

---

[16] By embracing ineffability, this presents a better version of the idea that the BIV scenario presents a metaphysical hypothesis (see §12.6). Chalmers (2005) might be read as presenting a version of metaphysical scepticism, since he does not regard the BIV hypothesis as sceptical, and he recognizes (2005: §5, §9 note 11) that it is not straightforwardly effable. Nevertheless, Chalmers does hold that it might be literally true that the world is part of a 'computer-an-sich'.

[17] Ebbs (1992b: 258; see also 1992a: 17; 2012: §4.6). Ebbs is criticizing Nagel (1986: 73).

have realized that all parties agree on this point, we shall find that we are able to pass over metaphysical scepticism in silence.

By its own admission, metaphysical scepticism presents us with nothing more than a nebulous sense that the world is mysterious, and in such a way that we cannot even begin to glimpse its mysteries. In so far as we feel that we *can* glimpse its mysteries, it is because we feel that our phrase 'the nature of things' might briefly acquire the magical ability to talk about the *meta*physical nature of things, even though in the main it latches onto their physical nature. The ineffable worry, as usual, hankers after magic (see §13.4).

Moreover, since the metaphysical sceptic admits that we shall never be able to say anything about what *meta*physics might amount to, the metaphysical sceptical hypothesis amounts to nothing more than a *bare formal possibility*. We cannot force the metaphysical sceptic to contradict herself, in the narrow deductive sense. But this is not to admit that the metaphysical sceptic has really *said* anything about how the world might be. (One way to put this point is to emphasize that she has not even tried to say something about how the *physical* world might be, but only about how the *meta*physical world might be.)

Finally, whatever she supposes herself to have said, by whatever magical means necessary, it is unclear what the metaphysical sceptic's *worry* is. We are not to worry, as the dead-sober sceptic does, that we are *deluded*. We are not to worry, as the bubble sceptic does, that we are out of touch with the world. The metaphysical sceptic thinks that we are in touch with the world, and that our beliefs are mostly true. She just tells us that the '*meta*physical nature of the world'—whatever that is—'might lie beyond our ken'.

Chapter 13 ended with the suggestion that Cartesian angst is like the fear of ghosts. The metaphysical sceptic's anxieties are more like the feeling that you sometimes have, just before falling asleep, of having just had a *tremendously important thought*. You might try to stir yourself awake to bring it into focus, but by the time you are sufficiently awake to think about things clearly, the content of the thought has evaporated. If indeed it was ever there. Often, I hazard, there was nothing more than the *feeling* of having had a thought. Such a feeling certainly need not keep us awake long into the night.

15

Vat variations

The BIV argument shows that there is nothing to fear: from night-marish Cartesian scepticism that can be articulated; from nightmarish Cartesian scepticism that cannot be articulated; nor from any other ineffable scepticism.

In this chapter, I want to start to explore the limits of BIV-style arguments as a response to scepticism. I shall do this by investigating several putative sceptical scenarios. Each presents a way in which a theory could be undetectably false, but less than nightmarishly so. A BIV-style reply can be given to each. My aim in this chapter is to demonstrate that whether BIV-style arguments succeed or fail is often vague.

The initial reason for doing this is to show that internal realism—the position which holds that *every* Cartesian sceptical scenario can be defeated—is untenable. This means that we shall need to locate ourselves somewhere *between* internal and external realism. However, this discussion will also provide the raw material for explaining, in Chapter 16, why we simply cannot hope to locate ourselves anywhere precise. That raw material, I am afraid to say, is your sheer and unmitigated sense of *frustration* as you read this chapter. You have been warned.[1]

15.1 Scepticism about space

A certain kind of sceptic might advance:

The space-1 scenario. The radius of the universe is just over one metre.

---

[1] Thanks to Michael Potter for fascinating discussion on vat variations.

I am meant to imagine a universe exactly like my own, except that everything (including space itself) more than one metre away from my navel has been obliterated. The actual world is a very narrow spacetime worm, containing me and some very peculiar, brute, unexplained stimuli.

The space-1 scenario is obviously very similar to the BIV scenario. The main difference is that, instead of imagining that my brain has been wired into a vat (perhaps with a radius of one metre), I retain my body together with (the surfaces) of the objects that come close enough for touch. But the space-1 scenario can be tackled along the same lines as the original BIV scenario:

(1a) The expression 'one metre', in the language of people living in the space-1 scenario, does not refer to distances of one metre.

(2a) My expression 'one metre' refers to distances of one metre.

(3a) So: the universe does not have a radius of one metre.

As in the original BIV argument, premise (2a) is justified by disquotation. Premise (1a) is again to be justified by rejecting all magical theories of reference. Suppose Dot lives in a universe with a radius of just over one metre. Dot opens his mouth and produces words which sound exactly like English constructions about distances. But unless space and the objects in it *cry out* to be named by the phonemes that actual English speakers use, this gives us no reason to think that Dot's utterance 'one metre away' refers to locations one metre away.

So far, everything has proceeded just as in the BIV argument. Now things change. For every non-negative real number δ, we can offer:

The space-δ scenario. The radius of the universe is just over δ metres.

(A particularly interesting example is the space-0 scenario, which is realized by Descartes's *malin genie* scenario.)[2] This will meet with a BIV-style argument:

(1a:δ) The expression 'δ metres', in the language of people living in the space-δ scenario, does not refer to distances of δ metres.

---

[2] Bouwsma (1949) offered a BIV-esque argument against *malin genie* scepticism; Van Inwagen (1988: 98) notes the parallel.

(2a:δ) My expression 'δ metres' refers to distances of δ metres.
(3a:δ) So: the universe does not have a radius of δ metres.

Premise (2a:δ) should cause no particular problems, as we allow δ to vary. (Of course if our universe has a large but finite radius, then for some δ there will be no locations that far away, but this is immaterial, for pedantic reasons explained at the start of §12.5.)

The real problem is the acceptability of premise (1a:δ), which clearly depends upon the value of δ. The radius of the visible universe is several billion light years. Let the *space-v scenario* be the hypothesis that the radius of the entire universe is (what we currently believe to be) its visible radius. This is a relatively credible scientific hypothesis, not a sceptical hypothesis. So, at some point between (1a:1) and (1a:v), we would be crazy to rest an argument for a cosmological hypothesis on semantic grounds. *What is that point?*

Our internal realist, aiming to reject all sceptical hypotheses, might argue that the difference comes down precisely to the fact that the space-v scenario is obviously not meant as a *sceptical* scenario. The idea would be that semantic considerations become irrelevant precisely when the scenarios in question cease to be *sceptical*. To explore this suggestion, let us consider the avowedly sceptical hypothesis that the universe ends just beyond what we currently believe to be the outermost boundaries of the Milky Way. Call this *the space-g scenario* (evidently 1 < g < v). In accordance with the internal realist's strictures, the space–g scenario is intended as a purely *sceptical* scenario. That is, we should not suppose that, if we just investigated *harder*, we would realize that the rest of the universe does not exist after all, or that everything is much closer to us than we previously thought, or anything of that nature. Rather, our current theory is just undetectably wrong. (So, for example: if we were to send out a probe to 'explore beyond the Milky Way', the probe will simply cease to exist, but we will continue to 'receive signals from it'.) Now, imagine Lot. Lot lives in the space–g scenario and thinks that his universe is much larger than it actually is. The question is whether the internal realist can demonstrate that Lot's use of 'g metres' does not refer to distances of g metres.

If Lot says 'my house is just down the road', or 'Berlin is the capital city of Germany', or 'Neil Armstrong landed on the moon', then what he says is true when interpreted disquotationally. Conversely, if Lot says 'the Andromeda Galaxy is a spiral galaxy', then what he says is false when interpreted disquotationally, since the Andromeda Galaxy is no part of his universe. If the internal realist wants to argue that Lot's use of 'g metres' does not refer to distances of g metres, she will have to argue that we must focus on our inability to disquote some of Lot's recherché astrophysical utterances, rather than on our ability to disquote *everything else* that he says.

It is very hard to see why we should have to do this. After all, we are under no obligation to make *everything* that Lot says true. Indeed, surely a *good* interpretation of the practice that Lot and his worldmates call 'astrophysics' is *that it is astrophysics*, but that these astrophysicians are sadly being deluded.

The general question that we have hit upon is: How much *space* does someone need to be swimming around in, before their words link up with *space*? Maybe a few metres; maybe several billions of kilometres—I have literally no idea how to even make a start with this question. The only obviously correct thought I can grasp is the following: the larger the universe described in a putative sceptical scenario, the more obviously coherent the sceptical worry.

15.2 Scepticism about the past

I now turn from scepticism about spatial distances to scepticism about temporal durations. Many of the same points apply. However, the fact that time has a *direction* adds an additional layer of complexity.

A sceptic about the past might ask us to consider, for any δ:

The past-δ scenario. The universe began just over δ seconds ago.

It is easy to see the worry here. In the past-δ scenario, any evidence that we have *now* to suggest that the universe is much older than δ seconds is simply deceptive.[3]

A BIV-style argument against past-δ scepticism would run thus:

(1b:δ) The expression 'δ seconds ago', in the language of people living in the past-δ scenario, does not refer to events δ seconds ago.

[3] Russell (1921: 159–60) considers $\delta = 300$.

($2b:\delta$) My expression 'δ seconds ago' refers to events δ seconds ago.
($3b:\delta$) So: the universe did not begin just over δ seconds ago.

As usual, premise ($2b:\delta$) is justified by a principle of disquotation. Premise ($1b:\delta$) is to be justified by rejecting all magical theories of reference. With $\delta = 1$, this is plausible, though it is far from straightforward. Suppose Neo lives in a universe which began one second ago. Neo produces words which sound exactly like English past-tense constructions. But unless the past *cries out* to be named by those phonemes that actual English speakers use, this fact alone provides no reason to think that Neo's utterance 'one second ago' refers to events one second ago.

The origins of this BIV-style argument lie with Norman Malcolm, who defends ($1b:1$) as follows.[4] Since Neo is a thinker, and since his thoughts 'about the past' must be mostly true, Neo must not be talking *about* the past, but about something else. After all, if we interpreted Neo disquotationally, then we would interpret Neo as making 'judgments about the past, all of which are false',[5] and Malcolm claims that there is no 'criterion' for doing that.

For now, I shall suppose that Malcolm is right about this (though I revisit this later). However, Malcolm's argument certainly breaks down as δ grows. (Again, we are to imagine that all of the different hypotheses are proposed as purely *sceptical* hypotheses. We are not to imagine that, if only we did more scientific research, we might find out that all the fossils are hoaxes, or that dinosaurs walked the earth only a few thousand years ago, or anything of that nature.)

It is obviously coherent to imagine that the universe began several billion years ago; and it is incoherent to suppose that the universe began one second ago; and at some point in between things will go awry. Where, exactly, I am not sure. But let us imagine Eoin, in a universe that is tens of millennia old. If it was perverse to deny that Lot can talk *about* space, it is surely even more perverse to deny that Eoin cannot talk *about* the past, given a background of tens of millennia of people using past-tense language to deal *with* their past.

---

[4] More accurately, Malcolm (1963: 254ff.) considers ($1b:300$) as a riposte to past-300 scepticism; Van Inwagen (1988: 98) notes the parallel between Malcolm's argument and Putnam's BIV argument.
[5] Malcolm (1963: 258).

The case of time, however, gives rise to a complication that does not arise in the case of space. We can raise fresh mischief by stipulating that Eoin is one of Neo's *descendants*, so that they live in the same universe, but are separated by tens of millennia. The interesting question is whether this fresh stipulation should give us any reason to think that Neo can talk about his past after all.

From the point of view of anyone in the Neo–Eoin universe, there may be no (relevant) change in *practice*, in the use of past-tense language, at any stage between Neo and Eoin. Since there is no apparent change in practice, an obvious thought is that Neo and Eoin speak the same language. Since we are clear that Eoin's expression 'one second ago' refers to events one second ago, the same will then be true of Neo, contradicting premise (1b:1). We might yet be in a universe which came into existence just one second ago.

I just appealed to an 'obvious thought', but here is an equally 'obvious' alternative.[6] We might maintain that Neo cannot talk about his past, that Eoin can talk about his past, and that there is some (vague) transition which is undetectable to anyone in that universe. And if *this* is the right approach, then we have found a further way in which the coherence of a sceptical worry—that is, its dependence upon a magical theory of reference—can be vague. One year ago, it was absolutely incoherent for me to worry that the universe only just came into existence. Now, it is slightly more coherent for me to suppose that the universe came into existence just over one year ago. A year from now, it will be slightly more coherent still. So it goes.

We have two approaches to interpreting Neo and Eoin. Which is *right*?

15.3 Scepticism about the future

Before attempting to answer that, we must throw a second consideration into the mix, relating to the directionality of time. We have considered scepticism about the *past*, but we could equally well consider, for each δ:

The future-δ scenario. The universe will end just over δ seconds from now.

---

[6] In §17.3, these two alternatives are played out in a more humdrum setting, concerning zebras.

This is just the reverse of the past-δ scenario. The sceptical problem is essentially the same: in the future-δ scenario, any evidence that we have *now* to suggest that the universe is going to continue for much more than δ seconds is simply deceptive.

The crucial premise in a BIV-style argument against future-δ scepticism will be:

(1c:δ) The expression 'δ seconds from now', in the language of people living in the future-δ scenario, does not refer to events δ seconds from now.

Many of the same considerations that apply to the space-δ and past-δ scenarios apply to the future-δ scenario. But the big question is whether the BIV-style argument gets off the ground *at all*. To give it the maximum chance of success, we shall focus on the case $\delta = 1$. As usual, (1c:1) is to be justified by rejecting certain magical theories of reference. We are to imagine a character, Dom, living in the future-1 scenario, blissfully unaware of the impending fate of his entire universe. If we interpret all of his apparently future-tensed utterances disquotationally, then almost everything Dom thinks about the future is just plain *false*. So we might be tempted, Malcolm-style, to say that there is no 'criterion' for saying that Dom has a future in his language.

That would be wrong. Plenty of people in Dom's past used language exactly like Dom—including earlier time slices of Dom himself—and it would surely be reasonable to say that they talked about their future. In particular, they said 'one second from now' to refer to events one second from *then*. So the 'obvious thought' that we should interpret Dom in line with his predecessors—who clearly can talk about their futures—gives us at least some 'criterion'.

Is it a sufficient 'criterion'? The 'obvious' alternative is to say that, as the apocalypse looms, the people in Dom's universe gradually lose the ability to talk about the future, until Dom himself is utterly unable to articulate his impending doom.

How are we to judge these issues? Dom's predecessors in the future-1 scenario and Neo's descendants in the past-1 scenario all act as ballast, weighting down purely disquotational interpretations. Perhaps the ballast is insufficient; perhaps some of it weighs more heavily than the rest; but how could we begin to judge such things? The curious cases of Neo and Dom, and all the cases in between, are genuinely *messy* cases.

15.4 Vats in space

We have considered various putative sceptical scenarios in which we are wrong about *many* (perhaps most) of our specific claims about the world. The upshot is that we are not sure what to say in many (perhaps most) of those cases. This does not resurrect the possibility of nightmarish Cartesian scepticism—the possibility supposedly exemplified by the BIV scenario. However, it does demonstrate the slipperiness of more tempered forms of Cartesian scepticism. For the second half of this chapter, I want to tinker with the BIV scenario, to highlight how slipperiness can arise there too.

Consider the following scenario:[7]

> **The Vat Earth scenario.** Earth has a distant neighbour, Vat Earth. This is a planet whose only inhabitants are eternally envatted brains. There is no relevant causal link between Earth and Vat Earth, but it so happens that, for every brain on Earth, there is a brain on Vat Earth in exactly the same state, and vice versa.

Our sceptical worry ensues: am I an embodied creature on Earth, or an envatted brain on Vat Earth? The crucial premise of our inevitable BIV-style response to the sceptic will be:

(1d) A vat-earthling's word 'brain' does not refer to brains.

If there is never any connection between Earth and Vat Earth, we might be inclined to say that there is no reason to interpret vat-earthlings as speaking a language that is any different from Brian's language. In which case, we will embrace (1d) for the same reason that we embrace the original premise (1) of the BIV argument.

Granting this, if only temporarily, we can simply change the scenario slightly. Let us move Earth closer to Vat Earth (metre by metre, if it matters). Let us imagine that earthlings visit Vat Earth (in ones, or twos, or threes, if

---

[7] This is a mash-up of the BIV scenario and Putnam's Twin Earth scenario; I discuss the latter in Chapter 17.

the number of visitors will make a difference). Let us imagine that the earthlings tap on the glass walls of the vats. They pity the state of the 'deluded' brains. And let us suppose now that some native vat-earthlings, and an equal number of visitors from Earth, simultaneously think the following words:

If I were envatted and someone were looking at me right now through the glass walls of my vat, I would want to be judged according to the language of the embodied, in thinking 'I am envatted'.

Does this really make no difference? Again, I boggle at the attempt to *start* answering that question. And if you have clear intuitions concerning its answer, I leave it to you to play with the scenario, decreasing or increasing the level of interaction between earthlings and vat-earthlings, until your intuitions shatter.

15.5 Vats in time

Just as we considered scenarios in which someone is spatially outside the vat, so we can consider temporal scenarios in which someone leaves or enters the vat. Consider:[8]

> **The release scenario.** Up until some moment, all sentient creatures are envatted brains. But then everyone is released, and housed in new bodies.

Once again, this is presented as a *purely* sceptical scenario which no amount of investigating could uncover. (We are to imagine that even on release from their vat, no one is or could be aware that any change has taken place, since the vat systems have been destroyed without trace and and the universe has been reconstructed to be exactly as it appeared to be.)

Attempts to rule out the hypothesis that all sentient creatures *were* freed δ seconds ago will encounter many of the same issues as attempts to rule out past-δ scepticism (see §15.2). The crucial premise of our BIV-style argument will be:

---

[8] Putnam (1981c: 16n3) notes but avoids passing comment on this scenario; Jackman (2001: 462ff.) holds that this undermines Putnam's original BIV argument; Farrell (1986: 149–50) offers a mash-up of the Vat Earth scenario and the release scenario.

> (1e:δ) The word 'brain', as used by someone who was freed from a vat fewer than δ seconds ago, does not refer to brains.

In defence of (1e:δ), we might regard a community which has only *just* been released from the vat as on a par with Neo in his new world. That is: just as Neo plausibly cannot talk about the past, very recently freed speakers plausibly cannot refer to brains, vats, trees, holes, and so forth, since they do not have enough history of interaction with these things. Thus, they would be no more right to say 'we were envatted' than Neo would be right to say 'I have no history of which to speak'.

Recall, though, that Eoin (Neo's descendant) certainly has the ability to talk about the past, and would be right to say 'Neo had no history of which to speak' (though it will, of course, never even occur to Eoin to say this). Similarly, we might hold that a descendant from the freed community will be right to say 'I descended from an envatted community' (though again the thought will never occur). And just as the existence of Eoin might be relevant to our interpretation of Neo, so the existence of the descendants might be relevant to our interpretation of the recently freed. I now boggle at the interpretative task.

There is, though, a difference between Neo's universe and the universe in which creatures were only recently freed: there were times before the moment of release. Indeed, we can also consider the putative sceptical hypothesis that we are all brains in vats, about to be released. The crucial premise will be:

> (1f:δ) The word 'brain', as used now by someone who will be freed from a vat just over δ seconds from now, does not refer to brains.

Can those brains who still dwell within their vat, with the moment of release just around the corner, speak in the same way as their free descendants, who can speak about the world beyond the walls of the vat? Again, I do not know how to begin to answer the question.

To drive this point home, note that the release scenario has a natural dual:[9]

---

[9] See Glymour (1982: 173–5), Smith (1984: 117), Farrell (1986: 150), Tymoczko (1989: 294–5), Wright (1992a: 89–90), Christensen (1993: 314–5), Forbes (1995: 207), Brueckner (1999: 237).

The capture scenario. Up until some moment, all sentient creatures are free people. But then everyone is captured, and placed eternally in a vat, where they receive electronic signals from an infernal machine.

If a deeply paranoid speaker were to say, just before the envatting event, 'I will soon be captured and envatted', presumably he says precisely *that* he will be captured and envatted, and so says something true. (Compare Dom, announcing 'my time is short'.) In the immediate aftermath of envatting, a less paranoid speaker would presumably be being *deluded* by the electronic signals he receives from the infernal machine. Very likely the language of the captured person gradually drifts towards Brian's. But God only knows when the switch occurs. Indeed, the idea that there is a *moment* at which the languages switch just seems faintly ludicrous.

15.6 Chaos unleashed

Now that we know what to do, we can multiply sceptical scenarios indefinitely. Consider:

The television scenario. All sentient creatures, including me, are eternally envatted brains, with our eyes still attached by our optic nerves. All sensory stimulation, other than visual stimulation, comes from a cunning computer which feeds electronic signals directly into our brains. However, our retinæ are stimulated by two tiny television screens positioned just in front of each eye. (Sensations of focusing, eye movement, eye strain, and so forth, are still controlled by direct stimulation.)

In the television scenario, our eyes *really* peer through space. Would this suffice to give us a genuine concept of space, rather than of space-in-the-image? Does it matter much that the machine stimulates our retinæ, rather than stimulating our brain directly? What if we considered other sense organs instead of (or as well as) our eyes? What if the television screens are wired up to cameras in such a way that, whenever I have visual sensations as of looking at a brain, in fact those cameras are pointed to a brain which looks exactly like that?

If these questions are deemed *too easy*, an arbitrary recombination of earlier scenarios may help to defeat that thought:[10]

> **The unfathomable scenario.** For an eternity, our universe was a swirling vortex of inductive chaos. A few seconds ago, the laws of nature settled down. The universe crystallized in such a way that every sentient creature in it is a brain in a vat. At some point soon, we shall be released from our vat, into a universe that is oddly smaller than it seems to be. Some time later, we shall all be recaptured, and envatted. This time, though, our eyes will be retained exactly as in the television scenario . . .

Now, if you please: determine the referents of my words 'brain', 'distance', and 'duration', at every stage in the scenario.

I hope that both your intuitions, and your patience, are beginning to fail. Where does this chaos leave us with regard to the original BIV argument? More importantly, where does it leave us with the debate between internal and external realism? That is the theme for the next chapter.

---

[10] I doff my hat to Patton (1988).

16

Mitigated aporia

The preceding chapters presented a mass of sceptical challenges. We started with a nightmarish Cartesian scepticism. Here, internal realism seemed on strong ground. We then considered a series of ineffable sceptical challenges. These may have applied some pressure to the internal realist, but nothing she could not resist. Finally, we considered a series of less nightmarish, more local sceptical scenarios. Somewhere along the line, it just becomes crazily dogmatic to say that *every* undetectable sceptical possibility depends upon a magical theory of reference.

My hope is that the preceding chapter has induced a state of aporia: a (metalevel) scepticism about our ability to answer Cartesian scepticism. Since our reaction to Cartesian scepticism determines our location on the realist spectrum—with external realism at one pole and internal realism at the other—this aporia infects our ability to choose where to position ourselves on that spectrum. In this chapter, my aim is to free us from the felt obligation to make that choice, without collapsing into either external realism or internal realism.

16.1 Clashing intuitions and trolley problems

The aporia can be presented as arising from a clash of intuitions. I am not using the word 'intuition' in any technical sense; it is simply a placeholder for a certain nebulous cluster of background thoughts, some of which may look philosophically neutral, some of which may not.

External realism may be grounded simply in a *metaphysical* intuition that the world is in principle *utterly* independent from human thought, so that Cartesian scepticism is always an unanswerable possibility. Alternatively, it might be grounded in an *epistemic* intuition concerning how we come to know about empirical objects, which leaves the BIV scenario as an unanswerable sceptical possibility. Internal realism combats this with a *semantic* intuition, that magical theories of reference should be banned. Our present state of aporia reflects the fact that these families of intuitions do not collectively determine a reaction to every single BIV-style scenario. This is likely to leave us with methodological worries concerning the way in which we have appealed to intuitions, whether epistemological, metaphysical, or semantic. *What*, we might wonder, *are we to do with this mess of intuitions and arguments?*

To answer this question, I intend to compare the plethora of BIV-style sceptical scenarios with problems from a rather different body of literature: the *trolley problems* in ethics. Trolley problems provide a series of 'intuition pumps' regarding ethical decision-making. At one extreme, we have:[1]

> **Trolley problem α.** Edward is the driver of a trolley, whose brakes have just failed. On the track ahead of him are five people; the banks are so steep that they will not be able to get off the track in time. The track has a spur leading off to the right, and Edward can turn the trolley onto it. Unfortunately there is one person on the right-hand track. Edward can turn the trolley, killing the one; or he can refrain from turning the trolley, killing the five.

At the opposite extreme, we have:[2]

> **Trolley problem ω.** David is a great transplant surgeon. Five of his patients need new parts—one needs a heart, the others need, respectively, liver, stomach, spleen, and spinal cord—but all are of the same, relatively rare, blood-type. By chance, David learns of a healthy specimen with that very blood-type. David can take the healthy specimen's parts, killing him, and install them in his patients, saving them. Or he can refrain from taking the healthy specimen's parts, letting his patients die.

Many people have relatively clear ethical intuitions about what Edward and David should do. But there are myriad cases in between that involve 'killing

---

[1] Thomson (1976: 206); the scenario is a verbatim quote from Thomson, which I have displayed in keeping with the other scenarios; it was first introduced by Foot (1967).

[2] Thomson (1976: 206); again, the scenario is a verbatim quote from Thomson.

one to save five'. At some point, there is a strong urge to throw up your hands and declare: *I have no idea what to do! My moral compass only guides me so far!* This is very like the situation we found ourselves in, at the end of Chapter 15.

Various responses have been offered to the trolley problems. What interests me is their parallels in the case of BIV-style arguments, and I shall explore these parallels over the next three sections. My ultimate focus, of course, is on how we might respond to BIV-style scenarios, so I will inevitably be a little brisk in my discussion of the trolley problem literature; my apologies to trolleyologists.

16.2 Selecting preferred intuitions

An initial response to aporia is to demand a radical rethink of our intuitions.

In the case of trolley problems, Peter Singer has stated that he wants to reject any appeal to ethical intuitions, preferring instead a pure form of consequentialism. This faces an immediate difficulty: if he bans *all* appeal to intuitions, then on pain of hypocrisy Singer must not appeal to intuitions when he attempts to motivate his own consequentialism. Really, then, Singer is asking us to distinguish between *good* intuitions (to be saved from aporia) and *bad* intuitions (to be damned).[3] Singer claims that *bad* intuitions are non-rational, highly particular moral judgements, which are spurious spandrels thrown up by our evolutionary past. *Good* intuitions— such as 'the intuition that five deaths are worse than one'—are 'rational intuition[s], something like [Sidgwick's] three "ethical axioms"'.[4] But to defend this stance, Singer needs to explain why an intuition's particularity, or its specific purported evolutionary history, should undermine its ethical authority, and that would seem to require an ethical argument.

In the case of BIV-style scenarios, we can equally imagine a philosopher who claims that she wants to reject any appeal to intuitions, preferring instead a pure form of external realism. Again, this faces an immediate difficulty: if she bans *all* appeal to intuitions, then on pain of hypocrisy she cannot appeal to intuitions when she attempts to motivate her own external realism. This external realist would need to explain why *her* metaphysical

---

[3] As Lillehammer (2011: 179) explains.   [4] Singer (2005: 350–1).

(or epistemological) intuitions are dependable. The arguments of Parts A and C indicate that this is an impossible task.

16.3 Navigating intricate intuitions

A second response to aporia is to embark upon an intricate process of discovering the *correct* reaction to every problem variant.

In the case of trolley problems, Frances Kamm holds that there is no simple universally acceptable answer to trolley problems (e.g. 'always save the many over the few'). Instead, Kamm asks us to consider trolley problem after trolley problem, working out exactly what to say in each case, feeding this back into our reasoning about trolley problems, coming up with new variants, working out exactly what to say, until we have reached the correct ethics. To this end, Kamm's *Intricate Ethics* (2007) lists around 120 trolley problem variants.[5]

The worry is, though, that no single set of intuitions *will* prove victorious; or, perhaps more significantly, that no single set of intuitions has any *right* to do so. This worry is particularly stark, since our ethical intuitions are simply too *humble* to be reliable when handling increasingly exotic trolley problems. Hallvard Lillehammer puts the problem well:

It is natural to expect that intuitions about cases are reliable, if at all, roughly in proportion to how similar the cases responded to in those intuitions are to cases in response to which intuitions of that kind have developed. Moral intuitions have not on the whole developed in response to highly unrealistic and complex cases. Lack of realism and complexity can therefore detract from reliability.[6]

This may lead us to doubt *any* reaction that we might end up offering in the face of a particularly unrealistic and complex trolley problem.

In the case of the BIV-style arguments, the analogous 'intricate' reaction would have the following form.[7] We would admit that there is no universally acceptable answer to BIV-style scenarios (e.g. 'all BIV-style arguments fail'). Instead, we must consider BIV-style scenario after BIV-style scenario, working out exactly what to say in each case, feeding this back into our reasoning about BIV-style scenarios, coming up with new scenarios, and

---

[5] Arithmetic by Lillehammer (2008: 456).   [6] Lillehammer (2008: 457).
[7] Warfield (1998: 143) comes close to advocating it.

so on. The (continuum-)many sceptical scenarios presented in Chapter 15 might form the starting point for such work.

I fervently hope that they do not. It is odd to expect that there should be any unique point of convergence for our intuitions concerning all the BIV-style scenarios. As I hinted in Chapter 15, our semantic intuitions are simply too humble to be reliable when handling increasingly exotic BIV-style arguments. We begin with everyday language use. Here, we are dealing with plants rooted in the deep soil of *practice*. By less-than-everyday reflections on this language use, we move to principles. These are cuttings curated by philosophers, and they are unlikely to capture perfectly the complexities of our ecosystem. These principles are then applied to a plethora of increasingly extraordinary sceptical scenarios. The cuttings are planted, far away from where they evolved, in the abstract atmosphere of thought experiments. They are expected to bear their ordinary fruits; they might equally well wither, or mutate into triffids.

It is not just semantic intuitions that have been transplanted beyond their natural home. We must face up to the worry that our metaphysical intuitions are similarly tainted. A certain kind of external realist strongly *intuits* that the world is in principle utterly independent from human thought. This may simply be a cutting taken from the humdrum observation that the objects of the world sometimes surprise and frustrate our abilities to understand them. Perhaps all that underpins the Independence Principle is the thought 'that there is something in every experience that escapes our arbitrary control'.[8] Equally, though, the opposing 'metaphysical intuition' of a certain kind of internal realist—that the world is in principle accessible to human thought—may simply be a cutting taken from the humdrum observation that we are normally able to find out more about the world when we try *really* hard.

In addition to the homely nature of our intuitions, it is also worth noting that our intuitions can be extremely *fragile*. It is well documented that various framing effects taint our reaction to trolley problems. If we consider a plethora of trolley problems and *happen* to reach some point of reflective equilibrium, we cannot in good conscience maintain that this point unproblematically reflects our invariant ethical inclinations, let alone the ethical facts. We must recognize that the kinds of answers that we

---

[8] James (1904: 464).

are inclined to offer, and the kinds of ethical arguments that we will be inclined to accept in the future, have been shaped by sheer contingencies of presentation, which are obviously ethically irrelevant.

Such framing effects may equally taint our discussion of BIV-style scenarios. I started Part C with Putnam's BIV argument. (Although if you read this book in order, this came after a part considering external realism, and a failed part exploring various attempts to deal with Cartesian angst; and prior to that, you had probably read various papers and books on these and related themes.) Appropriately primed, I moved to consider ineffable sceptical scenarios. After this, I investigated continuously varying sceptical scenarios, always starting at the 'small' end (a tiny universe, or a very young one) and moving outwards (a relatively large universe, or an ancient one). I have no confidence that the *order* of presentation has no effect on the kinds of answers that one is inclined to offer, and on the kinds of arguments that one will be inclined to accept in the future.

It gets worse. It is not clear how we might (in practice) test whether our discussion of BIV-scenarios was tainted by framing effects. We can ask a non-philosopher for her reaction to various trolley problems, and we can vary the framing of these problems across a population of non-philosophers in a controlled fashion.[9] By contrast, it can be extremely hard to bring non-philosophers (or philosophers, for that matter) to the point where they understand how Putnam's BIV argument is meant to work in the first place. By the time they *get* the argument—if they ever do—their intuitions have already been either beautifully honed or brutalized, depending upon one's point of view. So an experimental determination of the reactions of non-philosophers to various BIV-style scenarios is unlikely to provide much useful information. At best, we can only hope to examine the relevant metaphysical, epistemological, and semantic intuitions as they occur in more natural environments. But this leads straight back to the problem of *transplanting* them outside that environment. All this may be to say that *our present considerations depend upon intuitions that only a philosopher could truly have or really trust.* This should only make us more worried about the role they play.

---

[9] Though Berker (2009: 305–14) raises excellent concerns about current experimental design for experimental ethicists.

For all of these reasons, I am unable to take seriously the project of discovering the intricate principles that will deliver a precise verdict on every single BIV-style argument. Moreover, even if someone did think that they had landed somewhere in particular on the spectrum between internal realism and external realism, and could offer us a very precise verdict on exactly how much scepticism to take seriously, I would urge them to treat their own reaction with a heavy dose of ironic detachment.

16.4 Surrendering totally to aporia

If we cannot distinguish between the merits of different intuitions, perhaps we should surrender totally to the aporia.

One might draw the following moral in the case of trolley problems. Whenever there is a trolley variant, there are two sides to the argument, neither of which can claim victory. The only appropriate response to this is to suspend judgement in such cases; or at least, to suspend judgement about whether the beliefs that one ends up forming are justified. There is something very tempting about this reaction, but it is deeply risky. You may easily find yourself convinced that, for *any* ethical question, there is an appropriately associated trolley problem. But to surrender your ability to make any ethical judgement, or to give up on the idea that ethical beliefs can ever be justified, is to surrender an awful lot.

A similar moral might be drawn in the case of BIV-style arguments. Since there are two sides to every BIV-style argument, neither can claim victory. The only appropriate response to this would be to suspend any judgement about the coherence of the BIV-style scenario. Again, this is very tempting, but it is risky. You may find yourself convinced that we have no idea what to say about *any* questions about metaphysics or semantics, these being two of the key levers in the BIV-style arguments. At this point, you have surrendered rather a lot.

In particular, Part A contained a sustained argument for the inadequacy of external realism. If we surrender *totally* to aporia, then our only response to the earlier chapters of this book will have to be an ambivalent shrug. This is simply unacceptable. If someone suggests that reference is indeterminate, so that our words may fail to be about anything at all, an incredulous stare is the right response. If someone says that the objects of the world cry out to be named with English phonemes (or by our qualia, or by certain strings in the language of thought), a clenched fist is infinitely better than a shrug.

16.5 Connections with other anti-sceptical arguments

None of the three responses that I have surveyed is an adequate reaction to aporia. We cannot simply brush aporia aside by isolating the *good* intuitions. We cannot hope to navigate an intricate path through a morass of competing intuitions. And we cannot surrender totally to aporia and give up on all of our intuitions. The correct reaction is surely to cherish a certain amount of aporia, without surrendering to it across the board. We must respect the extent of the mess that we find ourselves in, whilst acknowledging that such messiness is not ubiquitous. To do otherwise would be to act in bad faith. It would either be to pretend that our intuitions are valueless, or to pretend that our intuitions have powers that they lack. We can defeat the sceptic sometimes, but not always, and we must abandon the idea that there is a precise point at which we are able to defeat the sceptic.[10]

Of course, there is a gap here, since there are anti-sceptical arguments other than Putnam's BIV argument (or Davidson's Cogito). Bringing them in might allow us to brush aside certain sceptical possibilities that BIV-style arguments leave vaguely lingering. But these arguments, too, will inevitably have vague limits. To explain why, I shall consider two examples of anti-sceptical strategies.

Charles Sanders Peirce attempts to rebut Cartesian scepticism by distinguishing 'real and living doubt' from what one might call *merely philosophical* doubt.[11] Peirce claims that only the former is coherent, for 'the whole function of thought is to produce habits of action'.[12] Thus Peirce entreats us: 'Let us not pretend to doubt in philosophy what we do not doubt in our hearts.'[13] Suppose we follow Peirce in drawing a distinction between *living* and *philosophical* doubt. Such a distinction might be useful in a particular context of enquiry, and in that context we shall be allowed to bury some of the *dead* sceptical concerns without much mourning. However, the distinction that we draw will surely not serve as a once-and-for-all dichotomy.

---

[10] For what it is worth, I urge the same reaction to trolley problems.

[11] Peirce (1868: 140–1; 1877: 6, 12). Putnam (1995b: 20–1; 1998: 524, 527n20) endorses something in this 'ballpark'.

[12] Peirce (1878: 292).   [13] Peirce (1868: 141).

In particular, it would surely be hopeless to think that one could precisely demarcate where living doubt ends and philosophical doubt begins. Philosophy has no sharp edges, and nor does merely philosophical doubt.

In a similar vein, consider Wittgenstein's discussion of 'hinge propositions'.[14] Wittgenstein's contention is that our ability even to make sense of justification (or the lack of it) turns on these hinges. He suggests that the Moorean claim 'Here is a hand' typically functions as a hinge, for if I attempt to doubt it, I lose any sense of what doubt even *is*.[15] Suppose that we go along with Wittgenstein here, accepting a particular rough-and-ready distinction between hinges and other propositions in a particular context of enquiry. Still, there is no sharp once-and-for-all dichotomy between hinges and other propositions. This is a point that Wittgenstein himself makes. We are asked to consider two claims:

'At this distance from the sun there is a planet' and 'Here is a hand' (namely my own hand). The second can't be called a hypothesis. But there isn't a sharp boundary between them.[16]

The point is precisely that Wittgenstein's hinges offer some protection against scepticism, but it would be nonsensical to ask exactly how much.

16.6 Virtues in vats

To press this point, I want to discuss something which might initially seem disconnected: the role that *ethical* values ought to play in our assessment of various sceptical scenarios. In a slightly different context, Robert Nozick claims that:

we want to *be* a certain way, to be a certain sort of person. Someone floating in a tank is an indeterminate blob. There is no answer to the question of what a person is like who has long been in the tank. Is he courageous, kind, intelligent, witty, loving? It's not merely that it's difficult to tell; there's no way he is.[17]

---

[14] Wittgenstein (1969).

[15] This connects with justificationism (see Chapter 11), and Putnam (1981c: 56, 83–4; 1986b: 114; 1987a: 21–5; 1988: 115; 1990b: viii; 1991c: 403; 1995a: 299; 1995b: 12; 2002a: 84–5, 166) has tended to sympathize with the idea.

[16] Wittgenstein (1969: §52).

[17] Nozick (1974: 43), Nozick's italics; Nozick is discussing whether or not to plug into his experience machine.

This consideration initially seems bizarre. It is not hard to imagine a scenario in which we would have good grounds for saying that an envatted brain is witty and courageous. Suppose that someone is envatted for a long period, and then released. During his envatting, the brain can continue to be shaped as a person, so that when he is at last released, he is witty or dull, brave or cowardly.

If there is anything to Nozick's remark, it comes through in his claim that 'we want to *do* certain things, and not just have the experience of doing them'.[18] Allow me to present a reading of this claim. At the somewhat shallow end: my well-being may not merely consist in my having sensations *as if* I have perfected some craft (such as lutherie), but in my *actually perfecting* that craft (in actually building musical instruments). Moving towards the rather deeper end, Putnam jokes:

> if we were two lovers making love, rather than just two people carrying on a conversation, then the suggestion that it was just two brains in a vat might be disturbing.[19]

There is a serious point to this. The value of (making) love consists in more than the sum of the first-person experiences of the two individuals involved. Indeed, Putnam's choice of locution—'it was just two brains'— raises a point that is obscured by the more obvious choice, 'we were just two brains': the very notion of personhood can be threatened by the BIV scenarios. To make this clear, I shall consider a final sceptical scenario that brings home, as deeply as I know how, Nozick's point that there is more to life than mere experience.

The isolated-BIV scenario. I am an eternally envatted brain who is *isolated*. That is, every other sentient creature in my world (if there are other sentient creatures) is an eternally envatted brain, but none of them share my vat-image.

To discuss the coherence of this scenario, let Sol be such an isolated BIV. Sol is in no causal contact with other humans, and cannot be unless he is rehoused in a human body. Sol therefore has no obligations, nor duties, to any other people. Indeed, I want to maintain that Sol cannot *be* a good

[18] Nozick (1974: 43), Nozick's italics.   [19] Putnam (1981c: 7).

man, but can only have experiences *as of* being a good man. And this gives us a way to understand Nozick's earlier claim that an envatted brain is not a 'certain sort of person'. Sol cannot be a *true friend*, for example, since Sol will never have interacted with other people who might have been his friends.

The foregoing might be summarized by saying that *the sceptical scenarios do not merely delude us perceptually; they can delude us ethically.* This formulation is expedient, since it suggests exactly how an internal realist—who wants to reject *all* sceptical challenges—would respond. I shall focus particularly on the case of Sol, since his ethical delusion is most complete.

The internal realist can agree that it is impossible for Sol to be a true friend. The internal realist may even agree with the more contentious claim that it is impossible for Sol's life to go well. But, the internal realist continues, it is not merely impossible for Sol to *be* a true friend; Sol also cannot posses the *concept* of true friendship. Just as Brian and Sol cannot refer to brains or vats, so Sol cannot refer to friends.[20] Neither can he refer to any of the various ways in which one can support a friend, nor the ways in which one can let down a friend. The entire ethical apparatus simply lies beyond Sol's ken. Thus, the internal realist simply offers us an ethically thick version of the BIV-argument:

(1g) An isolated BIV's expression 'true friendship' does not refer to true friendship.

(2g) My expression 'true friendship' refers to true friendship.

(3g) So: I am not an isolated BIV.

As before, it is only because I am not in Sol's situation that I am able to pity Sol's inability to understand true friendship.

However, the isolated-BIV scenario has interesting ramifications concerning interpretation. These can be brought out by considering Davidson's Cogito again. Recall from §14.1 that Davidson's Cogito has the form: *I think, therefore I am generally right.* Its immediate upshot is (supposedly) that no sceptical scenario leaves me with mostly false beliefs, so that no sceptical scenario can present a genuine Cartesian nightmare. However, sceptical scenarios can present what we might describe as an *ethical Kantian nightmare.* Though Sol is left with the ability to think thoughts—indeed, though most

---

[20] *Pace* Chalmers's (2005: §7 Objection 7, §9 Note 1) claim that 'friend' is 'semantically neutral'.

of Sol's thoughts will have to be *true*, if Sol is even to be a thinker—Sol's thoughts do not engage with anything of *value*.

What would be needed is an argument of the form: *I think, therefore I am a lover of the good*. In one place, Davidson himself seems to suggest precisely that there is such a constraint:

> In our need to make [the man we are interpreting] make sense, we will try for a theory that finds him consistent, a believer of truths, and a lover of the good (all by our own lights, it goes without saying).[21]

This sits strangely with Davidson's suggestion that, to make Sol a consistent believer of truths, we should interpret his thoughts as being about electronic signals (or similar; see §14.1). In particular, Sol's word 'friend' would then refer to certain electronic signals. But these electronic signals cannot plausibly be said to be *thinkers*. The problem is not the chauvinistic concern that they are not flesh-and-blood humans. The problem is that they are too *insubstantial* to qualify as thinkers (even for a very generous interpretationist). To be sure, they 'engage' with Sol from time to time. But nothing much persists of them when they are not 'engaging' with Sol. They have no lives beyond their brief 'encounters' with Sol. They are not thinkers, and so it is difficult to think that Sol could be the true friend of these patterns of electronic signals, any more than a man on LSD can be true friends with those chemicals responsible for his 'friendly' hallucination.

In short, if we interpret Sol to make him a consistent believer of truths, then what Sol calls 'friends' are not his friends, let alone his true friends. The issue which now arises is that 'friend' should be a *thick* term—its content is simultaneously descriptive and ethical—and the notion of being a 'true friend' is similarly thick. But we, who are not envatted, assign no value to the relationship which Sol calls 'true friendship' (except in the limited sense that it may give Sol some hedonic pleasure). We are able, therefore, only to assign a (relatively) thin content to Sol's words 'true friends'. Otherwise put, to make Sol's thoughts about 'true friends' true, we deprive them of value.

Matters are equally bad if we turn our attention from thick terms, such as 'friend', to ethically thin terms, such as 'good' and 'right'. Suppose, in an effort to make Sol a lover of the good (per se), we offer an account of

---

[21] Davidson (1970: §II).

reference to the good which does not go via paradigmatically good *things*. This will just sound like a magical theory of reference if anything does. It will be to say that thinkers possess the ability to refer to the good and the right because these values *cry out* to be so named.

Here, then, is the problem. *If we make Sol a believer of truths, we do not make him a lover of the good.* To be clear, I am not offering this as a rebuttal to Davidson's Cogito, for Davidson can either deny that Sol is a thinker at all, or drop the requirement that thinkers must be lovers of the good. In fact, Davidson clearly does the second. He later recommends that an interpreter should ascribe

beliefs that are mostly true and needs and values the interpreter shares or can imagine himself sharing if he had the history of the agent and were in comparable
circumstances.[22]

Davidson's constraint is not, after all, that we must regard every agent as a lover of *the* good. Rather, it is just that an agent must take some things as *her* goods. Otherwise put: to be a *thinker*, one must also be a *desirer*. (This is plausibly motivated by his belief–desire–action conception of psychology.) Now, there is no barrier to our imputing both beliefs and *desires* to Sol. If nothing else, his hormone levels give us some indication of which situations he prefers over others. But one cannot make Sol a lover of *the* good.

I am not a BIV, so in particular, I am not an isolated BIV. I have not, then, discussed Sol's predicament because I worry about my own. The reason I have discussed Sol is that the ethical considerations that I have raised are almost certain to feed into our attempts to assess the pleth-ora of BIV-style arguments considered in Chapter 15. Indeed, they *ought* to. Our desire to interpret people as even capable of moral agency, and as potential lovers of the good, will affect our judgement concerning exactly where BIV-style arguments break down. Let me offer some concrete examples.

At the shallow end: consider the variant on the Vat Earth scenario (see §15.4). An earthling is tapping on the walls of some vat-earthling's vat, and at just that moment, the earthling and a vat-earthling simultaneously think:

---

[22] Davidson (1985: 92).

If I were envatted and someone were looking at me right now through the glass walls of my vat, I would want to be judged according to the language of the embodied, in thinking 'I am envatted'.

The pressure that this variant applies is primarily one of *empathy*.

Getting deeper: consider the future-1 scenario (see §15.3). Dom's entire universe is about to be obliterated. If we interpret Dom's language as lacking a future, we leave him incapable of even beginning to articulate the horror of the extinction of *everything*.

Deeper still: consider the capture scenario (see §15.5). Here there is some pressure to allow the community, after the moment of envatting, to drift gradually towards speaking a language like Brian's. This will make them believers of more *truths*. However, it strips them of their ability to remain lovers of the *good*. Indeed, it will deprive them of their desire to *be* a certain sort of person. Suppose I have been captured, and envatted in an *isolated* fashion (as Sol is). Before I was envatted, I loved my partner; my well-being involves my continuing to love *him*, and his continuing to love *me*. You destroy something of me (and him) when you interpret me as loving-in-the-image him-in-the-image.

There is, then, an *ethical* significance to the judgement that a certain BIV-style scenario is incoherent, on the grounds that it would require a *magical* theory of reference. For this reason, ethical considerations both can and (morally) *should* be brought to bear upon the question of where to place ourselves on the spectrum between external and internal realism. An internal realist, who wants to write off *all* sceptical scenarios, must equally write off these considerations as mere *sentimentality*. To do so surely requires an *ethical* argument.

With all of this in mind, I want to revisit the temptations towards ineffable scepticism, discussed in Chapters 13 and 14. I have repeatedly emphasized that Brian's word 'brain' could only refer to brains by magic. I also suggested that ineffable scepticism arises from continuing to contemplate magic. Let me offer an ethically charitable diagnosis of why it is so hard to let go of magic: we are unwilling to regard Brian as someone so far beyond our community that he is unable to love the good, or to pursue it. Perhaps knowing that our nightmares have a noble source will help us to overcome them.

16.7 Letting go

We have seen that putative sceptical scenarios slide from an incoherent dependence on magic to an unanswerable epistemic possibility.[23] But by now I hope that we have given up on the idea that there is some *precise* point at which they flip. For which considerations are we to adduce to determine that point, in any given scenario? How are metaphysical, epistemological, semantic, and (now) ethical intuitions to be played off against each other, and brought into a precise equilibrium? They have been transplanted from their natural homes into the most extreme environments possible. The order in which they have been adduced is liable to influence our future judgement. We simply cannot trust any answer that we might ever be inclined to give.

Of course, the significance of this discussion is not particularly connected to the various sceptical scenarios. The (putative) point of trolley problems is to illuminate ethics more broadly. Equally, the (putative) point of discussing BIV-style scenarios is to illuminate the debate between internal and external realism.

We have found that the only way to make sense of the debate surrounding external realism is via an attitude towards scepticism. The external realist embraces the Cartesianism Principle, endorsing the possibility of nightmarish Cartesian scepticism. The internal realist rejects any and all forms of Cartesian angst. So to choose between them—or, indeed, to place ourselves somewhere on a spectrum with external realism at one pole, and internal realism at the other—we would need to answer the following question: *which sceptical possibilities should we entertain?*

That question was raised in §12.1. We now have an answer to it: *Shut up!* There is no hope of trying to answer how much scepticism we should or should not entertain. Rather than trying to determine exactly where to position ourselves between internal and external realism, the felt obligation to choose between these two poles must simply be *surrendered*. We should accept that *radical* scepticism is incoherent. We should accept that *radical* external perspectives leave us radically alienated from the world. But our ability to defend ourselves against radical scepticism is as vague as the term 'radical' itself. Our grasp on precisely where we should position ourselves

---

[23] Wittgenstein (1969: §54) notes something similar in connection with his 'hinges'.

between the twin poles of internal and external realism is equally vague. In a sense, the thing to do is to place ourselves somewhere between the external and the internal realist, but we should not aim to be any more specific than that. We are too human to say much more.

16.8 Internal and external as a distinction rather than a dichotomy

This observation has several consequences for recent debates in metaphysics and metametaphysics. I shall explore these in Part D. However, I shall close Part C by explaining an immediate consequence for some recent attempts to attack metaphysics by means of Carnap's dichotomy between 'internal' and 'external' questions.[24]

Internal sentences are formulated within a particular theoretical vocabulary.[25] An example of such a sentence might be 'the temperature at this spacetime region is 200 Kelvin'. Internal sentences are perfectly meaningful, for Carnap, since they are perfectly scientific. They are to be evaluated according to standard scientific practice.

On the other hand, *external* sentences go beyond any particular theoretical vocabulary.[26] They have a 'metaphysical' feel about them. For example, they might ask after the 'essence' of some kind of entity, or ask whether any such entity 'really' exists. In the *Aufbau*, and more firmly in *Scheinprobleme* (Carnap 1928b), Carnap dismisses these as nonsense. But Carnap's later writings treat such sentences more sympathetically. Carnap treats a claim like 'there are not *really* any electrons' as a pragmatic proposal to adopt a framework which contains no primitive word 'electron' (and which lacks axioms relevantly like those governing 'electron' in our current theory). And, regarded *as* proposals, 'there is no question of right or wrong, but only a practical question of convenience or inconvenience of a system form, i.e. of its suitability for certain purposes'.[27]

---

[24] As Friedman (1992: 22) notes, Carnap draws such a dichotomy as early as the *Aufbau*, but his most famous presentation of the internal/external dichotomy is Carnap (1950).

[25] In the *Aufbau*, these are sentences within a constitution-system; Carnap (1937: 3) then calls them sentences of the 'first kind'.

[26] In the *Aufbau*, these are called 'metaphysical'; Carnap (1937: 3–4) then calls them sentences of the 'second kind'.

[27] Carnap (1937: 3–4; see also 1950: 30–3; 1956: 44–6; 1963: 871–3).

For Carnap, then, the decision to embrace a framework cannot be guided by any question of *truth*—indeed, the question of *truth* does not even make sense—but must rather simply be guided by the question: 'are our experiences such that the use of the linguistic forms in question will be expedient and fruitful?'[28] Carnap, then, would have had very short shrift with the external realist's Cartesianism Principle. To call a theory false is at worst nonsense, and at best a practical suggestion to spurn the theory. But to describe the theory as ideal is surely to recommend its adoption. To call a theory *ideal but false* is then just garbled. Hence Huw Price explains:

In effect, the traditional metaphysician wants to be able to say, 'I agree it is useful to say this, but is it true?' Carnap rules out this question.[29]

The key idea here is simply the rejection of all sceptical possibilities. Put this way, it does not depend upon drawing a sharp analytic/synthetic dichotomy. For this reason, Price completes the preceding quote by adding 'and Quine does not rule it back in'. This is the background to *neo-Carnapian* approaches to metaphysics.

As mentioned in §8.3, attacks on metaphysics (*tout court*) can be rather blustering. Sometimes we are instructed to avoid adopting a distinctively metaphysical attitude. Other times, we are told that we must only ask what there is, without falling into the trap of asking what there REALLY IS. Left to themselves, these images are utterly empty. But neo-Carnapians characterize the difference between themselves and their opponents in terms of their respective attitude towards scepticism. This is sufficiently concrete to debate. Indeed, it connects directly with the themes of Parts A–C. The neo-Carnapian is evidently an internal realist, and since we cannot be internal realists, we cannot be neo-Carnapians.

It is worth spelling out the problem for neo-Carnapians in their own terminology. Whatever neo-Carnapians take a framework to be, we must ask the neo-Carnapian: *From which framework is it appropriate to reject all sceptical possibilities?* We can take our pick from the examples of Chapter 15, but let us focus on Dom, in a universe doomed to extinction one second from now (see §15.3). We must admit that Dom's way of speaking is useful. Indeed, it is hard to see how it could be any *more* useful. Now, perhaps I might waver on exactly how to interpret Dom. But the disquotational interpretation is

[28] Carnap (1950: 29–30).   [29] Price (2009: 326).

surely a reasonable interpretation—I certainly do not see that I can 'rule it out'—even though it entails that everything that Dom believes about the future is false. So I cannot rule out that Dom's way of speaking is useful but false. More generally, we cannot altogether rule out the question 'I agree it is useful to say this, but is it true?' (I should add that I am interpreting Dom, not from *nowhere*, but from within my *own* framework; where else?)

I cannot, then, join with the neo-Carnapians in embracing the dichotomy between internal and external questions. But I should immediately add that I do not thereby 'rule in' *all* questions that neo-Carnapians would characterize as 'external': BIV scepticism is, indeed, ruled out. And it is worth noting that when neo-Carnapians draw their line between internal and external questions, they are not much concerned with the gerrymandered sceptical hypotheses of Chapter 15. They are instead concerned with the question of whether rather sweeping 'discourses'—perhaps physics, ethics, or mathematics—could be useful but false. So in some fights, I may yet be on their side. (I shall say more about this in Part D.)

When, then, is the question of 'traditional metaphysics' to be tolerated, and when is it to be ruled out? To demand a *precise* answer to that question is to demand that we position ourselves somewhere *precise* between the two poles of external and internal realism. And I have argued that we cannot do that.

The same point could be expressed as follows: *We must collapse the dichotomy between internal and external questions.* Not because the analytic/synthetic dichotomy has collapsed (the Quinean objection to Carnap) but because the dichotomy between representable and unrepresentable sceptical possibilities has collapsed. It may sometimes be useful to think of certain questions as more internal or more external, but there is no sharp line, drawn once and for all, where internal ends and external begins. The very idea of an internal/external dichotomy must be surrendered, for it is a *meta*metaphysical bogey.[30]

---

[30] So I am adding *internal/external* to Putnam's (1987b: 1, 20–1, 26–40) bonfire of dichotomies that have become 'metaphysical bogey[s]' (2002b: 11).

Part D
Realism within Limits

17

Semantic externalism

We have overthrown the debate between internal and external versions of realism. If asked whether we are realists, we shall reply: *Yes*. But we might well add, *for what that is worth*. If asked what sort of realists we are, we shall simply shrug. There is little more we can say than: *The realist sort of realists*.

Still, having recognized both the limits of the realism debate and the limits of our ability to articulate the limits of our realism, it is worth pausing to take in the view. In this final part of the book, I want to explain that there is now a slightly hazy gap between earth and sky, as it were, where before there was a crisp horizon. To show this, I shall explore two long-standing Putnamian themes in some detail. In Chapters 18 and 19 I shall explore conceptual relativism. My concern in this chapter is with semantic externalism.

According to semantic externalism, "'meanings' just ain't in the *head*!'[1] I have already leaned upon some version of semantic externalism in defending premise (1) of the BIV argument. But in this chapter, I want to explore it in its own right. I shall maintain that a (messy) kind of semantic externalism falls out of our own *practices* of investigation and referring. This is no surprise: Putnam's advocation of semantic externalism was always distinctly un-metaphysical. Indeed, semantic externalism per se is ultimately neutral with respect to the realism debate, in just the way that the Independence and Correspondence Principles are. Consequently, external realists, internal realists, and everyone in-between can accept semantic externalism. However, when pushed on just *how* external our semantic externalism should be, we find that we are being asked where precisely to locate ourselves on the spectrum between internal and external realism. Given the discussion of Chapter 16, there is little we can say.

---

[1] Putnam (1973: 704; 1975b: 227; essentially repeated in 1981c: 19).

17.1 Two principles of Putnam's semantic externalism

The first component of Putnam's semantic externalism is:

The Hidden-Structure Principle. Many of our words do not simply abbreviate a long list of superficial properties, but (rigidly) pick out exactly those things with a certain 'general *hidden structure*'.[2]

As examples of phrases governed by the Hidden-Structure Principle, Putnam suggests 'water', 'elm', 'gold', 'aluminum', 'this substance', and 'this liquid'. The Hidden-Structure Principle might initially sound worryingly metaphysical. Certainly, it is easy to imagine it being advanced by an external realist, who treats the 'hidden structure' in question in terms of Natural (with a capital 'N') reference magnets that are *required* to forestall the model-theoretic arguments (see §§3.2 and 7.5). But Putnam's motivations for advancing the Hidden-Structure Principle are much more mundane, as indeed is the notion of 'hidden structure' that it invokes. Even when Putnam first presented the principle, Putnam claimed to be doing little more than reconstructing our *actual* practices concerning the relationship between our use of language and our scientific investigations of the world.[3]

The best illustration of this comes from Putnam's discussion of the ancient Greek word 'χρυσός', which we typically translate as 'gold':

Unless we say that what the ancient Greeks meant by 'χρυσός' was *whatever has the same essential nature* as the paradigmatic examples, then neither their search for new methods of detecting counterfeit gold (which led Archimedes to the density test) nor their physical speculations will make sense.[4]

The task facing Archimedes was to determine whether something superficially like χρυσός was, indeed, χρυσός. We therefore cannot make sense of this, or of his eureka moment, if 'χρυσός' abbreviates a list of superficial properties. Instead, the word must pick out things with a certain hidden structure. The Hidden-Structure Principle is, then, motivated just by the way in which we use words in the context of scientific discovery.

---

[2] Putnam (1975b: 235); compare Kripke (1972) on natural kinds.

[3] Putnam (1992b: 349; see also 1982c: 220–1; 1990a; 1994b: 187). Ebbs (1992a: 2, 6, 10–12) is excellent on this. Putnam (1992b: 349) notes that the gist of his (1975b) was clear to him as early as 1966–7.

[4] Putnam (1981c: 103–4; 1981a: 200), Putnam's italics, though I have replaced 'chrysos' with "'χρυσός'", for uniformity. See also Putnam (1975b: 235–8; 1979a: 285; 1988: 36–7).

These internal motivations for the Hidden-Structure Principle tend, however, to be obscured by focusing on Putnam's famous science fiction:[5]

> **The Twin Earth scenario.** It is the year 1750, and Earth has a distant neighbour, Twin Earth. This is a planet just like Earth, except that wherever there is H_2O on Earth, there is XYZ on Twin Earth. XYZ is indiscernible from H_2O without post-Daltonian chemistry.

Putnam holds that earthlings in 1750 use 'water' to mean something like 'this liquid' (pointing to a paradigmatic sample). The idea is that they pick out everything which is the *same liquid* as the indicated sample, where liquids count as the *same* just in case they have the same hidden structure.[6] Putnam therefore concludes that the earthling word 'water', in 1750, was governed by the Hidden-Structure Principle, and refers *only* to H_2O, even though H_2O and XYZ are superficially similar.

I have a confession to make: I am unsure about Putnam's diagnosis of the Twin Earth scenario.[7] But, the vast literature on Twin Earth notwithstanding, it is deeply unimportant whether or not the word 'water', in 1750, in a thought experiment, falls under the Hidden-Structure Principle. The case study of χρυσός is much clearer, it is far from being an isolated example, and it demonstrates that our own practices mandate the Hidden-Structure Principle.

Putnam also brings out a second aspect of our referential practices. As a community, we acknowledge that some people are *experts*. In particular, they are experts at recognizing (or knowing how to recognize) whether or not something is gold. To acknowledge this is to acknowledge that we (typically) use the word 'gold' in the same way as experts, so that we can (typically) accept at face value the answers that experts give to the question 'is this thing gold?' Putnam called this the *division of linguistic labour*.[8]

The most straightforward cases of division of labour will require that some people are reasonably well positioned to recognize whether or not

---

[5] Putnam (1973: 700–3; 1975b: 223–7; 1981c: 22–5; 1986b: 109–11; 1986a: 287–8; 1988: 30–6; 1990a: 59–70).

[6] Putnam (1973: 708–9; 1975b: 232–3). Putnam (1975b: 239; 1990a: 69; 2002c: 101–4) notes that this is sensitive to *context*, which I fully endorse, but it would lead me too far afield to explore this.

[7] I am quite moved by Hacking (2007), and will offer a few further comments on this later.

[8] Putnam (1973: 704–6; 1975b: 227–9). In discussing the division of labour, Ebbs (2000: 257–8) rightly stresses the importance of taking 'each other's words at face value'.

something falls under a certain kind. Thus Putnam says that 'we could hardly use such words as "elm" and "aluminum" if no one possessed a way of recognizing elm trees and aluminum metal'.[9] Since both 'elm' and 'aluminum' featured on Putnam's list of words that are governed by the Hidden-Structure Principle, this suggests that Putnam might think that our referential practices mandate a second principle:

> **The Recognizability Principle.** In order for us to have a word that picks out exactly those things with a certain hidden structure, we must be able to recognize things with that structure.

However, there is an apparent tension between the Hidden-Structure Principle and the Recognizability Principle. If a kind term picks out *hidden* structure, then it seems that we could use that kind term whilst being completely ignorant about *what* structure the predicate picks out. This tension can be explored via the Twin Earth scenario. In 1750, neither earthlings nor twin-earthlings are able to tell the difference between H_2O and XYZ. Thus the Recognizability Principle seems to suggest that 'water' cannot refer *only* to H_2O. This would contradict Putnam's own diagnosis of the Twin Earth scenario.

If we are to avoid this tension, we shall evidently have to take more care over what it takes to 'be able to recognize things with that structure'. This will occupy us for the remainder of the chapter.

17.2 Brown on recognitional capacities

I can recognize zebras when I see them. That said, I lack this ability when I am taken to the Zoo of Deception, where most of the things which superficially seem to be zebras are cunningly painted mules.[10] Nonetheless, since there are few such zoos, I can indeed recognize zebras. The moral is that whether I have a recognitional capacity or not depends upon my powers of discrimination in my environment.

Jessica Brown has applied this line of thought to the Twin Earth scenario.[11] Oscar the pre-Daltonian earthling can recognize largish, liquid samples of H_2O when confronted by them. Of course, Oscar lacks this

---

[9] Putnam (1973: 704; 1975b: 227).   [10] Dretske (1970: 1015–16).
[11] Brown (1998: 285–91).

ability when he is placed in a room where samples of XYZ are scattered among the samples of H_2O. Nevertheless, since Oscar lives on Earth, where there is no XYZ, it remains the case that Oscar can recognize H_2O. The tension between the Hidden-Structure Principle and the Recognizability Principle dissolves, at least in this case. More generally, Brown maintains that reference is 'fixed directly by recognitional capacities',[12] that is, by our powers of discrimination within our environment.

Immediate caution is required. The sorts of recognitional capacities that Brown has highlighted respond very rapidly to environmental changes: place me in the Zoo of Deception, and I (immediately) lack the ability to recognize zebras. The referent of my kind terms does not shift so quickly: place me in the Zoo of Deception, and my word 'zebra' still refers to zebras. That, after all, is why I say something *false* when I point to a cunningly painted mule and say 'that's a zebra'. So when Brown says that reference is 'fixed directly by recognitional capacities', we should read her as saying that reference is fixed directly by the powers of discrimination that people in our community have had over a vaguely determined but suitable period of our history.[13]

Unfortunately, even this is wrong. To show why, I shall present a scenario that grows out from one of Putnam's discussions of Archimedes.[14]

The Sicilian fake-gold scenario. It is the third century BCE, and Archimedes has not yet developed the density test. As it happens, there is a substance, *fake gold*, which is superficially very similar to gold but somewhat less dense. Indeed, prior to developing the density test, neither Archimedes nor anyone else has the ability to discriminate between fake gold and (genuine) gold. Worse: there are a few samples of fake gold in Sicily. But, by sheer good luck, none of these are amongst the paradigms of what the Sicilians call '$\chi\rho\upsilon\sigma\grave{o}\varsigma$'. Archimedes comes across one of these fake-gold samples, X, and says quite reasonably 'X is $\chi\rho\upsilon\sigma\grave{o}\varsigma$'.

Prior to developing the density test, fake gold is to Archimedes's ability to recognize gold as cunningly painted mules are to my ability to recognize

---

[12] Brown (1998: 300).

[13] Many thanks to Rob Trueman for suggestions here.

[14] Putnam (1975b: 237–8). Collins (2006: 63) offers a similar criticism of Brown, adopting Ebbs's (2000: 248ff.) discussion of the ability in 1650 to distinguish gold from platinum.

zebras. However, since fake gold occurs in Sicily in small quantities, it is not as if we have suddenly taken Archimedes to the equivalent of the Zoo of Deception. So, before developing the density test, Archimedes (and everyone else) lacks the ability to recognize gold. Brown's account therefore tells us that Archimedes's word 'χρυσός' refers to *both* gold and to fake gold. This verdict is a little worrying, and we can make it more worrying by following Archimedes's progress:

> The very next day, Archimedes has his eureka moment. He develops the density test and applies it to all of his paradigm χρυσός-samples satisfactorily. He applies it further afield, with great success. And then he applies it to X, yielding a very different result. He says, quite reasonably, 'maybe I was *wrong* when I said that X is χρυσός'.

I claim that we should share Archimedes's last thought.[15] To be clear: I am not claiming that, in the Sicilian fake-gold scenario, Archimedes's word 'χρυσός' definitely did not apply to fake gold before his development of the density test. My claim is only that it is not *certain* that his word 'χρυσός' then applied to fake gold as well as gold. Since Brown's account renders it certain, her account must be rejected.

Brown has focussed our attention on something that is undoubtedly very important in determining the reference of our words. My claim is just that other things can also be relevant. And for that reason, the tension between the Hidden-Structure and the Recognizability Principles is not yet resolved. We shall have to read talk of 'what we are able to recognize' in the Recognizability Principle somewhat more broadly than Brown would allow.

17.3 Continuity of reference over time

In discussing the Sicilian fake-gold scenario, I hinted that the reference of Archimedes's word 'χρυσός' *prior* to his development of the density test might depend upon the fact that he will *later* develop the density test. This sort of claim is characteristic of *temporal* semantic externalists, who hold

---

[15] So I am echoing Putnam's (1975b: 238) sentiment: 'This may not *prove* that it isn't gold, but it puts the hypothesis that it may not be gold in the running.'

that the reference of a word at a time can depend upon what will happen after that time. Temporal semantic externalism merits our investigation, since we might be able to smooth over the tension between the Hidden-Structure and the Recognizability Principles by considering what powers of discrimination we *will* develop.

In one discussion of Twin Earth, Putnam issues a challenge to those who want to say that, in the Twin Earth scenario, an earthling's word 'water' in 1750 refers to both H_2O and XYZ:

Should we then say the reference *changed* when chemistry was developed?.... [If so,] then we will have to say that almost every scientific discovery changes the reference of our terms.... To me this seems clearly wrong.[16]

Putnam's argument is as follows: there has been no change in the reference of 'water' since 1750 (only new discoveries with the development of science); 'water' now only refers to H_2O (thanks, perhaps, to our powers of discrimination); so 'water' referred only to H_2O in 1750. This argument is utterly germane to temporal semantic externalism. Moreover, temporal semantic externalists might hope that it enshrines a general pattern of reasoning which they can employ.

The main weakness in the argument (pattern) is its first premise. Certainly there was no *sudden* shift in the reference of 'water' with the discoveries by Lavoisier and company. But perhaps there was a *gradual* shift in meaning, as the new science *gradually* exerted its influence on the meaning of the word 'water' in the ordinary vernacular. Even granting everything said so far, one could coherently believe the following: in 1750, most earthlings' uses of 'water' are indeterminate between picking out hidden structure and abbreviating a list of superficial properties (that would encompass both H_2O and XYZ); in 2012, it is wholly unambiguous that 'water' picks out things with a certain hidden structure; and there is a gradual transition between these two states.

To explore this further, I will retreat from the Twin Earth thought experiment, and instead discuss a case study which is closer to real life. The case study concerns zebras, and has been suggested by Henry Jackman

---

[16] Putnam (1981c: 24), developing some earlier (1973: 702–3; 1975b: 225) remarks.

in an effort to motivate temporal semantic externalism,[17] although I have changed the example slightly to reflect recent zoology.[18]

The plains zebra, *Equus quagga*, is one of three species of zebra. There are six subspecies of plains zebra, the southernmost of which, *Equus quagga quagga*, became extinct in the latter half of the nineteenth century. All six subspecies 'interweave geographically and grade morphologically into one [an]other'.[19] So now consider a story, describing how the quagga got its name.[20]

The quagga-naming scenario (near-actual version). It is the 1770s, and European zoologists have encountered plains zebras for the first time, starting with the southernmost subspecies, *Equus quagga quagga*. Adopting a Khoikhoi word, they name this animal the 'quagga', probably aiming to pick out an entire species.

Throughout the nineteenth century, zoologists encounter morphologically distinct groups of plains zebras in various locations from southern to eastern Africa. Believing these to be of different species, both from one another and from the animals they call 'quaggas', they introduce new names (e.g. 'Burchell's zebra', 'Grant's zebra') for these purportedly new species. Meanwhile, the animals they have been calling 'quagga' are hunted to extinction. Much later, biologists determine that all of these animals belong(ed) to a single species.

By the end of this (near-actual) story, it is clear that the word 'quagga' picks out an extinct subspecies (*Equus quagga quagga*). That is, indeed, how the word is used today. But now consider an alternative story, where the word 'quagga' is introduced in the same way, but where differences soon arise.

The quagga-naming scenario (merely possible version). It is the 1770s, and European zoologists have encountered plains zebras for the first time, starting with the southernmost subspecies, *Equus quagga quagga*.

[17] Jackman (1999: 159–60). Ebbs (2000: 248ff.) presents similar examples to the same end.
[18] Groves and Bell (2004) and Lorenzen et al. (2008).
[19] Lorenzen et al. (2008: 2821).
[20] The extremely complicated actual history of taxonomy is mapped by Groves and Bell (2004: 182–3, 193–5).

Adopting a Khoikhoi word, they name this animal the 'quagga', probably aiming to pick out an entire species.

Throughout the nineteenth century, zoologists slowly move from southern to eastern Africa, on a grand expedition to catalogue the zebras of Africa. They encounter hundreds of thousands of plains zebras as they go, with no sharp morphological differences that cannot be written off as natural variance. The zoologists therefore (correctly) believe that they are always encountering animals of a single species. Accordingly, they continue to use the word 'quagga' to refer to all of the animals they encounter. Much later, genetic evidence confirms that there is just a single species.

By the end of this (merely possible) story, it is clear that the word 'quagga' picks out an entire species of zebra (*Equus quagga*). But in neither story does it feel like there is any change in the reference of the word 'quagga' (only new discoveries). So Jackman holds that there *is* no change of reference in either story. Jackman concludes that an utterance in 1780 of the sentence 'the quagga form a distinct species' *was* therefore false (in 1780), given what *actually happened* in the nineteenth century. However, if events in the nineteenth century *had been* different, that very same utterance *would have been* true (in 1780). Jackman therefore takes it that these two stories vividly illustrate temporal semantic externalism.

However, there is an equally good diagnosis of this case study that does not lead to temporal semantic externalism.[21] In the late eighteenth century, the word 'quagga' certainly applied to all members of the subspecies *Equus quagga quagga*, but it was simply indeterminate whether or not it applied to the remaining plains zebras. Different future use throughout the nineteenth century will resolve this indeterminacy in various different ways, making the word 'quagga' increasingly precise in its application. But this will not affect what the word referred to in the late eighteenth century. Finally, since the application of the term is only *gradually* made more precise, we can indifferently describe this as a gradual change of practice, or as a gradual sharpening of a single practice. Either way, however, it will not seem to those involved as if there is a *change* in application of the word 'quagga'. So

---

[21] McLeish (2009: 71–9) explores this diagnosis. Interestingly, Wilson (1982: 572–3) is the first philosopher to discuss zebras in this sort of context, and this is roughly the diagnosis that he offers.

we can preserve the undeniable feeling that there is continuity of reference without resorting to temporal semantic externalism.

In maintaining that both diagnoses are acceptable, I am not claiming that later events could not possibly play any role in determining earlier reference. On the contrary, if Archimedes is just hours away from his eureka moment, perhaps this contributes to fix his current use of the word 'χρυσός', for in that case it is very hard to say that there has been any *change* (noticed, or incremental) in his reference in the intervening minutes. Nevertheless, sometimes the best interpretation of past speakers will be that they failed to recognize distinctions that we now recognize (or recognized more distinctions than we now trace). As at the end of §17.2, we may not have not exhausted all the factors that are relevant in fixing reference.

17.4   Temporal and modal deference

There is, however, a second supposed motivation for temporal semantic externalism. It comes out of considering what a speaker *would have deferred to*. To illustrate the idea, let us return to the Sicilian fake-gold scenario. An important point of this scenario, as Putnam notes, is that even before Archimedes develops his density test:

> there are a host of situations that *we* can describe (using the very theory that tells us that X isn't gold) in which X would have behaved quite unlike the rest of the stuff Archimedes classifies as gold. . . . If we had performed the experiments with Archimedes watching, he might not have known the theory, but he would have been able to check the empirical regularity that 'X behaves differently from the stuff I classify as χρυσός in several respects'. . . . If, now, we had gone on to inform Archimedes that gold had such and such a molecular structure (except for X), and that X behaved differently because it had a different molecular structure, is there any doubt that he would have agreed with us that X isn't gold?[22]

Another way to gloss this is to suggest that Archimedes would be willing to defer to better-informed scientists from the future, on questions of the form 'is this χρυσός?' He might even make this explicit, saying 'I reckon that this is χρυσός, and may future experts judge me right or wrong.' This would be to make explicit an attitude that is already implicit in our scientific

---

[22] Putnam (1975b: 237–8), Putnam's italics; I should be clear that the Sicilian fake-gold scenario, as I have presented it, adds several details to the scenario that Putnam is discussing.

practices: if we want future generations to stand on our scientific shoulders for the view, we also want them to see the mistakes that we made in raising them.[23] Thus we seem to admit the possibility of the 'division of labor *across time*'.[24]

I am happy to grant that, to some extent, we ask that our present practices be judged by scientists who come after us, and that such deference helps to link our reference to theirs. Nevertheless, we would rightly be unwilling to defer, if we discovered that science was about to enter a dark age, so that our successors will be spectacularly *less* well informed than we are now. So, when we consider how Archimedes might have reacted to better-informed scientists from the future, the point is not that the scientists are *from the future*, but simply that they are *better informed*.[25] Indeed, a similar point applies to more straightforward (synchronic) cases of (putative) division of labour. When I defer to the folks in white coats, I hope that it is not just *because* they are in white coats, but because they are indeed *better* informed than me.

The cases just mentioned therefore lend no further weight to temporal semantic externalism. They do, however, suggest that there is a further element which might bear on the question of what fixes reference. If Archimedes was on the verge of developing the density test, but instead suddenly died, did he refer to gold with '$\chi\rho\upsilon\sigma\grave{o}\varsigma$', given that he would have done so if he had lived and so become better informed? I have no idea, but I do not want to say that what he would have done is utterly irrelevant. So I am willing to countenance a *modal* dimension of deference, to better-informed possible people. That said, I am under no illusions that our actual discriminatory powers are rather more important than what we would do if we knew vastly more about the world.

(A digression is perhaps necessary here, to explain how modal deference affects the BIV argument of Chapter 12. Given the strictures of the BIV scenario, no one is outside Brian's vat. However, it is undoubtedly physically possible that someone should be outside Brian's vat. And, intuitively, such a person would be better informed about the world than Brian is. So one might think that, if we allow Brian to defer to *possible* people, then we

---

[23] Thus I side with Jackman (2005: 370) and McLeish (2009: 76) against Brown (2000: 186–7).

[24] Putnam (1975b: 229); Putnam noted that one could view the Twin Earth scenario in this way, but did not himself pursue the idea.

[25] Thanks to Tim Storer for discussion on this.

run the risk of allowing Brian's word 'brain' to refer to brains after all, thereby undermining all of Part C. Fortunately, this is not the case. The motivation to embrace modal deference might be put roughly as follows: if we had worked harder than we actually did, then we would have come to a better understanding of the structure of the world, and would have moulded our language accordingly; and our actual language is to be judged by the standards that we would have attained. But no matter how cunning Brian had been, or how hard he had worked, he would still have been hoodwinked by the infernal machine into which he is wired. To the extent that modal deference can be motivated at all, then, it is inadequate *in kind* to allow Brian to refer to the wider world.)

17.5 Messy semantic externalism

Over the past few sections, we have adduced a number of considerations that might figure in fixing reference. None were found *trumping*, and none were ruled out altogether. All told, then, we are left with a fairly nebulous list of factors to bear in mind when considering reference. We should advance something like:

> **Messy semantic externalism.** Reference depends upon many things, including: the environment you are in; your intentions and interests; your past, present, and future powers of discrimination; what people did before you, are doing now, and will do in the future; and what better-informed people (would) do.

I am deliberately leaving open the question of how much weight to assign to each of these factors, and would recommend that it should simply be approached case by case. This might seem like a tremendous cop-out, but I would suggest that this is a *feature* rather than a flaw. The messiness of meanings is sometimes just a datum to be acknowledged, rather than a problem to be solved.[26] Semantic externalism was motivated by our practices. Well then: *messiness is a feature of our own practices.* We humans are mucky beasts.

We should cheerfully admit that there might be multiple different ways to interpret a practice that is extended in time, without much to choose between them. But, to be absolutely clear, acknowledging this does *not*

---

[26] We can draw this moral from Putnam (1975b: 242–5; 1986a: 292–5); see also Ebbs (1992a: 15, 21).

amount to accepting the kind of radical referential indeterminacy that is characteristic of the model-theoretic arguments. We are wondering whether 'water' referred only to H_2O or to XYZ as well; or whether 'quagga' referred to a subspecies or a species. There is no threat here that 'water' picked out certain natural numbers, that 'quagga' refers to cherries, or that every word is equally about every thing.

17.6 Kinds beyond all recognition?

I shall close this chapter by revisiting the tension between the Hidden-Structure and Recognizability Principles. The Recognizability Principle was originally motivated by the practical fact that what we refer to very often depends upon the actual and concrete division of labour in our present community, which in turn depends upon the fact that some people actually have the ability to distinguish gold from clever fakes, beeches from elms, and so forth (all in our actual environment, of course). But, although such matters are *extremely important* in determining reference, they do not *exhaust* all relevant factors. Thus, over the course of this chapter, we have success-ively widened the notion of 'what we are able to recognize', as it features in the Recognizability Principle. Our referential powers may be able to out-strip our present powers of discrimination, for we can sometimes refer to kinds that no one can *yet* recognize. Indeed, perhaps we are occasionally able to refer to kinds that no one ever *will* recognize. This thought might prompt us to read the Recognizability Principle extremely broadly, and as follows: our referential powers cannot (in principle) outstretch what it is (in principle) possible for someone like us—only better-informed and perhaps in better circumstances—to recognize.

Reading the Recognizability Principle in this way tears it loose from its moorings in 'everyday' division of linguistic labour. Even so, some philosophers will maintain that there is *still* a tension between the Hidden-Structure Principle and the Recognizability Principle. Here is a nice example of the supposed tension, due to Sanford Goldberg:[27]

---

[27] Goldberg (2008: 152).

Goldberg's bloofer scenario. *A* and *B* are distinct natural kinds. However, it is in principle impossible for us to discriminate between *A*s and *B*s. We do not even suspect that they form two distinct natural kinds. Accordingly, we use the same word, 'bloofer', in the presence of both *A*s and *B*s. As it happens, we encounter *A*s extremely regularly, and encounter *B*s only very rarely.

According to Goldberg, semantic externalists should maintain that the word 'bloofer' is governed by the Hidden-Structure Principle and refers only to *A*s.[28] But since there is no way for us to distinguish *A*s from *B*s, even in principle, this is incompatible with the Recognizability Principle, no matter how weakly it is read.

More is at stake than the Recognizability Principle. Goldberg's bloofer scenario presents us with a mild instance of unanswerable Cartesian scepticism. As Goldberg points out, if 'bloofer' does not refer to *B*s, then people will make (rare) false assertions of the form 'that thing is a bloofer', where 'that thing' picks out some *B*. Such assertions will be as justified as any assertion can be; indeed, by hypothesis it will be *impossible* for anyone to come to a justified belief that such assertions are false. Thus we have a (putative) instance of an indefeasible but justified *falsehood*.

A very mild version of Cartesian angst looms. The external realist will embrace such angst. The internal realist will brush it aside. What should *we* do, who are neither external nor internal realists?

It will help to start by drawing a parallel between Goldberg's bloofer scenario, and the Sicilian fake-gold scenario. We were prepared to countenance that Archimedes's word 'χρυσός' refers only to gold, and not to *X*, so that he will have said something false if he says '*X* is χρυσός'. But as Putnam emphasizes, *we*, who come after Archimedes and are better informed than him, are in a position to judge that *X* was fake gold rather than gold.[29] Moreover, nothing prevents us from worrying (nor, indeed, from expecting) that better-informed scientists might stand to us as we stand to Archimedes,

---

[28] Goldberg (2008: 152). There is a nuance here: Goldberg (2008: 152*n*8) acknowledges that *Davidson's* semantic externalism might not regard 'bloofer' as referring only to *A*s, but explicitly holds that *Putnam's* semantic externalism is so committed.

[29] Putnam (1975b: 237).

and might tell similar stories in the future about us. But in the case of Gold-berg's bloofer scenario, all of this is ruled out by hypothesis. No one will stand to us as we now stand to Archimedes; indeed, no one *possibly could*.

With this distinction between the two cases in mind, we must ask whether Goldberg is right that the word 'bloofer' refers only to *A*s. He cannot simply appeal to an analogy with the Sicilian fake-gold scenario, since we have just broken the analogy. And it would be somewhat dog-matic to insist that 'bloofer' must refer only to *A*s, on the grounds that we encounter *A*s much more frequently than *B*s.

A more interesting thought arises from the fact that we might both *intend* for 'bloofer' to be a natural kind term, and *justifiably believe* that it is such. So we seem to face a dichotomy: *either* our intentions are respected, in which case the word 'bloofer' refers only to *A*s and we say something false when we say 'that is a bloofer' (pointing to a *B*); *or* our intentions are overriden, in which case the word 'bloofer' refers to both *A*s and *B*s so that we say something false when we say 'the bloofers form a natural kind'. On either horn, there is an indefeasible but justified falsehood, and (mild) Cartesian angst remains.

However, this dichotomy is posed too quickly. It assumes that our expres-sion 'natural kind' refers to natural kinds in the sense employed by the story. Obviously our expression 'natural kind' refers to natural kinds. So the question is simply whether the world's natural kinds could be as described by Goldberg's bloofer scenario. That is, we are forced to ask whether the scenario is even *coherent*.

Evidently, the scenario cannot be narrated as known fact. But we know that this alone is insufficient grounds for dismissing a scenario (recall the discussion of §§8.4, 11.5, 12.5, and 13.1). The question is whether we can *represent* the scenario. This is not straightforward, and a comparison will help us see why.

In Chapter 11, I presented several scenarios in which there are truths that transcend our ability to recognize them. With Putnam, I emphasized that such unjustifiable truths are not 'external' impositions, but something that arise within our physical theories (which are themselves well justified). By contrast, Goldberg's bloofer scenario requires that the kinds *themselves* tran-scend our ability to recognize them, no matter how ingeniously we develop our physical theories and experimental techniques. It is difficult to see how we could *ever* be pressed to adopt a physical theory that countenances (the physical possibility of?) such kinds. Goldberg's bloofer scenario therefore involves an 'external' imposition,[30] in the sense that it comes from outside the realm of all possible physical theorizing.

But is that sufficient grounds for dismissing the scenario? Can we not give some sense to the notion of 'natural kind' that Goldberg's bloofer scenario invokes? If all of the world's natural kinds are discernible from one another except for *A* and *B*, then might not the expression 'natural kind' transcend the limits of our mere physical *theorizing* and possess a content that is more than barely formal?

I have no more idea of how to arbitrate this debate than I have of how to arbitrate the various scenarios discussed in Chapter 15. For that reason, I recommend regarding Goldberg's bloofer scenario as just another imponderable vat variation. But if your intuitions tell you firmly that the scenario is coherent, I would recommend that you vary the case, following the template of Chapter 15. In the extreme case, consider the sceptical worry that *no* two objects are of the same natural kind, but that this is utterly undetectable, so that we shall still (usefully) classify things as 'gold', 'zebra', 'electron', or whatever. Hopefully you will worry what the phrase 'natural kind' could even *mean* in this extreme case. But at some point between this extreme case and the case of Goldberg's bloofers, I trust your intuitions will wave the white flag of surrender.

There are, then, two morals to this chapter. First, that any realist (internal, external, or something in between) can and should adopt some form of semantic externalism, since it is mandated by our own practices. Second, that our intuitions concerning the 'extent' of semantic externalism disintegrate at precisely the point where we are asked to adopt a precise position between internal and external realism.

---

[30] Compare Ebbs's (1992a: 13) claim that, for Putnam, 'our ontological conceptions are not available independently of the norms underlying the linguistic practices in which we participate'.

18

Conceptual relativism

Putnam's commitment to semantic externalism is matched in duration by his commitment to conceptual relativity. As with semantic externalism, his first statement of the idea precedes his discussion of 'internal realism'. Moreover, conceptual relativity became increasingly important during his 'internal realist period'. Where conceptual relativity had initially been an optional component of 'internalist' philosophy,[1] Putnam started to say that 'internal realism is, at bottom, just the insistence that realism is *not* incompatible with conceptual relativity'.[2] Whilst he now rejects 'internal realism', he continues to stand by conceptual relativity. Indeed, Putnam now traces the contours of the realism debate, less by following the trail of scepticism (as I have done in Parts A–C), and more by one's commitment to conceptual relativity.[3]

My initial challenge is to make sense of what 'conceptual relativity' might even be. In Chapter 19, I shall consider a moderate doctrine that might answer to the name. But in this chapter, I shall define *conceptual relativism* as the radical doctrine that objects and kinds are scheme-relative. If correct, this doctrine would pose a serious challenge to metaphysics. Unfortunately, it is untenable. Indeed, its problems are essentially those of nonrealism (as explained in Chapter 9).

18.1 The conceptual relativist manifesto

Conceptual relativism presents us with a manifesto, whose first pledge is:

The Pledge to Tolerate. There is more than one way to approach the world, with no unique best way.

---

[1] Putnam (1980a: 100; 1981c: 49).
[2] Putnam (1987b: 17; see also 1991c: 404; 1994b: 178).
[3] See in particular Putnam (2012b: 62–4).

The various different approaches will apparently mention different objects and different natural kinds. If we have pledged that no approach is best, we may well think that there is no question of which objects and natural kinds *really exist*. And this thought motivates the scandalous central claim of conceptual relativism:

> **The Pledge to Relativize.** The objects that we talk about and the kinds that they fall under are relativized to conceptual schemes.

This poses a challenge to certain branches of philosophy. In particular, consider some paradigmatically metaphysical questions, such as: *which objects really exist? are there really any objects of this kind?* and *what is the essence of that object?* If objects and kinds are always relativized to conceptual schemes, then all such questions can only be asked from *within* a conceptual scheme. Deep confusion will be engendered if they are asked from a scheme-transcendent, metaphysical perspective. Accordingly, we arrive at the third and final manifesto pledge of conceptual relativism:

> **The Pledge to Liquidate.** Certain contemporary metaphysical debates are bankrupt and must be liquidated.

An immediate question is whether, in advocating 'conceptual relativity', Putnam is advocating what I have called *conceptual relativism*. Certainly he has sometimes strayed close to the doctrine. For example, in *Reason, Truth and History*, he comes very close to an explicit endorsement of the Pledge to Relativize:

'Objects' do not exist independently of conceptual schemes. *We* cut up the world into objects when we introduce one or another scheme of description.[4]

However, in later work Putnam both offers an extremely clear criticism of the Pledge to Relativize and explicitly rejects that Pledge.[5] So Putnam's 'conceptual relativity' should not simply be equated with what I am calling *conceptual relativism*. I shall say more on what it might amount to in Chapter 19. In this chapter, I shall continue the task of exploring conceptual relativism.

---

[4] Putnam (1980a: 101; 1981c: 52; see also 1980a: 101, 102; 1981c: 52, 54; 1983c: 230–1).
[5] Most clearly in Putnam (2012b: 63–4).

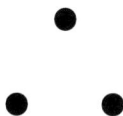

Figure 18.1 Rudy and Stan's mini-world.

18.2 Rudy and Stan on mereology

Putnam's work presents us with several putative examples of conceptual relativity. In the foundations of mathematics, Putnam observes that we can either construct modality from primitive sets, or construct set theory from primitive modality.[6] Equally, we could start with sets, or start with functions.[7] In topology, we may treat either points or regions as primitive.[8] Newtonian physics can be formulated either with or without fields.[9] So it goes. But Putnam's favourite example of conceptual relativity concerns *mereology*,[10] and this will be the focus of my discussion.

Putnam asks us to imagine two characters, Rudy and Stan, confronted by the *miniworld* depicted in Figure 18.1. Rudy claims that there are three objects in the mini-world: the three dots. Stan claims that there are seven objects in the miniworld: three dots, three *duos* of dots, and one *trio* of dots. More generally, whenever Rudy claims that there are n objects, Stan claims that there are $2^n - 1$ objects.

Resolving this apparent disagreement may seem easy enough. As Frege noted, we count things under concepts:

if I give [someone] a deck of playing cards with the words 'determine the number thereof', he does not thereby know, whether I want to find out the number of cards, or of the complete games [one could play with the deck], or perhaps of the point-cards in skat. . . . I must add a word: card, game, or point-card.[11]

One might think that disagreement has arisen between Rudy and Stan simply because we have given them a mini-world with the ambiguous

---

[6] Putnam (1967; 1975c: 70–2; 1977: 492; 2004: 67).

[7] Putnam (1979a: 287–8).

[8] Putnam (1977: 489–92; 1978a: 42–3; 1987b: 19; 1987c: 71; 1992a: 115–20; 2004: 46–7; 2012b: 58); see also Goodman (1978: 99–100, 114–16).

[9] Putnam (1977: 492; 1978a: 44–5; 1979b: 613; 1981c: 73; 1983c: 230).

[10] Putnam (1987b: 18–20; 1987c; 1988: 110–16; 1993c: 308–9; 2004: 37–46; 2012b: 57–8, 63). Putnam attributes the example to Carnap 'in the early nineteen fifties', and calls the protagonists 'Carnap' and 'the Polish Logician'.

[11] Frege (1884: §22); the point-cards in skat are 10, J, Q, K, A.

words: 'determine the number thereof'. That disagreement is then to be dissolved simply by adding some words: 'determine the number *of dots*'.[12]

Correct though it is, Frege's observation needs to be reconciled with our ability to offer numerically definite sentences in first-order logic. For example, to specify that there are exactly three things, I can simply produce the sentence:

$$\exists x \exists y \exists z (x \neq y \wedge y \neq z \wedge x \neq z \wedge \forall w(x = w \vee y = w \vee z = w))$$

This is a sentence of pure first-order logic. So it seems perfectly possible to act on the command 'determine the number thereof', so long as we treat this as the command 'determine the number *of things falling under any concept whatsoever*'. Moreover, Rudy thinks that this quantified sentence is true of the mini-world, whereas Stan thinks that it is false. So the disagreement between Rudy and Stan is visible at the level of which first-order sentences they accept and reject. If we follow Quine in thinking that to be is to be the value of a variable in our best (first-order) theory of the world,[13] then Rudy and Stan will seem genuinely to disagree about what there is. Now, *perhaps* Frege's observation somehow holds the solution to their apparent disagreement, but we cannot know this merely by quoting a few lines from the *Grundlagen*. We need to find out for ourselves what that solution is.

If we *do* suppose that Rudy and Stan genuinely disagree, then we shall want to know who is right. It is at this point that conceptual relativism is supposed to kick in. According to Putnam: Rudy's sentence is true *relative* to his conceptual scheme, and Stan's sentence is true *relative* to his conceptual scheme, and 'the mini-world itself does not *force* us to talk one way or to talk the other way'.[14]

It is easy to see how this case study of the mini-world is supposed to exemplify the manifesto of conceptual relativism. Regarding the Pledge to Tolerate, conceptual relativists will hold that Rudy and Stan have different conceptual schemes which are equally good responses to the mini-world. Now, if objects were not relativized to conceptual schemes, then Rudy would be wrong to say that there are only three objects; but a conceptual relativist will argue that Rudy can hardly be regarded as *mistaken*: his approach is, after all, as good as Stan's. Accordingly, conceptual relativists

---

[12] Dorothy Edgington has suggested this in conversation; also compare Blackburn (1994: 17–18).
[13] Quine (1948: 32; 1951a: 67; 1957: 17).
[14] Putnam (1994a: 245), Putnam's italics.

will say that this example realizes their Pledge to Relativize. Finally, conceptual relativists will say that this reveals the pointlessness of contemporary debates about mereology. They will therefore claim to have delivered part of their Pledge to Liquidate.

Despite all this, a *hardcore* realist might staunchly maintain that there is a uniquely correct description of the (mini-)world.[15] Such a hardcore realist therefore buys into an extraordinarily strong version of the correspondence theory of truth, namely, that 'there is just One True Theory of the fixed mind-independent Reality.'[16] Even the external realist regards this as pious legend, rather than Credo-enshrined orthodoxy (see §1.2), and indeed there is an obvious connection between hardcore realism and external realism. Suppose we challenge the hardcore realist to say which (if either) of Rudy's or Stan's is the uniquely correct description of the (mini-)world. If the hardcore realist cannot answer this question, then some degree of Cartesian angst looms threateningly nearby,[17] for it seems that a perfectly justifiable theory (either Rudy's or Stan's) will be undetectably but systematically mistaken. Hardcore realism, then, would seem to sit firmly towards the externalist pole of the continuum between internal and external realism.

However, we have not yet offered any argument that the hardcore realist *cannot* say which scheme is correct. On her behalf, I shall now consider an argument which seems to count against Rudy's scheme. It does not do that, exactly, but it does serve to undermine conceptual relativism.

18.3 The behind-the-schemes argument

One might diagnose the apparent disagreement between Rudy and Stan by invoking

The cookie-cutter metaphor. 'There is a single world (think of this as a piece of dough) which we can slice into pieces in different ways.'[18] To be an object in a conceptual scheme is to be a chunk of that dough, sliced out by the scheme's cookie cutters.

---

[15] Van Inwagen (2009) embodies Putnam's (1977: 490–1; 1978a: 43) 'hardcore' realist.

[16] Putnam (1989: 352; see also 1979a: 288; 1980a: 100; 1981c: 49; 1982a: 30).

[17] See Putnam (1978a: 43; 1994a: 248–9).

[18] Putnam (1987b: 19; 1987c: 70; see also 1982a: 31; 1987b: 33–6; 1988: 113–14).

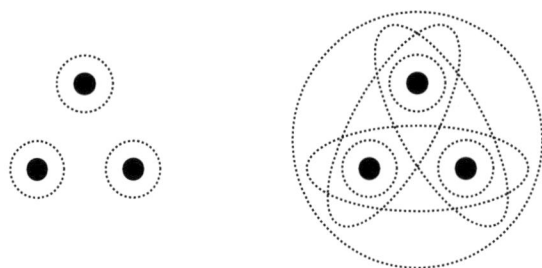

Figure 18.2 Cut along the dotted lines: instructions for Rudy (left) and Stan (right).

The general idea here is that the world supplies us with a lump of dough, from which we can slice out objects of various shapes. It is easy to apply this idea to our case study: Rudy's and Stan's different ways of slicing the same dough of the mini-world are illustrated in Figure 18.2. More generally, the cookie-cutter metaphor promises to realize the Pledge to Relativize since, in the statement of the metaphor, the notion of an 'object' is clearly relativized to a conceptual scheme.

Unfortunately, other central notions in the cookie-cutter metaphor are *not* relativized to conceptual schemes. In particular, the notion of *the single world* (thought of as a piece of dough) transcends any particular conceptual scheme. This is ultimately the undoing of the cookie-cutter metaphor, as Putnam himself came to explain a few years after (apparently) endorsing it.

Putnam asks a question about the cookie-cutter metaphor: 'What are the "parts" of this dough?'[19] In a context when someone is arguing that different *mereological* schemes are equally acceptable, it might come across as hopelessly question-begging to ask about *parts*. However, no one who advocates the cookie-cutter metaphor can raise this objection. The advocate of the cookie-cutter metaphor herself suggests that the world is a piece of dough, and she quantifies over the parts of the dough when she explains what it is to be 'an object in a conceptual scheme'. For just this reason, she is committed to the view that to be (simpliciter) is to be a part of the dough. So Putnam's question is a fair one.

His question, however, is barbed. Suppose we think that Rudy and Stan have adopted equally acceptable conceptual schemes, and we want to explain this in terms of the cookie-cutter metaphor. In that case, we must

---

[19] Putnam (1987b: 19; 1987c: 70). Case (1997: 5–9) offers an interesting discussion of the cookie-cutter metaphor, and its appeal.

think that Rudy and Stan have both successfully sliced out various parts of the single dough that is the world. But then we must acknowledge that Stan makes all the slices in the dough that Rudy makes, and many more besides (just look again at Figure 18.2). This means that the world has more parts than Rudy acknowledges. So, if Rudy takes himself to be speaking unrestrictedly about *all* the parts of the world, Rudy is just wrong. To save Rudy from this fate, we must interpret him as speaking with restricted quantifiers, as not attempting to talk about *all* the parts of the world.

This undermines the Pledge to Relativize: we have merely *restricted* Rudy's quantifiers, and restriction surely fails to qualify as relativization in any interesting sense. Equally, it undermines the Pledge to Liquidate: the idea that we sometimes employ restricted quantifiers surely poses no threat to any metaphysical debate. Putnam concludes, correctly, that the cookie-cutter metaphor is a dead end.

The discussion of cookie-cutting should help us to understand one of Davidson's (briefer) criticisms of the very idea of a conceptual scheme. One might try to explain conceptual relativism by invoking the metaphor that there are many different ways to *organize* the world. Davidson rejects this:

> We cannot attach a clear meaning to the notion of organizing a single object (the world, nature etc.) unless that object is understood to contain or consist in other objects. Someone who sets out to organize a closet arranges the things in it.[20]

The organizing-the-closet metaphor faces the same problem as the cookie-cutter metaphor. To make sense of the idea that different schemes can organize the world in different ways, we must assume that the objects of the world are ready and waiting for the schemes to come along and organize them.

A third attempt to understand conceptual relativism might draw inspiration from:

The quantifier-variance thesis. Rival conceptual schemes employ quantifiers with different meanings.

This thesis has been advanced by Eli Hirsch.[21] Hirsch himself rejects the Pledge to Relativize,[22] and so is not a defender of conceptual relativism

---

[20] Davidson (1973: 14).

[21] Hirsch (2002; 2008: 373ff.; 2009: 231n2, 248); see also Putnam (2004: 37–8).

[22] Hirsch (2002: 55–6; 2005: 92–3; 2009: 231).

(I discuss Hirsch's own views in Chapter 19). Nonetheless, the quantifier-variance thesis seems promising for conceptual relativists. If the quantifiers of different schemes have different meanings, then perhaps it will be impossible to offer a neutral comparison between objects from different conceptual schemes. This will allow us to realize the Pledge to Relativize.

However, to assess the quantifier-variance thesis, we need to understand what the 'meaning' of a quantifier might be. (What follows picks up on an argument advanced by John Hawthorne and Matti Eklund.)[23] One obvious component of the 'meaning' of a quantifier is its introduction and elimination rules in a natural deduction system. But this will not account for the supposed difference between Rudy's and Stan's quantifiers, since both (presumably) employ the standard rules of classical first-order logic. The only other component of a quantifier's 'meaning' would seem to be the *domain* over which it ranges. The quantifier-variance thesis, then, seems to require that we regard rival conceptual schemes as operating with different domains of quantification. This thought is easily applied to our case study: Rudy and Stan produced two different 'models' of the mini-world, which neither share a domain nor satisfy the same first-order theory. (Contrast this with the permutation argument of §2.1, where two models are produced which share a single domain and satisfy exactly the same theory.) But to talk about competing domains is no better than talking about different ways to slice a single piece of dough. According to our understanding of the quantifier-variance thesis, when we encounter an instance of conceptual relativism, we are given two different domains of quantification, A and B. If these are legitimate domains of quantification, then their union, C, is also a legitimate domain of quantification. Then since $A \subseteq C$ and $B \subseteq C$, what looked like a potentially interesting instance of quantifier variance turns out just to be a thoroughly humdrum instance of quantifier *restriction*. Indeed, in the specific case of Rudy and Stan, we find that Rudy's domain is a proper subset of Stan's. As in the cookie-cutter metaphor, we have interpreted Rudy as speaking with restricted quantifiers.

Three attempts to understand conceptual relativism have fallen to three successive arguments. The arguments share a common core. In Putnam's reflections on cookie cutters, the dough sits behind any particular scheme.

---

[23] Hawthorne (2006) and Eklund (2006: 104–5; 2008a: 204–7; 2008b: 386–9; 2009: 150). Eklund explained the argument in this way at seminars in Harvard in Spring 2009. Compare Hirsch (2002: 64) and Putnam (2004: 39–40).

Scheme A's model   Scheme B's model   Scheme C's model

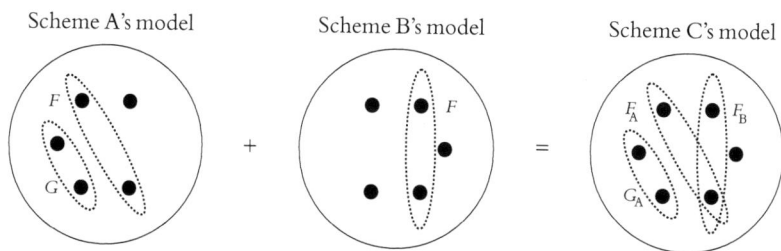

Figure 18.3 The behind-the-schemes argument. The objects recognized by two schemes, A and B, are represented by black blobs. Note that A and B recognize many of the same objects, but that each scheme recognizes an object that the other scheme omits. The predicate-extensions (or cookie jars) recognized by each scheme are represented by dotted lines. Note that the two schemes have 'orthogonal' predicate-extensions (and that the two schemes have different jars with the same label 'F'). Nonetheless, the two schemes can easily be combined into a single scheme: C includes all the objects recognized by either scheme, and incorporates the predicate-extensions of both schemes (with predicates indexed to their original schemes, to ensure consistency).

In Davidson's comments on organization, the objects in 'the closet of nature'[24] do not belong to any particular scheme. In considering the domains of quantifiers, those domains and hence the objects in them do not belong to any particular scheme. In short, every attempt to explain conceptual relativism ends up invoking objects that sit behind any particular scheme, thereby undermining the Pledge to Relativize. I shall therefore call this the *behind-the-schemes argument* against conceptual relativism.

It is worth noting that the disagreement between Rudy and Stan is artificially limited, since I have assumed that their languages contain no predicates.[25] However, the behind-the-schemes argument readily generalizes. All we need to do is group cookies together into 'cookie jars', labelled with predicates. The idea is illustrated in Figure 18.3.

For all its generality, the behind-the-schemes argument operates only at the level of truth, reference, and correspondence, and not at the level of meaning (speaking broadly and informally). To see this, consider two schemes, Gothic and Bauhaus. Suppose that Gothic countenances a person so strong she can lift anything, whilst Bauhaus countenances an object so heavy it cannot be lifted. The scheme obtained by the behind-the-schemes

[24] Davidson (1973: 14).
[25] Putnam (1987b: 33–4; 1987c: 72–3) allows the schemes to include monadic colour predicates, but does not consider relational predicates, or collective predicates (such as '____ comprise a kettle').

argument cannot consistently countenance the existence of both objects when described *as such*. Instead, the Gothic-predicate '___ can lift anything' and the Bauhaus-predicate '___ cannot be lifted' acquire different subscripts during the behind-the-schemes argument (see Figure 18.3). This preserves consistency, but it sacrifices the original meanings of the predicates. Accordingly, there are deep questions concerning the extent to which expressions from different schemes can share meanings.[26] But these questions are separable from the behind-the-schemes argument, and unless we can address the behind-the-schemes argument we shall have to give up on conceptual relativism.[27]

18.4 The syntax-first thesis and idealism

The behind-the-schemes argument will arise whenever the conceptual relativist employs an image which starts with objects and then brings schemes to bear upon them. If she wants to deliver on the Pledge to Relativize, she will instead have to start with schemes and maintain that objects follow in their wake. Thus she must employ something like:

> **The syntax-first thesis.** Certain sentences express propositions. Objects then fall out of the syntax of the sentences that we use to express propositions. But the syntax of our language comes first.

To see how this would help the conceptual relativist, suppose that we are confronted with two theories which apparently countenance different ontologies. Since both theories are (presumably) consistent, they have models, M_1 and M_2. Applying a behind-the-schemes argument, we can generate a new model, N, and from this we can read off a third theory. Now, the behind-the-schemes argument is supposed to have some *bite* because N is supposed to represent more of the very same world than either M_1 or M_2. But if syntax somehow 'comes before' the objects, then all we have is three different models that reify the (inferential) connections between propositions, as they are expressed by three different theories. There is no longer any a priori reason to favour any one of these models or any one of these theories.

---

[26] See Putnam (1978a: 38–40; 1992a: 118–19; 1994a: 246) and Case (1997: 13–15).
[27] Eklund (2008a: 205) directs a point like this against Putnam.

It is noteworthy that the syntax-first thesis is somewhat similar to the neo-Fregean metaphor that objects 'are no more than *shadows* cast by the syntax of our discourse'.[28] However, there is a potentially significant difference. Neo-Fregeans are aiming to use a claim which is already understood (perhaps 'line *x* is parallel to line *y*') to introduce abstract objects ('the direction of *x* = the direction of *y*'). For these purposes, it might be sufficient to claim that we come to know about certain objects (directions) by developing new syntactic forms for already-understood expressions that make explicit reference to other objects (lines). The conceptual relativist needs much more than that. If syntax precedes objecthood in a merely *epistemological* sense, then we will still be able to run the behind-the-schemes argument. The conceptual relativist who wants to invoke the syntax-first thesis has to be saying that the *existence* of objects (somehow) depends upon syntax. This is what I find problematic.

In §8.1, I argued that everyone should be able to accept the Independence Principle. In particular, everyone should be able to accept that 'human minds did not create the stars or the mountains'.[29] The syntax-first thesis threatens precisely this claim. If I understand any of the metaphor of directionality that it invokes, it claims that there would be no stars or mountains if there had not been a *language* in which one 'speaks of stars' or 'speaks of mountains'. This is obviously false, at least when read 'internally', as part of our best broadly empirical theory (see §8.1 again). The proponent of the syntax-first thesis must, then, intend for it to be read 'externally'. At this point, alarm bells should start to ring.

In Chapter 9, I discussed Putnam's early nonrealism. The nonrealist holds that we must first *understand* sentences, in terms of 'inner' sensations alone, whereafter external objects come swimming into view. I rejected this picture, on the grounds that it assumes an unacceptably external perspective, from which it then denies the Independence Principle. The syntax-first thesis is guilty of exactly the same mistakes. It requires that we first *understand* propositions, in a way that does not depend upon the existence of objects, and that we then carve out objects from the syntax that we used to

---

[28] Wright (1992b: 181–2); Eklund (2006; 2009: 153–4) is particularly keen to explore neo-Fregeanism in this regard.

[29] Putnam (1982a: 30).

express those propositions. This is nothing but external subjective idealism, all over again.[30]

18.5 The demise of conceptual relativism

The syntax-first thesis can only be affirmed from the external perspective of a subjective idealist. The same is true of conceptual relativism itself. Crucially, it cannot be affirmed from *within* any conceptual scheme.

The basic problem is very simple. From whatever perspective it is right to affirm that two rival schemes both succeed in talking about certain objects, *that* perspective countenances both kinds of objects without relativizing them to the two rival schemes. Otherwise put: the behind-the-schemes argument can be run *within* any conceptual scheme, and so conceptual relativism cannot be affirmed from within any conceptual scheme. But the conceptual relativist herself denies the existence of any scheme-transcendent perspective. In short, conceptual relativism is as dead as nonrealism, and it has died for much the same reason.

Nevertheless, hardcore realists cannot afford to relax. Although we have rejected the scandalous doctrine of conceptual relativism, the possibility of a multiplicity of conceptual schemes still poses a threat to metaphysical debates. That is the theme of Chapter 19.

---

[30] Putnam (2012b: 61, 64) detects idealism in his 'internal realist' approach to conceptual schemes; however, given his natural realism, he frames this criticism in terms of 'intermediaries'.

19

Conceptual cosmopolitanism

In Chapter 18, I explained that conceptual relativism must be rejected. My aim, in this chapter, is to save everything that was good about conceptual relativism whilst avoiding its problems. To this end, I shall draw on Hirsch's discussion of shallow debates and Putnam's discussion of people who are equally at 'home' in multiple conceptual schemes. I call the resulting position *conceptual cosmopolitanism*. This disavows the Pledge to Relativize but retains the Pledge to Tolerate and the Pledge to Liquidate. Consequently, it presents a serious threat to metaphysics. However, given the mitigated aporia that I have recommended in this book, it is hard to say exactly how much of a threat it poses.

19.1 Hirsch on shallow debates

The stance I shall outline has two active ingredients. The first is the notion of a *shallow* debate.

It is surely a general truism that, if the parties to a debate do not actually disagree, then their debate is not worth having. Metaphysical debates are no exception to this rule, and Hirsch therefore proposes

The shallowness criterion. If participants to a debate should both regard each other as making true statements, then their debate is shallow and should be liquidated.[1]

The difficulty, of course, concerns how to map uninterpreted strings of letters—'there are three objects' versus 'there are seven objects'—to *statements* that might be true or false. Hirsch's suggestion is roughly as follows.

---

[1] Hirsch (2002: 68–9; 2005: 70–2; 2009: 238–9).

Rudy's description	Possible mini-worlds	Stan's description
there are three objects		there are seven objects
there are two objects		there are three objects
there is one object		there is one object
there are no objects		there are no objects

Figure 19.1 Rudy and Stan countenance the same eight possible mini-worlds, but describe the worlds using different sentences.

To determine whether metaphysicians are simply talking past each other—using different words to say the same things—we first need to consider the truth conditions of the various sentences that metaphysicians utter. Hirsch asks us to do this by assigning a class of possible worlds to each sentence, namely, those worlds in which the sentence is to count as *true*.[2] So, when one utters a sentence, one makes a statement roughly to the effect that the actual world belongs to the class of possible worlds assigned to that sentence.

Hirsch's suggestion applies straightforwardly to the debate between Rudy and Stan.[3] When I explained the case of Rudy and Stan, I pointed out that Rudy says 'there are n objects' iff Stan says 'there are $2^n - 1$ objects'. It is therefore reasonable to assign exactly the same class of possible (mini-)worlds to these different strings of letters and to hold that Rudy and Stan make the very same *statement* with different words. (This is depicted in Figure 19.1.) But then Rudy and Stan should regard each other as making true statements. Their debate is therefore shallow, and should be liquidated.

Hirsch's idea runs into difficulties, however, because metaphysicians do not merely debate about what is actual. As Hawthorne points out, they debate about *which* possible worlds there are.[4] We can bring this out, just by thinking more about the case study of the mini-world.

Rudy thinks that the three objects in the mini-world are all metaphysically independent. Rudy therefore countenances eight possible mini-worlds, obtained by removing objects one-by-one from the original mini-world: the eight mini-worlds depicted in Figure 19.1.

---

[2] Hirsch (2005: 72, 78; 2009: 234); the assignment is to be charitable and performed in a context.
[3] Many thanks to Adam Caulton for discussion on this, particularly on metaphysical dependence and independence.
[4] Hawthorne (2009: 220–4).

Stan, by contrast, holds that complex objects metaphysically depend upon their parts. He therefore believes that if you remove an object from a world, you also thereby remove all complexes of which that object is a part. (So if you remove a dot from the mini-world, you must also remove all associated duos and trios of dots.) Accordingly, Stan also countenances the eight possible mini-worlds depicted in Figure 19.1.

Tara agrees with Rudy that there are only three objects in the mini-world. Moreover, Tara agrees with Rudy that it is possible to remove any of the three objects from the mini-world. However, Tara does not think that it is metaphysically possible for there to be an empty (mini-)world.[5] So Tara countenances only *seven* possible mini-worlds; she disregards the bottom row of Figure 19.1.

Quin also agrees with Rudy that there are only three objects in the mini-world. However, Quin holds that there is no more to being an object (in the mini-world) than fulfilling a certain structural role (in the mini-world). For this reason, Quin thinks that there are (typically) no transworld identity facts. In particular, Quin thinks that there is only *one* mini-world obtained by removing just one object, because there is no (transworld identity) fact telling us *which* object was removed.[6] So Quin countenances only *four* possible mini-worlds: one world for each row in Figure 19.1.

If we follow Hirsch in assigning classes of possible worlds to sentences, then we cannot get any grip on the (apparent) disagreement between Rudy, Tara, and Quin. Indeed, we might well worry that Hirsch's approach automatically entails that their debate is metaphysically serious.[7] That would be disastrous. Anyone who wanted to liquidate the debate between Rudy and Stan should also want to liquidate the debate between Rudy, Tara, and Quin.[8] For this reason, we must reject Hirsch's suggestion that we should determine the statement a sentence makes by assigning a class of possible worlds to that sentence. That suggestion is simply inadequate when the sentences in question involve modal language.

---

[5] Tara thus sides with D. Lewis (1986: 73–4) against Baldwin (1996).

[6] Quin is inspired by Leitgeb and Ladyman (2008).

[7] Hawthorne (2009: 224, 227) suggests so. Compare Case's (1997: 8) claim that to think of Rudy and Stan as expressing different propositions 'would amount to the metaphor of the cookie cutter all over again, with a propositional dough and sentential cookie cutters'.

[8] So I would now advocate tolerance, where before (2006) I argued for a position that was incompatible with Quin's.

If we drop that suggestion, then we can continue to use the shallowness criterion in an effort to liquidate the debate between Rudy and Quin (for example). Rudy says to himself that there are eight relevant possible worlds. But he can still understand Quin as uttering truths: he can work out what Quin will say by mentally 'factorizing' through the modal space. Quin says to herself that there are four relevant possible worlds. But she can still understand Rudy as uttering truths: she can work out what Rudy will say by 'de-factorizing', postulating 'specious differences' which are easy to anticipate. (Note that Rudy faces roughly the same issue in understanding Quin as Stan faces in understanding Rudy; and that Quin faces roughly the same issue in understanding Rudy as Rudy faces in understanding Stan.)

Of course, this is merely a sketch of how Rudy and Quin might interpret each other. Once we start to deal with more complicated (mini-)worlds, mutual interpretation will become trickier. However, my aim is not to say, of any particular metaphysical debate, that the shallowness criterion applies. It is simply to outline a tenable general stance, given that conceptual relativism is untenable. To this end, the shallowness criterion is perfectly in order.

19.2   Cosmopolitans and their many languages

The second active ingredient in the stance that I am outlining comes directly from Putnam.[9] It is the notion of a *cosmopolitan*: someone who is fully at 'home' in two or more conceptual schemes. A cosmopolitan might, for example, be equally happy chatting with Rudy as she is with Stan. Crucially, though, this is not because she has just one 'home' scheme into which she interprets all of Rudy's and Stan's utterances. Rather, a cosmopolitan is *fully* and *equally* at 'home' in multiple different schemes.

It is helpful to think of the cosmopolitan as the perfect bilingual. And this way of thinking presents me with the opportunity to discuss the relationship between languages and conceptual schemes. Putnam has always maintained that two languages can express different schemes even though they are intertranslatable[10]—indeed, almost all of his examples of rival

---

[9] Putnam (1987c: 77).
[10] Here he parts company with Davidson (1973: 7). This explains how Putnam (1981c: 114–19; 1984b: 232–3) can embrace Davidson's (1973) attack on conceptual relativism, at the same time as he embraced some doctrine of 'conceptual relativity'.

conceptual schemes have conformed to this pattern[11]—and I shall simply follow Putnam here. So my typical cosmopolitan will be completely bilingual in two (or more) languages which express different schemes but are intertranslatable.[12]

But when *do* different intertranslatable languages express different schemes? Putnam answers that the languages in question must '*appear* to be contradictory'.[13] This will raise a further question: appear contradictory *to whom?* My answer is simple: to metaphysicians. For so long as metaphysicians think that there is some (metaphysical) incompatibility between Rudy's and Stan's ways of talking, I shall classify Rudy and Stan as adopting different schemes. If every metaphysician were one day to agree that Rudy and Stan are simply talking past each other, then the question of whether their languages give voice to one scheme or two will cease to matter very much.

It might help to contrast my attitude here with that of Jennifer Case,[14] particularly since Putnam has embraced some of Case's suggestions.[15] Case also rejects Davidson's stipulation that a scheme is a set of intertranslatable languages.[16] However, she does so by distinguishing 'optional' languages from 'natural' languages. As an illustration: Rudy and Stan may both speak the same 'natural' language (perhaps German) despite adopting different 'optional' languages for developing mereology ('es gibt drei Dinge'; 'nein, es gibt sieben'). For Case, someone who is at home in many conceptual schemes is simply someone who speaks many 'optional' languages.

I agree with Case that it is helpful to think of Rudy and Stan as pursuing different 'options' for extending a 'natural' language. But I would caution against leaning too heavily on the distinction between 'optional' and 'natural' languages, for two reasons. First, as Putnam notes, different 'natural' languages (perhaps English and Shawnee) can seem to enshrine

---

[11] See Putnam (1967: 19–21; 1978a: 38–9; 1979a: 287–8; 1981c: 73; 1987b: 33–4; 1987c: 72–6; 1994a: 246; 2001a; 2012b: 57, 65). The notable exception concerns the phenomenon which he mistakenly called 'conceptual relativity' but now (2001a; 2004: 46–9; 2012b: 64–5) terms 'conceptual pluralism'.

[12] If you are a die-hard Davidsonian, replace 'conceptual scheme' with 'language' in everything that follows and you will not be much disappointed.

[13] Putnam (2004: 46, Putnam's italics; see also 2001a; 2004: 48–9; 2012b: 64–5). Note that Putnam regards this only as a *necessary* condition.

[14] Case (1997; 2001).

[15] Putnam (2001a; 2004: 43, 49–51).

[16] Indeed, I believe that Case (1997: 9–13; 2001: 428–30) was the first philosopher to note explicitly that Putnam and Davidson use different notions of conceptual schemes.

very different ontologies before any 'optional' accretions (such as the axioms of mereology) are made.[17] Second, what starts as an 'optional' addition to a language can gradually become 'natural', as that addition becomes entrenched through repeated use. The collective moral of these two points is simply that what counts as 'natural' (or 'common sense') is sensitive both to cultures and to times. But we can easily imagine metaphysicians disagreeing about which of two 'natural' schemes is *right*.

For this reason, my attitude is fundamentally more *ad hominem* than Case's. I am interested in cosmopolitans because I want to reanimate the Pledge to Liquidate various metaphysical disputes. So I am willing simply to wait for metaphysicians to decide whether two ways of speaking are incompatible. At that point, I will attempt to pose a challenge for them by considering someone who is fluent in both ways of speaking. At the risk of repetition: whether or not we think that these give voice to different 'schemes' does not much matter.

To see how this challenge might work, in the next section I shall describe a confrontation between a cosmopolitan and a hardcore realist over some shallow debate. Before that, let me repeat an important reminder. I am *not* trying to resurrect the Pledge to Relativize. Conceptual relativism cannot be affirmed from within any scheme (see §18.5). It follows that a cosmopolitan cannot affirm conceptual relativism from within *any* of her 'home' schemes. Conceptual relativism is genuinely dead, and nothing is going to bring it back.

19.3 The cosmopolitan and the hardcore realist

Poly is a cosmopolitan, at home in two conceptual schemes: Bauhaus and Gothic. Poly regards both Bauhausers and Goths as only ever making true utterances. Thus, invoking the shallowness criterion, she thinks that any metaphysical debate between Bauhaus and Gothic is not worth having.

Along comes Meryl, a hardcore realist. Meryl asks Poly which of her schemes is *really* correct. Poly replies that both are rather wonderful. Meryl says that this is not what she was getting at; she wants to know which one *really* delivers the objects of the world. Poly is a little perplexed by this, but has most recently been working within Bauhaus. For this reason she

---

[17] Putnam (2004: 49–50), referencing Whorf (1956: 234–5).

answers—with some hesitancy—that Bauhaus is the correct scheme. Meryl thanks her and goes away to work on metaphysics.

But a few days later, Meryl experiences a pang of disquiet. Meryl visits Poly again, wanting to know which scheme is *really* correct. Their discussion plays out just as before, except that this time, Poly has most recently been working within Gothic. So Poly now says—with some hesitancy—that Gothic is the correct scheme.

This confirms what Meryl feared, that Poly had failed to understand what '*really*' means in the questions 'which scheme is *really* correct?' or 'which objects are there *really*?' Meryl tries to explain what she means. She points out that this is the ontology classroom, and not the Clapham omnibus. She says that '*really*' should be read as italicized, or with a capital-R, or in SHOUTING-CAPSLOCK. She thumps the desk. But no amount of emphatic force helps Meryl here. Poly says to Meryl:

What exists is what really exists, is what *really* exists, is what *Really* exists, and so forth. And I am *not* claiming, in either this scheme or in any of my 'home' schemes, that what (really, *really*, *Really*) exists is scheme-relative. But you are just going to have to learn to live with the fact that, if you catch me at different moments, I will give different answers to the question 'what (really, *really*, *Really*) exists?'

Poly has pointed out that she will indifferently give different answers to the question 'what exists?' at different times, since she speaks different languages at different times.

Meryl insists that Poly must choose one of her languages as *the* language within which to describe the world. Poly replies that both languages describe the world, and insists on her freedom to use different languages at different times.

Meryl tells Poly that this is unacceptable. She insists that the chosen language is to be *the world's language*, Ontologese, perfectly suited for describing the joints of the world (see again §1.2), and the world hardly changes its language from time to time in the way that Poly does. Pushing the metaphor, Meryl tells Poly that everyone has to declare a single scheme as *home* for tax purposes, so that her ontological debts can be properly assessed. Poly simply does not understand these images. The world does not speak in any language, and Poly is happy to take her chances with the ontological bailiffs.

Somewhat frustrated, Meryl asks Poly how to *interpret* both Bauhaus and Gothic. However, this gets Meryl no further, for the issue 'simply reproduces itself at a metalinguistic level'.[18] Just as Poly speaks different languages at different times, so she offers different interpretation manuals at different times. When she is speaking in Bauhaus, she gives a disquotational interpretation of Bauhaus but a fancier interpretation of Gothic (and conversely). (She did, after all, think that the Bauhaus/Gothic debate was shallow.)

Exasperated, Meryl tries to run the behind-the-schemes argument against Poly.[19] She aims to push Poly into accepting a single scheme, *Rococo*, which countenances the objects of both Bauhaus and Gothic. But Poly simply thanks Meryl for supplying her with a third way of speaking about the world. Meryl will insist that only Rococo allows Poly to speak unrestrictedly. But Poly will demur. When she adopts Rococo, of course, Poly interprets both Bauhaus and Gothic by the simple expedient of restricting her quantifiers. But when she adopts Bauhaus, Poly claims to be speaking unrestrictedly and offers a somewhat fancy interpretation of Rococo (in much the way that she offers a somewhat fancy interpretation of Gothic). Meryl will insist, nevertheless, that Bauhaus does not *really* allow Poly to speak unrestrictedly. But now we are back where we began. So it goes.

19.4 Conceptual cosmopolitanism

I am at last in a position to describe the stance of *conceptual cosmopolitanism*. Conceptual cosmopolitanism has two active ingredients: the notion of a shallow debate, and the notion of a cosmopolitan. It is committed to the Pledge to Tolerate: indeed, we are encouraged to become cosmopolitans and to roam freely from scheme to scheme. It rejects the Pledge to Relativize: objects and kinds are *not* scheme-relative. But it retains the Pledge to Liquidate various metaphysical disputes: faced with Poly's cosmopolitan attitude, Meryl's hardcore realism is exposed as nothing other than parochial huffing and puffing.[20]

Conceptual cosmopolitanism helps us to offer a deflationary gloss on Putnam's claim that 'what is factual and what is conventional is a matter

---

[18] Putnam (1987c: 77; see also 1993c: 309).

[19] Compare Eklund (2008a: 206–7), who suggests that the behind-the-schemes argument forces a maximally generous metaphysics upon those who adopt a semantic approach to conceptual schemes.

[20] In Button (2010), I explain how a *dadaist* attempts to confound the absolute generalist's attempt to talk about 'absolutely' everything. Conceptual cosmopolitanism is to conceptual relativism what dadaism is to restrictivism.

of degree'.[21] If this is the claim that our conventions somehow shape the world, then it must be rejected along with the Pledge to Relativize. Equally, we cannot accept any talk about the 'interpenetration of fact and convention',[22] if this is meant to suggest that the world is much affected by how we choose to talk. But purged of any hint of idealism, claims like this will end up deflating down to two simple truisms. First, that we cannot state the facts without speaking a language; second, that there are many different languages that we might choose to speak.

Indeed, these truisms are all that we *should* mean,[23] for in philosophy even truisms can have claws. The hardcore realist is inclined to ask which of the many possible languages *really* tells us what there is, or which language *really* enables her to speak with no restrictions on her quantifiers. But in asking these questions, she has simply forgotten the first truism.[24] Her questions must *themselves* be fielded within a language, and so can receive no answer that will satisfy her. (Recall the debate between Meryl and Poly.) Conceptual cosmopolitanism thus gives both sense and claws to Putnam's cryptic claim that we can describe the world 'as it really is', whilst holding that it is senseless to ask for a description of the world 'as it is "independent of perspective," or "in itself"'.[25]

19.5 The slippery slopes of metaphysics

In this chapter I have claimed that conceptual cosmopolitanism poses a coherent challenge to metaphysics. The extent of this challenge will depend upon the plausibility of saying, of any two particular 'rival' schemes, that they can both be simultaneously regarded as true. And here there is a deep connection with the themes discussed earlier in this book. To explore this connection, I shall consider a challenge that Hawthorne has laid down against anyone who holds that certain metaphysical debates are shallow. (His particular target is Hirsch, but the challenge applies equally to a conceptual cosmopolitanist.)

---

[21] Putnam (1987a: 28; 1988: 113; see also 1987b: 33; 2004: 43–5).

[22] As Case (2001: 419–24, 429–30) does; I am not sure how to read her, given her endorsement of Putnam's (1981c: xi) Hegelian metaphor.

[23] They also seem to be all that Putnam (2012b: 64) means.

[24] So this is my response to Eklund's (2008a: 207) worry that Putnam's position reduces to truisms.

[25] Putnam (1994a: 243; see also 1992b: 368; 1995b: 40; 2004: 43).

Hawthorne begins his challenge by presenting a series of metaphysical disagreements, one of which is as follows:

One physicist adopts the special theory of relativity for standard reasons. Another clings to Euclidean geometry and...holds that physical reality is confined to a sphere in Euclidean space, with a deforming force operating on its inhabitants in such a way that they decrease in size as they move towards the edge (tending towards zero as the edge approaches).[26]

Of course, a certain kind of verificationist will maintain that these two physicists are simply talking past each other. Hawthorne contends, however, that *only* a verificationist would think this, since it is just obvious (to Hawthorne) that these physicists are engaged in a serious metaphysical debate. And now he claims that the conceptual cosmopolitanist, who wants to claim that some debates are shallow, is in a tight spot. She has no precise list of principles that govern interpretation. Consequently, she has no neat formula that will determine precisely when metaphysicians are simply talking past each other. So it is 'unclear' how she will 'motivate [her] view in a way that preserves reasonable distance from ... verificationism'.[27]

Hawthorne's choice of example should not be allowed to slip past without comment.[28] If the worst that can be said of the conceptual cosmopolitanist is that she has to regard Hawthorne's two physicists as talking past each other, that is a long way from a *reductio* of conceptual cosmopolitanism.[29] Indeed, I cannot even see that it is a *reductio ad verificationism*.

The only genuine threat of a *reductio* is raised by a theme that has been familiar to us since Part A. If nothing constrains interpretation, then every consistent theory can be made true in infinitely many different ways, whereupon the very idea of truth and falsity floats away. For this reason, conceptual cosmopolitanists must think that there are *some* constraints on interpretation. But of course they *should* think this,[30] and assert it in (each of) their 'home' schemes. Their various schemes may advance causally-constrained correspondence theories of truth (for words from multiple

[26] Hawthorne (2009: 214).   [27] Hawthorne (2009: 219–20).

[28] Hawthorne (2009: 214) provides three other examples. I feel similarly about one of them, and note that the remaining two plausibly raise non-trivial ethical issues, thereby carrying with them the complications discussed in §16.6.

[29] Indeed, compare Putnam's (1981c: 73) example of 'mathematically intertranslatable' but metaphysically 'incompatible' formulations of Newtonian physics.

[30] Compare Hirsch (2005: 72–3; 2009: 236).

schemes);[31] they may offer genealogies and etymologies explaining how words (from multiple schemes) came to acquire their meanings; and they may even advance some (messy) semantic externalism for natural kind terms (from multiple schemes).

Of course, none of this detracts from Hawthorne's point that no one has a precise list of principles that tell us exactly how to interpret anyone (ever). Indeed, a theme of Chapters 16 and 17 was that anyone who claimed to have such a list should be laughed out of town. But Hawthorne is mistaken if he means to suggest that this fact provides much defence of metaphysics. To see why, let us start from the opposite end than does Hawthorne. *Some metaphysical disputes are plainly silly.* Mereology is the stalking horse of our times, but if mereology strikes you as a serious matter, then start instead with an example from James:

Some years ago, being with a camping party in the mountains, I returned from a solitary ramble to find every one engaged in a ferocious metaphysical dispute. The *corpus* of the dispute was a squirrel – a live squirrel supposed to be clinging to one side of a tree-trunk; while over against the tree's opposite side a human being was imagined to stand. This human witness tries to get sight of the squirrel by moving rapidly round the tree, but no matter how fast he goes, the squirrel moves as fast in the opposite direction, and always keeps the tree between himself and the man, so that never a glimpse of him is caught. The resultant metaphysical problems now is this: *Does the man go round the squirrel or not?* He goes round the tree, sure enough, and the squirrel is on the tree; but does he go round the squirrel? In the unlimited leisure of the wilderness, discussion had been worn threadbare.[32]

James's camping colleagues were obviously talking past each other. Now: was their debate really very different from the debate between Hawthorne's two physicists? More generally, how will Hawthorne motivate his belief that *some* metaphysical debates are meaningful, in a way that preserves reasonable distance from the silly position that no metaphysicians have ever talked past each other?

The burden of proof might now be shuffled back and forth. However, as in earlier chapters, I recommend an attitude of mitigated aporia. I cannot say exactly when we should kill five to save one, but I can tell you that it is

---

[31] Hirsch (2002: 57; 2005: 77; 2009: 248–9) sometimes seems to be tempted towards rejecting the Correspondence Principle in favour of something like the syntax-first thesis. If so, this is a mistake, for reasons given in §18.4.

[32] James (1907: 25).

somewhere between the extremes of the trolley problems. I cannot supply you with particularly sharp principles that explain exactly which sceptical scenarios can be dismissed as depending on magic, but I can say that I am neither an internal nor an external realist. Similarly here. Not every apparent metaphysical debate is contentful, and not every debate is empty, but it is hard to say much more than that.

Coda

In this book, I have done my best to obliterate faith in external realism. But I have set up no new faith in its place. I have not painted a picture which rivals that of reasoning from a God's Eye point of view. I have found no salvation in any particular philosophy of perception. I have offered no comforting conceptual connection between truth and justification. I have provided no metaphor that explains the relationship of minds, words, and world. I have merely rejected external realism, on the grounds that it is ultimately incoherent.

But I have also rejected internal realism. Although all nightmarish Cartesian sceptical scenarios can be defeated with BIV-style arguments, some less global Cartesian sceptical scenarios remain standing. And since there is no sharp point at which we can say that a sceptic is invoking magic in defence of her sceptical scenarios, I cannot say precisely where I sit between external realism and internal realism.

Being a realist, I endorse a (messy) kind of semantic externalism. But it is quite messy. And I cannot recommend any particular attitude towards whether there are natural kinds that transcend our (in principle) abilities to recognize them.

Being a realist, I also deny that objects are scheme-relative. But the death of conceptual relativism does not mean that every metaphysical debate is deep. Some are; some are not. I cannot tell you precisely which is which.

The hope of this book is not, then, that we shall overcome metaphysics. Nor that we shall overcome metametaphysics and get back to doing metaphysics. Nor even that we shall overcome metametametaphysics. The hope of this book is simply that we shall become more aware of what we are asking when we pose philosophical questions, and thereby become more sensitive to the limits of our answers.

Appendices

Appendix I
Model theory primer

This appendix constitutes a not-too-rigorous overview of the (simple) model theory required for the model-theoretic arguments. My target audience is those people who have taken an introductory course in formal logic, and who have a little familiarity with elementary set-theoretic and functional notation.[1] (Note: to ward off a nasty rash of quotation marks, I shall be quite relaxed about quotation conventions in this appendix.)

I.1 Structures and permutations

Model theory relates languages with structures. So let us start with language.

Definition 1. A *language*, $\mathcal{L}$, is a collection of some symbols, of three basic kinds:

- *Constant symbols*, e.g. $c_1, c_2, c_3, \ldots$. These will be thought of as *names*.
- *Predicate symbols*, e.g. $R_1, R_2, R_2, \ldots$. These will pick out properties or relations. A two-place relation, such as the relation *x is larger than y*, will need to be associated with a two-place predicate symbol. More generally, each predicate symbol has an *arity*: a natural number indicating how many places it has.
- *Function symbols*, e.g. $f_1, f_2, f_3, \ldots$. These will pick out functions. A two-place function, such as *addition*, will need to be associated with a two-place function symbol. Accordingly, each function symbol also has an arity. □

---

[1] More mathematically inclined readers might prefer to turn immediately to Marker (2002: 7–48), and to Shapiro (1991: 61–95), to whom this appendix is heavily indebted.

We can now say what it is to be a *structure*; or, more accurately, what it is to be an $\mathscr{L}$-structure, since strictly speaking structures are relative to languages.

Definition 2. An $\mathscr{L}$-*structure*, $\mathcal{M}$, consists of:

- A non-empty set M, which is the *domain* of $\mathcal{M}$.
- An object $c^{\mathcal{M}} \in M$ for each constant symbol c of $\mathscr{L}$,
- A set $R^{\mathcal{M}} \subseteq M^n$ for each n-place predicate symbol R of $\mathscr{L}$,
- A function $f^{\mathcal{M}} : M^n \longrightarrow M$ for each n-place function symbol f of $\mathscr{L}$. □

A few comments on notation are in order. Throughout this book, I use swash-fonts for structures, thus: $\mathcal{A}$, $\mathcal{B}$, $\mathcal{C}$. I write the structure's domain in italics, thus: A, B, C. The symbols '$\in$' and '$\subseteq$' which feature in this Definition are just the ordinary symbols from set theory, with their standard meanings. Equally, A^n is the set of all n-tuples, each of whose members is in A, i.e.:

$$\{\langle x_1, \ldots, x_n \rangle \mid x_1 \in A \text{ and } \ldots \text{ and } x_n \in A\}$$

Let me emphasize that these bits of set-theoretic notation are *not* assumed to be $\mathscr{L}$-symbols. Rather, we *use* these set-theoretic symbols and employ some set theory when we do model theory. (By contrast, when we describe $\mathscr{L}$-structures in our model theory, we *mention* the $\mathscr{L}$-symbols.) Let me also emphasize that we shall need only extraordinarily minimal set theory.

Allow me to illustrate these ideas. Consider a language that contains two constant symbols c_1 and c_2, a single two-place predicate symbol R, and a single one-place function symbol f. I shall define a structure of this language, $\mathcal{G}$, by specifying a domain and interpretations for these three symbols:

$$G := \{\text{rock, paper, scissors}\}$$
$$c_1^{\mathcal{G}} := \text{rock}$$
$$c_2^{\mathcal{G}} := \text{scissors}$$
$$R^{\mathcal{G}} := \{\langle \text{rock, scissors} \rangle, \langle \text{scissors, paper} \rangle, \langle \text{paper, rock} \rangle\}$$
$$f^{\mathcal{G}}(\text{rock}) := \text{paper}$$
$$f^{\mathcal{G}}(\text{paper}) := \text{scissors}$$
$$f^{\mathcal{G}}(\text{scissors}) := \text{rock}$$

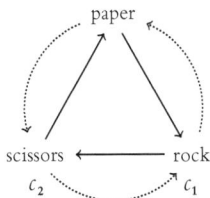

Figure I.1 The roshambo structure, $\mathcal{G}$. There are three elements in its domain: rock, paper, and scissors. The constant c_1 names rock, and the constant c_2 names scissors. Thick straight arrows symbolize the relation $R^{\mathcal{G}}$. Dotted curved arrows symbolize the function $f^{\mathcal{G}}$.

Our structure, $\mathcal{G}$, captures the game of *roshambo*. The domain contains the three objects a player can choose. The two constants have been interpreted as naming two of those objects. The two-place predicate symbol has been interpreted as standing for the relation which holds between x and y just in case x beats y (a two-place relation being, for model-theoretic purposes, just a set of ordered pairs). The one-place function symbol has been interpreted as mapping each object to the object that beats it. All this is depicted intuitively in Figure I.1.

Now that we know what structures are, we can explore how they might relate to each other. To do this, we shall consider certain kinds of functions *between* structures. (Note that a function $\sigma : A \longrightarrow B$ is a *bijection* **iff** for every $y \in B$ there is one and only one $x \in A$ such that $\sigma(x) = y$.)

Definition 3. Let $\mathcal{M}$ and $\mathcal{N}$ be $\mathcal{L}$-structures. A bijection $\sigma : M \longrightarrow N$ is an *isomorphism* **iff** all of the following conditions hold:

$$\sigma(c^{\mathcal{M}}) = c^{\mathcal{N}} \qquad \text{for all constant symbols } c$$

$$\langle a_1, \ldots, a_n \rangle \in R^{\mathcal{M}} \text{ iff } \langle \sigma(a_1), \ldots, \sigma(a_n) \rangle \in R^{\mathcal{N}} \qquad \text{for all } n\text{-place } R \text{ and all } a_1, \ldots, a_n \in M$$

$$\sigma\big(f^{\mathcal{M}}(a_1, \ldots, a_n)\big) = f^{\mathcal{N}}(\sigma(a_1), \ldots, \sigma(a_n)) \qquad \text{for all } n\text{-place } f \text{ and all } a_1, \ldots, a_n \in M$$

We say that $\mathcal{M}$ and $\mathcal{N}$ are *isomorphic* if there is an isomorphism between them. We can express this more briefly thus: $\mathcal{M} \cong \mathcal{N}$. $\qquad\square$

The idea of an isomorphism is central to the model-theoretic arguments. To illustrate the idea, I shall build a new structure, $\mathcal{H}$, which is isomorphic to our roshambo structure, $\mathcal{G}$. The domain of my new structure, H, will

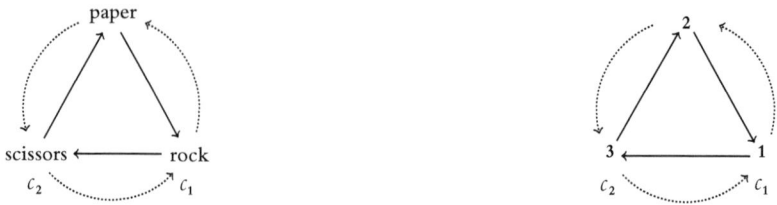

Figure I.2 The roshambo structure $\mathcal{G}$ (left), together with an isomorphic structure $\mathcal{H}$ (right). As in figure I.1, thick straight arrows symbolize the interpretation of R in each structure, and dotted curved arrows symbolize the interpretation of f in each structure. It is easy to see that the structures are isomorphic.

need to contain three objects; for lack of imagination, I shall choose the numbers 1, 2, and 3. I shall now define a bijection, σ, from G to H:

$$\sigma(\text{rock}) := 1$$
$$\sigma(\text{paper}) := 2$$
$$\sigma(\text{scissors}) := 3$$

And I can now use this bijection to define $\mathcal{H}$. All I need to do is replace rock with 1, paper with 2, and scissors with 3:

$$H := \{1, 2, 3\}$$
$$c_1^{\mathcal{H}} := 1$$
$$c_2^{\mathcal{H}} := 3$$
$$R^{\mathcal{H}} := \{\langle 1, 3 \rangle, \langle 3, 2 \rangle, \langle 2, 1 \rangle\}$$
$$f^{\mathcal{G}}(1) := 2$$
$$f^{\mathcal{G}}(2) := 3$$
$$f^{\mathcal{G}}(3) := 1$$

This is all depicted in Figure I.2. It is easy to check that σ is an *isomorphism* between $\mathcal{G}$ and $\mathcal{H}$, so that $\mathcal{G} \cong \mathcal{H}$.

We should pause to think about what just happened. I started with a given structure, $\mathcal{G}$. Then, armed with a fairly arbitrary bijection, I constructed a new structure, $\mathcal{H}$, that was isomorphic to the originally given structure. The method I followed should be easy to generalize, and indeed it is:

Construction 4 (The Isomorphism Construction). Let $\mathcal{M}$ be an $\mathscr{L}$-structure and π be any bijection $M \longrightarrow N$, for some N. For each individual constant symbol c, each n-place predicate symbol R, and each n-place function symbol f of $\mathcal{L}$, define:

$$c^{\mathcal{N}} := \pi(c^{\mathcal{M}})$$
$$R^{\mathcal{N}} := \{\langle \pi(x_1), \ldots, \pi(x_n)\rangle \mid \langle x_1, \ldots, x_n \rangle \in R^{\mathcal{M}}\}$$
$$f^{\mathcal{N}}(\pi(x_1), \ldots, \pi(x_n)) := \pi(f^{\mathcal{M}}(x_1, \ldots, x_n))$$

Taking N as the domain, this defines an $\mathcal{L}$-structure, $\mathcal{N}$, such that π is an isomorphism $\mathcal{M} \longrightarrow \mathcal{N}$. $\qquad\qquad\square$

If $N \neq M$ in the Isomorphism Construction, then the ensuing model $\mathcal{N}$ will be distinct from $\mathcal{M}$, just because they have different domains. We can apply this idea to the philosophical discussion of the permutation argument in §2.1 and §5.3. If the external realist presents us with a model $\mathcal{W}$, and we can find some set of objects which is distinct from W (but which is the same size as W), then we can run a version of the permutation argument, just by following the Isomorphism Construction.

This Construction provides the raw material for *Frege's* permutation argument which is, so far as I am aware, the first 'model-theoretic argument'.[2] However, our canonical version of the permutation argument—involving cats and cherries—sees Putnam focusing primarily on the case of the Construction when $N = M$. This is the case where we *simply* shuffle the objects of a given model around.

In this case, if we are not careful then we shall find that $\mathcal{N} = \mathcal{M}$. That will certainly happen if π is the identity function, for then we shall simply map each object to itself, and so will end up where we began. But it might also happen if $\mathcal{M}$ is a rather boring structure. To avoid this possibility, we need a definition.[3]

Definition 5. $\mathcal{M}$ is a *non-trivial* structure $\mathcal{L}$-structure **iff** it meets any of the following conditions:

(a) M contains more than one element and $\mathcal{L}$ contains at least one constant symbol.

---

[2] Frege (1893: §10).
[3] Definition 5 and Theorem 6 together improve on Button (2011: Lemma 2).

(b) there are $a_1, \ldots, a_n, b_1, \ldots, b_n \in M$, with $a_i = a_j$ iff $b_i = b_j$, such that $\langle a_1, \ldots, a_n \rangle \in R^M$ and $\langle b_1, \ldots, b_n \rangle \notin R^M$ for some $\mathscr{L}$-predicate symbol R.

(c) there are $a_1, \ldots, a_n, b_1, \ldots, b_n \in M$, with $a_i = a_j$ iff $b_i = b_j$, such that $f^M(a_1, \ldots, a_{n-1}) = a_n$ and $f^M(b_1, \ldots, b_{n-1}) \neq b_n$ for some $\mathscr{L}$-function symbol f.   □

Theorem 6. $\mathcal{M}$ is a non-trivial structure **iff** there is a structure $\mathcal{N}$ such that $\mathcal{N} \cong \mathcal{M}$ and $N = M$ but $\mathcal{N} \neq \mathcal{M}$.

Proof. Left-to-right. Let $\mathcal{M}$ be non-trivial. Define a bijection $\pi : M \longrightarrow M$ subject to the following constraint. If condition (a) of Definition 5 obtains then let $\pi(c^M) \neq c^M$, where c is the constant mentioned in condition (a); otherwise, with $a_1, \ldots, a_n, b_1, \ldots, b_n$ as in condition (b) or (c), let $\pi(a_i) = b_i$ for each $i \leq n$. Now apply the Isomorphism Construction.

Right-to-left. Let $\mathcal{N}$ be as described; since $\mathcal{N}$ and $\mathcal{M}$ are distinct but share the same domain, $\mathcal{N}$ and $\mathcal{M}$ must differ on the interpretation of some $\mathscr{L}$-symbol. If they differ on the interpretation of an individual constant, then condition (a) of Definition 5 obtains. If they differ on the interpretation of some predicate symbol then, without loss of generality, suppose $\langle a_1, \ldots, a_n \rangle \in R^M$ but $\langle a_1, \ldots, a_n \rangle \notin R^N$. Since they are isomorphic, there is some isomorphism $\sigma : \mathcal{N} \longrightarrow \mathcal{M}$. Since $\langle \sigma(a_1), \ldots, \sigma(a_n) \rangle \notin R^M$, condition (b) obtains. If $\mathcal{N}$ and $\mathcal{M}$ differ on the interpretation of some function symbol, condition (c) obtains similarly.   □

To illustrate this, let us again consider our roshambo structure, $\mathcal{G}$. This is clearly non-trivial, so by Theorem 6 it is possible to generate a distinct but isomorphic model with the same domain. Here is one way to do so. Define a function $\pi : G \longrightarrow G$ as follows:

$$\pi(\text{rock}) := \text{scissors}$$

$$\pi(\text{scissors}) := \text{rock}$$

$$\pi(\text{paper}) := \text{paper}$$

We can now plug $\mathcal{G}$ and π into the Isomorphism Construction, to induce a structure with domain $\{\text{rock}, \text{paper}, \text{scissors}\}$. I leave it as an exercise to verify that the constructed model, $\mathcal{P}$, is accurately depicted by Figure I.3.

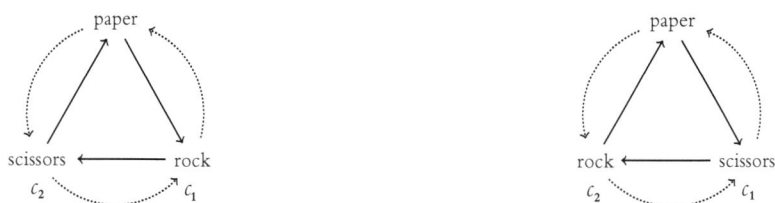

Figure I.3 The roshambo structure $\mathcal{G}$ (left), together with a permuted but iso-morphic structure $\mathcal{P}$ (right). The representation conventions are as for figures I.1 and I.2. The structures share a domain and are clearly isomorphic; however, it is also clear that they are *distinct*.

The reader may now wish to contemplate the full horror of a world in which scissors beats rock, rock beats paper, and paper beats scissors.

This example illustrates an important point concerning permutations. To generate a distinct but isomorphic model by a permutation, it is not in general necessary to shuffle all of the objects around. In this case, π held paper fixed. This observation underpins the discussion, in §5.3, of Permutation behind the veil.

I.2 First-order satisfaction

We know what structures are, and what it means to describe them as *iso-morphic*. Our next task is to relate structures to *formulæ*. I shall start with the formulæ of first-order logic. These are built from the primitive symbols of the language and all the apparatus of first-order logic, namely sentential connectives ($\neg$, $\wedge$, $\vee$, $\rightarrow$, $\leftrightarrow$), quantifiers ($\exists$, $\forall$), parentheses, the identity sign, and variables. I assume familiarity with the syntax of these symbols, and with the following notions.[4]

- A first-order $\mathscr{L}$-term is any $\mathscr{L}$-constant, any variable, or anything (recursively) constructed from other $\mathscr{L}$-terms using $\mathscr{L}$-function sym-bols. A closed term is a term containing no variables.
- A first-order $\mathscr{L}$-formula is either two terms connect by the identity sign, or an n-place $\mathscr{L}$-predicate symbol followed by n $\mathscr{L}$-terms, or anything

---

[4] For formal definitions, consult e.g. Boolos et al. (2002: 106–12) or Marker (2002: 9–10).

(recursively) constructed from other $\mathscr{L}$-formulæ using the symbols of first-order logic.

- A first-order $\mathscr{L}$-*sentence* is a first-order $\mathscr{L}$-formula containing no free variables, where a free variable is one not falling within the scope of any quantifier connected to that variable.
- A first-order $\mathscr{L}$-*theory* is a set of first-order $\mathscr{L}$-sentences.

The aim of this section is to make sense of the following notion: *the first-order sentence φ is true in the structure $\mathcal{M}$.* This will allow us to understand what it means when, in the course of an indeterminacy argument, we say that many different structures make exactly the same sentences true.

The formal relation that we are aiming to define—our surrogate for truth—is called *satisfaction*, and it will be expressed thus: $\mathcal{M} \models \varphi$. Satisfaction concerns sentences, and sentences are constructed recursively, so we shall define satisfaction recursively.

We start with atomic sentences. These consist either of an n-place predicate symbol followed by n closed terms, or of two closed terms linked by the identity sign. So we must first understand how to interpret closed terms in a structure. Closed first-order terms are constructed recursively, by compounding function symbols with constant symbols, so their interpretation is defined recursively. We know how $\mathcal{M}$ interprets constants. So all we require is a clause telling us how to deal with function symbols. We offer:

Definition 7. For any $\mathscr{L}$-structure $\mathcal{M}$:

- $(f(t_1, \ldots, t_n))^{\mathcal{M}} := f^{\mathcal{M}}\left(t_1^{\mathcal{M}}, \ldots, t_n^{\mathcal{M}}\right)$
  for any n-place $\mathscr{L}$-function symbol f and any closed $\mathscr{L}$-terms $t_1, \ldots, t_n$

Armed with an understanding of how closed terms behave, we can now define satisfaction for atomic sentences:

- $\mathcal{M} \models Rt_1 \ldots t_n$ **iff** $\left\langle t_1^{\mathcal{M}}, \ldots, t_n^{\mathcal{M}} \right\rangle \in R^{\mathcal{M}}$
  for any $\mathscr{L}$-predicate symbol R and any closed $\mathscr{L}$-terms $t_1, \ldots, t_n$
- $\mathcal{M} \models t_1 = t_2$ **iff** $t_1^{\mathcal{M}} = t_2^{\mathcal{M}}$
  for any closed $\mathscr{L}$-terms t_1 and t_2 □

It is worth pausing to check that this is intuitively correct. In the roshambo structure, $\mathcal{G}$, c_1 is interpreted to name rock, and c_2 is interpreted to name scissors. Since R is interpreted to stand for the relation x *beats* y, and since rock beats scissors, it should be the case that Rc_1c_2 is true in $\mathcal{G}$; so it should be the case that $\mathcal{G} \vDash Rc_1c_2$. According to our definitions, this holds just in case $\langle c_1^{\mathcal{G}}, c_2^{\mathcal{G}} \rangle \in R^{\mathcal{G}}$, i.e. just in case $\langle \text{rock}, \text{scissors} \rangle \in R^{\mathcal{G}}$, which is indeed the case.

For a slightly more interesting case, let us check whether $\mathcal{G} \vDash c_1 = f(f(c_1))$. We need to know whether $c_1^{\mathcal{G}} = (f(f(c_1)))^{\mathcal{G}}$. Evaluating our terms, $c_1^{\mathcal{G}} = \text{rock}$ and $(f(f(c_1)))^{\mathcal{G}} = f^{\mathcal{G}}((f(c_1))^{\mathcal{G}}) = f^{\mathcal{G}}(f^{\mathcal{G}}(c_1^{\mathcal{G}})) = f^{\mathcal{G}}(f^{\mathcal{G}}(\text{rock})) = f^{\mathcal{G}}(\text{paper}) = \text{scissors}$. Since rock $\neq$ scissors, it is not the case that $\mathcal{G} \vDash c_1 = f(f(c_1))$.

We have defined satisfaction for atomic sentences, so we must now define satisfaction for non-atomic sentences. The recursion clauses handling sentential connectives are straightforward:[5]

Definition 7 (continued). For any $\mathscr{L}$-structure $\mathcal{M}$:

- $\mathcal{M} \vDash \neg\varphi$ **iff** it is not the case that $\mathcal{M} \vDash \varphi$
- $\mathcal{M} \vDash \varphi \wedge \psi$ **iff** $\mathcal{M} \vDash \varphi$ and $\mathcal{M} \vDash \psi$
- $\mathcal{M} \vDash (\varphi \vee \psi)$ **iff** $\mathcal{M} \vDash \varphi$ or $\mathcal{M} \vDash \psi$ $\square$

However, there is a certain amount of trickiness regarding the quantifiers. Where $\varphi(v)$ is a formula with one free variable v, we want a clause that says something like the following: $\mathcal{M} \vDash \forall v \varphi(v)$ **iff** $\mathcal{M} \vDash \varphi(a)$ for every object $a \in M$. But there is an immediate problem: '$\varphi(a)$' *is not an $\mathscr{L}$-formula*, since a is an object rather than an $\mathscr{L}$-constant. Of course, if every object a in the domain is picked out by some $\mathscr{L}$-constant c, then we could simply consider $\mathcal{M} \vDash \varphi(c)$ (where $\varphi(c)$ is the formula obtained by replacing every instance of φ's free variable with c). But most structures contain unnamed objects. Indeed, no constant picks out paper in our roshambo structure, $\mathcal{G}$.

The way around the obstacle is intuitive: we consider what would happen if we were simply to name our unnamed object. To make this precise, though, is a little fiddly:[6]

Definition 7 (continued). Let $\mathcal{M}$ be an $\mathscr{L}$-structure, let $a \in M$, and let d be a constant not featuring in $\mathscr{L}$. We define $\mathcal{M}(d, a)$ to be the structure

---

[5] I assume that $\rightarrow$ and $\leftrightarrow$ are defined in terms of the other connectives.
[6] This follows Boolos et al. (2002: 117). The signature $\mathscr{L} \cup \{d\}$ is, of course, the signature formed by augmenting $\mathscr{L}$ with the constant d.

with signature $\mathscr{L} \cup \{d\}$ such that: (i) its domain is M; (ii) it agrees with $\mathcal{M}$ on the interpretation of all $\mathscr{L}$-symbols; and (iii) it assigns d to a, i.e. $d^{\mathcal{M}(d,a)} = a$. Armed with this notation, say that:

- $\mathcal{M} \vDash \varphi(a)$ **iff** $\mathcal{M}(d, a) \vDash \varphi(d)$ for any constant d not in $\mathscr{L}$

Here we also say that *a satisfies* φ in $\mathcal{M}$, or that φ is *true of a* in $\mathcal{M}$. □

Again, it will help to illustrate this. Since scissors beats paper in roshambo, it ought to be the case that Rc_2v is true of paper in $\mathcal{G}$. So suppose we add a new constant, d, to our language, and then consider the structure $\mathcal{G}(d, \text{paper})$ as earlier defined. We must check that $\mathcal{G}^{(d,\text{paper})} \vDash Rc_2 d$, i.e. that $\langle c_2^{\mathcal{G}(d,\text{paper})}, d^{\mathcal{G}(d,\text{paper})} \rangle \in R^{\mathcal{G}(d,\text{paper})}$. But $\mathcal{G}(d, \text{paper})$ agrees with $\mathcal{G}$ on the interpretations of c_2 and R. So this holds iff $\langle \text{scissors}, \text{paper} \rangle \in R^{\mathcal{G}}$. Since this obtains, Rc_2v is true of paper in $\mathcal{G}$, as we would hope.

We are now in a position to supply a recursion clause for the quantifiers:

Definition 7 (completed). For any $\mathscr{L}$-structure $\mathcal{M}$ and any $\mathscr{L}$-formula φ with one free variable, v:

- $\mathcal{M} \vDash \forall v \varphi(v)$ **iff** $\mathcal{M} \vDash \varphi(a)$ for all $a \in M$
- $\mathcal{M} \vDash \exists v \varphi(v)$ **iff** $\mathcal{M} \vDash \varphi(a)$ for some $a \in M$ □

Thus we now know what it means to say, of any sentence, that it is true in $\mathcal{M}$. This allows us to say that a structure is a *model* of a theory, if it makes all of the sentences of that theory true. More formally:

Definition 8. Let T be a first-order $\mathscr{L}$-theory, and let $\mathcal{M}$ be an $\mathscr{L}$-structure. $\mathcal{M}$ is a *model* of T **iff** $\mathcal{M} \vDash \varphi$ for every φ in the theory T. We can express this more briefly thus: $\mathcal{M} \vDash$ T. □

Generically, we can now understand the claim that an indeterminacy argument arises, whenever we can find more than one model for a theory.

Now, we already know from Theorem 6 that if we have a theory T with a non-trivial model, then there will be many structures that are isomorphic to that non-trivial model. To generate an indeterminacy argument, we just need to show that these isomorphic structures are all models of T. It suffices to prove:

Theorem 9. Let M and N be isomorphic $\mathscr{L}$-structures. Then for every first-order $\mathscr{L}$-sentence φ: $M \vDash \varphi$ iff $N \vDash \varphi$.

Proof sketch. By induction on complexity of φ. I shall indicate how to prove the most interesting case, namely, that of a quantified $\mathscr{L}$-sentence, like $\exists v \psi(v)$.

   The induction hypothesis will be that for any language $\mathscr{L}^*$ containing all the symbols of $\mathscr{L}$, any isomorphic $\mathscr{L}^*$-structures satisfy exactly the same $\mathscr{L}^*$-sentences of lower complexity than $\exists v \psi(v)$. So consider isomorphic $\mathscr{L}$-structures M and N, with some isomorphism $\sigma : M \longrightarrow N$. Note that, for any new constant d not occurring in $\mathscr{L}$ and any $a \in M$, σ is an isomorphism from $M(d, a)$ to $N(d, \sigma(a))$. Consequently, by the induction hypothesis:

$M \vDash \exists v \psi(v)$ **iff** $M \vDash \psi(a)$ for some $a \in M$
   iff $M(d, a) \vDash \psi(d)$ for some $a \in M$ and some constant d not in $\mathscr{L}$
   iff $N(d, \sigma(a)) \vDash \psi(d)$ for some $a \in M$ and some constant d not in $\mathscr{L}$
   iff $N \vDash \exists v \psi(v)$

I leave the remainder of the proof as an exercise for the reader.[7]   □

At last, we have arrived at the central plank of the permutation argument:

Theorem 10 (The Permutation Theorem). Any first-order theory with a non-trivial model has many distinct isomorphic models with the same domain.

Proof. Combine Theorems 6 and 9.   □

We also used the Completeness Theorem to generate model-theoretic arguments. Since we now understand the notion of a model of a first-order theory, we are in a position to understand the following result:

Theorem 11 (The First-Order Completeness Theorem). Any consistent, countable first-order theory has a model whose domain contains only natural numbers.   □

However, I shall not prove this result here. Most introductory logic books conclude with a proof of completeness for the deductive system (for

---

[7] For help, see Boolos et al. (2002: 140–2).

first-order logic) that they have introduced, and so I advise the interested reader to find a logic book that they are comfortable with.

We can, of course, combine these results. For example: if there are countably many concrete objects, then any consistent, countable first-order theory has a countable model whose domain contains only concrete objects. (This follows by applying an Isomorphism Construction to the model yielded by the Completeness Theorem.) This is the gist of Putnam's first presentation of the infallibilism argument.[8] A similar thought underpins the discussion, in §5.3, of Completeness behind the veil.

I.3 Second-order satisfaction

I now move from first- to second-order logic. Second-order logic differs from first-order logic in allowing second-order variables—both predicate variables and function variables—and allowing quantifiers to bind them. Thus it allows for sentences like: $\forall V^1 \exists x\, V^1 x$ (roughly, every monadic property is held by at least one object); or $\exists g^2 \forall x \forall y\, g^2(x, y) = c$, (roughly, there is a two-place function whose value for every input is c). The superscripts on the second-order variables indicate their required arity (in the sense of Definition 1).

As in the first-order case, we shall want to know what it means for a second-order sentence to be true in a structure. Since second-order sentences can contain second-order quantifiers, we shall need to expand Definition 7 with recursion clauses to govern the second-order quantifiers. I shall sketch two different approaches that we might adopt.[9]

I start with what is conventionally called *standard semantics* for second-order logic. The relation of *standard satisfaction*, to be symbolized by '$\vDash_s$', will inherit everything from Definition 7, but will add the following:[10]

Definition Sketch 12. Let $\mathcal{M}$ be an $\mathscr{L}$-structure, let $A \subseteq M^n$ (for some n), and let S be an n-place predicate symbol not featuring in $\mathscr{L}$. We define $\mathcal{M}(S, A)$ to be the structure with signature $\mathscr{L} \cup \{S\}$ such that: (i) its domain

---

[8] Putnam (1977: 485–6), although Putnam employs a very general version of the Completeness Theorem connected to the Upward Löwenheim–Skolem Theorem (see §I.4).

[9] Shapiro (1991: 62–5, 70–6) offers a completely rigorous presentation of the technicalities.

[10] This follows Boolos et al. (2002: 280).

is M; (ii) it agrees with $\mathcal{M}$ on the interpretation of all $\mathscr{L}$-symbols; and (iii) $S^{\mathcal{M}(S,A)} = A$. Armed with this notation, say that:

- $\mathcal{M} \vDash_s \varphi(A)$ **iff** $\mathcal{M}(S, A) \vDash_s \varphi(S)$ for any n-place predicate symbol S not in $\mathscr{L}$

A similar clause can be given for functions. These allow us to provide recursion clauses for the second-order universal quantifiers (existential quantifiers are treated similarly):

- $\mathcal{M} \vDash_s \forall V^n \varphi(V^n)$ **iff** $\mathcal{M} \vDash_s \varphi(A)$ for all relations $A \subseteq M^n$
- $\mathcal{M} \vDash_s \forall g^n \varphi(g^n)$ **iff** $\mathcal{M} \vDash_s \varphi(p)$ for all functions $p : M^n \longrightarrow M$ $\qquad\square$

The alternative to standard semantics is *Henkin semantics*. Whereas standard semantics just deals with structures as defined in Definition 2, Henkin semantics requires a slightly different notion of a structure. To offer a *Henkin* second-order structure, we require (as in the standard case) a domain and an interpretation of the symbols of the language. However, we *also* require what might usefully be regarded as domains for our second-order quantifiers. More precisely, for each $n < \omega$, we must supply:

- M_{rel}^n: a collection of n-place relations (i.e. subsets of M^n)
- M_{fun}^n: a collection of functions $M^n \longrightarrow M$

We then define *Henkin satisfaction*, symbolized by '$\vDash_h$', in exactly the way that we define standard satisfaction, except that we insist that any relation must come from some M_{rel}^n, and that any function must come from some M_{fun}^n. To highlight the contrast with standard satisfaction, compare Definition Sketch 12 with:

Definition Sketch 13. Let $\mathcal{M}$ be a Henkin $\mathscr{L}$-structure, let $A \in M_{rel}^n$ (for some n), and let S be an n-place predicate symbol not featuring in $\mathscr{L}$. We define $\mathcal{M}(S, A)$ to be the structure with signature $\mathscr{L} \cup \{S\}$ such that: (i) its domain is M and it retains M_{rel}^n and M_{fun}^n for all n; (ii) it agrees with $\mathcal{M}$ on the interpretation of all $\mathscr{L}$-symbols; and (iii) $S^{\mathcal{M}(S,A)} = A$. Armed with this notation, say that:

- $\mathcal{M} \vDash_h \varphi(A)$ **iff** $\mathcal{M}(S, A) \vDash_h \varphi(S)$ for any n-place predicate symbol S not in $\mathscr{L}$

A similar clause can be given for functions. These allow us to provide recursion clauses for the second-order universal quantifiers (existential quantifiers are treated similarly):

- $\mathcal{M} \vDash_h \forall V^n \varphi(V^n)$ **iff** $\mathcal{M} \vDash_h \varphi(A)$ for all relations $A \in M_{rel}^n$
- $\mathcal{M} \vDash_h \forall g^n \varphi(g^n)$ **iff** $\mathcal{M} \vDash_h \varphi(p)$ for all functions $p \in M_{fun}^n$ $\square$

Now, since our M_{rel}^ns and M_{fun}^ns act like domains for relations and functions, a fairly trivial modification of the proof of the First-Order Completeness Theorem allows us to prove:[11]

Theorem 14 (The Second-Order Completeness Theorem). Every countable, consistent set of second-order sentences has a Henkin model $\mathcal{M}$ in which M, M_{rel}^n, and M_{fun}^n are all countable (for each $n < \omega$). $\square$

By contrast, there is no completeness theorem for *standard* second-order satisfaction. This follows immediately from the fact that we can prove (for example) that any *standard* model of second-order real analysis has the cardinality of the continuum.[12] Of course, since second-order real analysis is a consistent theory, it must have a *Henkin* model, $\mathcal{H}$, with a countably infinite domain. But since H_{rel}^1 is countable and $\wp(H)$ is uncountable, $\mathcal{H}$ will violate the Fullness Constraint proposed in §3.3. Indeed, a Henkin model $\mathcal{M}$ will meet the Fullness Constraint just in case M_{rel}^n contains all subsets of M^n and M_{fun}^n contains all functions $M^n \longrightarrow M$ (for all $n < \omega$); at which point, one might as well consider only standard models and standard satisfaction, and forget about Henkin models and Henkin satisfaction.

However, it is worth emphasizing that the permutation argument is utterly unaffected by the move to standard second-order logic: Theorems 6 and 9 both hold in that setting.[13] (Theorem 6 is unchanged, and the proof of Theorem 9 is easily expanded.)

I.4 Löwenheim–Skolem results

I mentioned in §2.1 that indeterminacy arguments can be based upon various Löwenheim–Skolem results. I shall end this appendix by outlining the results, and explaining why I have largely ignored them in this book.

---

[11] Shapiro (1991: 89–91) offers a Henkin-style proof.
[12] Shapiro (1991: 82–4) offers a proof.
[13] As observed by Hale and Wright (1997: 451).

The canonical Löwenheim–Skolem results make use of the following:[14]

Definition 15. Let $\mathcal{M}$ and $\mathcal{N}$ be $\mathcal{L}$-structures. $\mathcal{N}$ is an *elementary extension* of $\mathcal{M}$ **iff** $M \subseteq N$ and for every first-order $\mathcal{L}$-formula φ and any $a_1, \ldots, a_n \in M$, $\mathcal{M} \vDash \varphi(a_1, \ldots, a_n)$ iff $\mathcal{N} \vDash \varphi(a_1, \ldots, a_n)$. We can express this more briefly thus: $\mathcal{M} \preccurlyeq \mathcal{N}$. □

And here are the two main results:[15]

Theorem 16 (Downward Löwenheim–Skolem Theorem). Let $\mathcal{M}$ be an $\mathcal{L}$-structure. For any subset $A \subseteq M$, there is an $\mathcal{L}$-structure $\mathcal{N}$ of cardinality no greater than $\max(|A|, |\mathcal{L}|, \aleph_0)$, such that $\mathcal{N} \preccurlyeq \mathcal{M}$ and $A \subseteq N$. □

Theorem 17 (Upward Löwenheim–Skolem Theorem). Let $\mathcal{M}$ be an infinite $\mathcal{L}$-structure. For any cardinal $\mathfrak{a} \geq \max(|M|, |\mathcal{L}|)$, there is an $\mathcal{L}$-structure $\mathcal{N}$ of cardinality $\mathfrak{a}$ such that $\mathcal{M} \preccurlyeq \mathcal{N}$. □

Since any *standard* model of second-order real analysis has the cardinality of the continuum (see above), these results do not apply to *standard* second-order logic. They do, however, apply for Henkin second-order logic. In that regard, the Löwenheim–Skolem results are similar to the Completeness Theorem.

The Löwenheim–Skolem results might generate the following sort of worry. Suppose the external realist's favourite theory is countable, and let $\mathcal{W}$ be an uncountable model of that theory. Using the Downward Löwenheim–Skolem Theorem, we will be able to find smaller models that elementarily embed into $\mathcal{W}$. Or, using the Upward Löwenheim–Skolem Theorem, we will be able to find larger models that elementarily extend $\mathcal{W}$. In both cases, as with the indeterminacy arguments generated using the Permutation or Completeness Theorems, there seems to be nothing to choose between letting truth, reference, and correspondence be given by one of these Skolemized models, rather than by $\mathcal{W}$.[16]

---

[14] I have not here defined the expression $\mathcal{M} \vDash \varphi(a_1, \ldots, a_n)$ when $n \geq 1$; but Definition 7 could be expanded in an obvious way. Alternatively, a different definition of satisfaction could be used from the outset, as in Marker (2002: 9–11).

[15] I write '$|X|$' for the cardinality of the set X, and '$|\mathcal{L}|$' for the number of $\mathcal{L}$-symbols.

[16] See Putnam (1980b: 465–6).

The question is whether this raises any difficulties for the external realist that are not essentially already raised by the Permutation and Completeness Theorems together. An obvious thought is as follows. If we generate some model S by applying the Downward Löwenheim–Skolem Theorem to W, then we will have:

$$S \subseteq W$$
$$c^S = c^W \qquad \text{for each constant } c$$
$$R^S = R^W \cap S^n \qquad \text{for each } n\text{-place predicate symbol } R$$
$$f^S = f^W \upharpoonright S^n \qquad \text{for each } n\text{-place function symbol } f$$

and 'conversely' if we apply the Upward Löwenheim–Skolem Theorem. Such an interpretation might be thought to be dialectically useful, since it would enable us to run an indeterminacy argument whilst conceding to the external realist that she can pin down rather a lot about reference and correspondence.

In the context of a philosophical discussion about the interpretation of formal mathematical theories, there is much to explore here. But in the context of a debate concerning realism *in general*, the concession just made to the external realist leaves the model-theoretic arguments toothless. The external realist about cats, cherries, and electrons has little to fear from Skolemized models, for there are (I hope) only finitely many cats. The dialectical concession would also be entirely unnecessary, for as shown in Part A, the Permutation and Completeness Theorems together provide enough ammunition to destroy our faith in external realism.

Appendix II

Fitch-style reasoning

In Chapter 11, I discussed an informal argument in favour of the Fitchian Unjustifiables scheme, i.e.:

$$\neg \Diamond \bigstar (\varphi \wedge \neg \bigstar \varphi)$$

The question is whether there is a *formal* argument that establishes this scheme.

Künne advocates the scheme. However, his formal argument for it is incomplete. With minimal rules, he proves that '$(\varphi \wedge \neg \bigstar \varphi)$' entails '$\neg \bigstar (\varphi \wedge \neg \bigstar \varphi)$'. However, we need to prove '$\neg \Diamond \bigstar (\varphi \wedge \neg \bigstar \varphi)$' unconditionally, and Künne does not specify how this is to be achieved.[1] I take it that he is implicitly relying upon the kinds of formal reasoning used in standard proofs of Fitch's *knowability* paradox. The question is whether any of these proofs apply in the context of *justifiability* (rather than knowability).

Before starting, we must unpack the quantification over people and times that is buried within our notion of justification. Specifically, we need a three-place device, to express that person p has a justified belief at time t that φ. For brevity, I shall write this as '$J_t^p \varphi$'.

It is clear that '$\exists p \exists t\, J_t^p\, \varphi$' is equivalent to '$\bigstar \varphi$'. If we can derive a contradiction from '$J_m^a (\varphi \wedge \neg \exists p \exists t\, J_t^p \varphi)$' without any further assumptions, then we shall be able to derive '$\Box \neg \exists q \exists u\, J_u^q (\varphi \wedge \neg \exists p \exists t\, J_t^p \varphi)$' by $\exists$-introduction and $\Box$-introduction, which is of course equivalent to '$\neg \Diamond \bigstar (\varphi \wedge \neg \bigstar \varphi)$'. So it suffices to derive a contradiction from '$J_m^a (\varphi \wedge \neg \exists p \exists t\, J_t^p \varphi)$'. I shall consider two salient attempts at a derivation.

---

[1] Künne (2002: 162).

Any attempted derivation will begin thus:

$$1 \quad \mathrm{J}_m^a(\varphi \wedge \neg\exists p\exists t\,\mathrm{J}_t^p\varphi) \qquad \text{Assumption}$$

$$2 \quad \mathrm{J}_m^a\varphi \wedge \mathrm{J}_m^a\neg\exists p\exists t\,\mathrm{J}_t^p\varphi \qquad \text{from 1}$$

$$3 \quad \mathrm{J}_m^a\varphi \qquad \text{from 2}$$

$$4 \quad \mathrm{J}_m^a\neg\exists p\exists t\,\mathrm{J}_t^p\varphi \qquad \text{from 2}$$

The rule invoked in the transitions from line 2 to lines 3 and 4 is just ∧-elimination. The rule invoked in the transition from line 1 to line 2 is eminently reasonable: if someone somewhen has a justified belief in a conjunction, then that person has a justified belief in either conjunct.[2] This establishes the trunk of our two attempts to derive a contradiction, on the assumption of line 1. I take it that both rules are acceptable.

The first attempt to derive a contradiction continues the trunk thus:

$$5 \quad \neg\exists p\exists t\,\mathrm{J}_t^p\varphi \qquad \text{from 4}$$

$$6 \quad \neg\mathrm{J}_m^a\varphi \qquad \text{from 5}$$

$$7 \quad \bot \qquad \text{from 3, 6}$$

The transition from line 5 to line 6 is given by ordinary logical manipulations. But the transition from line 4 to line 5 is highly suspicious. If justification were *factive* (as knowledge is), then this rule would be beyond reproach, but we know from §11.1 that it is not. Unsurprisingly, both the bouffant-pianist scenario and the opaque-justification scenario (discussed in §11.3) resist this argument by denying the inference from line 4 to line 5.

The second attempt to derive a contradiction attempts to track the informal reasoning I offered in §11.3. I suggested there that anyone who *did* count the number of hairs on my head would *no longer* be justified in believing that no one is justified in believing that the number of hairs on my head is even. My reason for suggesting this was that a moment's reflection would convince such a person that *they themselves* are justified in believing that the number of hairs on my head is even. This is not, though, to say that they actually *will* pause for a moment's reflection. Thus, to formalize the argument, I must introduce a second three-place predicate. Let '$\mathrm{H}_t^p\varphi$'

---

[2] Though Douven (2007: 155–7) contests this, by considering a probabilistic threshold for a belief's being justified.

express that person p at time t would (on a moment's reflection) in fact be justified in believing that φ. Armed with this, we might attempt to continue the proof as follows:

5′	$H^a_m \neg H^a_m \varphi$	from 4
6′	$H^a_m H^a_m \varphi$	from 3
7′	$\bot$	from 5′, 6′

The rule invoked in the transition from line 4 to line 5′ is the following: if someone is justified in believing that nobody ever has a justified belief that φ, then that same person would also be justified (on a moment's reflection about their own status) in believing that at that time they themselves lacked a justified belief that φ. This is reasonable. However, both of the other inferences can be contested. The supposed rule invoked in the transition from lines 5′ and 6′ to line 7 is: no one would ever (on a moment's reflection) be justified in ·believing contradictory propositions (here, that $H^a_m \varphi$ and that $\neg H^a_m \varphi$). The bouffant–pianist scenario rejects this inference. The supposed rule invoked in the transition from line 3 to line 6′ is the following: someone with a justified belief that φ would (on a moment's reflection) in fact be justified in believing that they themselves have a justified belief that φ. The opaque-justification scenario rejects this inference.

Bibliography

Armstrong, D. M. (1983). *What is a Law of Nature?* Cambridge: Cambridge University Press.

Auxier, R. E. and L. E. Hahn, eds. (2007). *The Philosophy of Michael Dummett*. La Salle, IL: Open Court.

Baghramian, M. (2008). 'Three Pragmatisms: Putnam, Rorty, and Brandom'. In Monroy et al. 2008, pp. 83–101.

Baldwin, T. (1996). 'There Might be Nothing'. *Analysis* 56.4, pp. 231–8.

Bays, T. (2001). 'On Putnam and His Models'. *The Journal of Philosophy* 98.7, pp. 331–50.

—— (2008). 'Two Arguments Against Realism'. *The Philosophical Quarterly* 58.231, pp. 193–213.

Ben-Menahem, Y. (2005). 'Putnam on Skepticism'. In *Hilary Putnam*. Ed. by Y. Ben-Menahem. Cambridge: Cambridge University Press, pp. 125–55.

Bennett, J. (1971). *Locke, Berkeley, Hume: Central Themes*. Oxford: Clarendon Press.

Berker, S. (2009). 'The Normative Insignificance of Neuroscience'. *Philosophy and Public Affairs* 37, pp. 293–329.

Blackburn, S. (1994), 'Enchanting Views'. In Clark and Hale 1994, pp. 12–30.

Boolos, G. et al. (2002). *Computability and Logic*, 4th edn. Cambridge: Cambridge University Press.

Bouwsma, O. K. (1949). 'Descartes' Evil Genius'. *The Philosophical Review* 58.2, pp. 141–51.

Brown, J. (1998). 'Natural Kind Terms and Recognitional Capacities'. *Mind* 107.426, pp. 275–303.

—— (2000). 'Against Temporal Externalism'. *Analysis* 60.2, pp. 178–88.

Brueckner, A. (1983). 'Transcendental Arguments I'. *Noûs* 17.4, pp. 551–75.

—— (1984). 'Putnam's Model-Theoretic Argument Against Metaphysical Realism'. *Analysis* 44.3, pp. 134–40.

—— (1986). 'Brains in a Vat'. *The Journal of Philosophy* 83.3, pp. 148–67.

—— (1992). 'If I Am a Brain in a Vat, Then I Am Not a Brain in a Vat'. *Mind* 101.401, pp. 123–8.

—— (1994). 'Ebbs on Skepticism, Objectivity, and Brains in Vats'. *Pacific Philosophical Quarterly* 75, pp. 77–87.

—— (1995). 'Trying to Get Outside Your Own Skin'. *Philosophical Topics* 23.1, pp. 79–111.

Brueckner, A. (1996). 'Modest Transcendental Arguments'. *Philosophical Perspectives* 10, pp. 265–80.

—— (1999). 'Transcendental Arguments from Content Externalism'. In Stern 1999, pp. 229–50.

—— (2001). 'A Priori Knowledge of the World Not Easily Available'. *Philosophical Studies* 104.1, pp. 109–14.

—— (2006). 'Johnsen on Brains in Vats'. *Philosophical Studies* 129, pp. 435–40.

—— and G. Ebbs, eds. (2012). *Debating Self-Knowledge*. Cambridge: Cambridge University Press.

Burge, T. (1988). 'Individualism and Self-Knowledge'. *The Journal of Philosophy* 85.11, pp. 649–63.

Button, T. (2006). 'Realistic Structuralism's Identity Crisis: A hybrid solution'. *Analysis* 66.3, pp. 216–22.

—— (2010). 'Dadaism: Restrictivism as militant quietism'. *Proceedings of the Aristotelian Society* 110.3, pp. 387–98.

—— (2011). 'The Metamathematics of Putnam's Model-Theoretic arguments'. *Erkenntnis* 74.3, pp. 321–49.

Byrne, A. and H. Logue (2008). 'Either/Or'. In Haddock and Macpherson 2008, pp. 57–94.

Camus, A. (1942). *Le mythe de Sisyphe*. Trans. by J. O'Brien. 1955 English translation.

Carnap, R. (1928a). *Der logische Aufbau der Welt*. Trans. by R. A. George (1967, London: Routledge & Kegan Paul). I have departed slightly from George's translation.

—— (1928b). *Scheinprobleme in der Philosophie: Das Fremdpsychische und der Realismusstreit*. Trans. by R. A. George (1967, London: Routledge & Kegan Paul).

—— (1931). 'Die physikalische Sprache als Universalsprache der Wissenschaft'. *Erkenntnis* 2.1, pp. 432–65.

—— (1937). 'Testability and Meaning—Continued'. *Philosophy of Science* 4.1, pp. 1–40.

—— (1950). 'Empiricism, Semantics and Ontology'. *Revue Internationale de Philosophie* 4, pp. 20–40.

—— (1956). 'The Methodological Character of Theoretical Concepts'. In *The Foundations of Science and the Concepts of Psychology and Psychoanalysis*. Ed. by H. Feigl and M. Scriven. *Minnesota studies in the philosophy of science 1*. Minneapolis: University of Minnesota Press, pp. 38–76.

—— (1963). 'Replies and Systematic Expositions'. In Schilpp 1963, pp. 859–1013.

Case, J. (1997). 'On the Right Idea of a Conceptual Scheme'. *The Southern Journal of Philosophy* 35, pp. 1–18.

Case, J. (2001). 'The Heart of Putnam's Pluralistic Realism'. *Revue internationale de philosophie* 218.4, pp. 417–30.

Chalmers, D. J. (2005). 'The Matrix as Metaphysics'. In *Philosophers Explore the Matrix*. Ed. by C. Grau. Oxford: Oxford University Press.

—— et al., eds. (2009). *Metametaphysics: New essays on the foundations of ontology.* Oxford: Oxford University Press.

Christensen, D. (1993). 'Skeptical Problems, Semantical Solutions'. *Philosophy and Phenomenological Research* 53.2, pp. 301–21.

Clark, P. and B. Hale, eds. (1994). *Reading Putnam.* Oxford: Blackwell.

Collins, J. M. (2006). 'Temporal Externalism, Natural Kind Terms, and Scientifically Ignorant Communities'. *Philosophical Papers* 35.1, pp. 55–68.

Conant, J. (2004). 'Varieties of Scepticism'. In McManus 2004, pp. 97–136.

—— and U. M. Żegleń, eds. (2002). *Hilary Putnam: Pragmatism and realism.* London: Routledge.

Davidson, D. (1970). 'Mental Events'. In *Essays on Actions and Events.* Oxford: Oxford University Press, pp. 170–86.

—— (1973). 'On the Very Idea of a Conceptual Scheme'. *Proceedings and Addresses of the American Philosophical Association* 47, pp. 5–20.

—— (1979). 'The Inscrutability of Reference'. In Davidson 1984, pp. 227–41.

—— (1983). 'A Coherence Theory of Truth and Knowledge'. In Davidson 2001, pp. 137–53.

—— (1984). *Inquiries into Truth and Interpretation.* Oxford: Oxford University Press.

—— (1985). 'A New Basis for Decision Theory'. *Theory and Decision* 18, pp. 87–98.

—— (1987). 'Knowing One's Own Mind'. *Proceedings and Addresses of the American Philosophical Association* 60.3, pp. 441–58.

—— (1988). 'Reply to Burge'. *The Journal of Philosophy* 85.11, pp. 664–5.

—— (1998). 'Replies to My Critics'. *Crítica* 30.90, pp. 89–112.

—— (2001). *Subjective, Intersubjective, Objective.* Oxford: Clarendon Press.

Davies, D. (1995). 'Putnam's Brain-Teaser'. *Canadian Journal of Philosophy* 25.2, pp. 203–27.

DeRose, K. (2000). 'How Can We Know that We're Not Brains in Vats?' *The Southern Journal of Philosophy* 38, pp. 121–48.

Devitt, M. (1983). 'Realism and the Renegade Putnam: A Critical Study of *Meaning and the Moral Sciences*'. *Noûs* 17.2, pp. 291–301.

—— (1984a). *Realism and Truth.* Princeton: Princeton University Press.

—— (1984b). 'Review of Putnam 1981c'. *The Philosophical Review* 93.2, pp. 274–7.

—— (1991). 'Aberrations of the Realism Debate'. *Philosophical Studies* 61.1, pp. 43–63.

Devitt, M. (2010). 'Postscript to Devitt 1991'. In *Putting Metaphysics First: Essays on metaphysics and epistemology.* Oxford: Oxford University Press, pp. 48–56.

Dewey, J. (1929). *Experience and Nature.* 2nd edn. London: George Allen & Unwin.

Doguoglu, U. (2008). 'Putnam Beyond Putnam: Understanding, pragmatism, humanism'. In Monroy et al. 2008, pp. 103–24.

Dorr, C. (2011). 'Physical Geometry and Fundamental Metaphysics'. *Proceedings of the Aristotelian Society* 111.1, pp. 135–59.

Douven, I. (1999). 'Putnam's Model-Theoretic Argument Reconstructed'. *The Journal of Philosophy* 96.9, pp. 479–90.

—— (2007). 'Fitch's Paradox and Probabilistic Antirealism'. *Studia Logica*, 86.2, pp. 149–82.

Dretske, F. I. (1970). 'Epistemic Operators'. *The Journal of Philosophy* 67.24, pp. 1007–23.

Dummett, M. (1963). 'Realism'. In *Truth and Other Enigmas* (1978). London: Duckworth, pp. 145–65.

—— (1979). 'Comments'. In Margalit 1979, pp. 218–25.

—— (1991). *The Logical Basis of Metaphysics.* London; Duckworth.

—— (2006). *Thought and Reality.* Oxford: Clarendon Press.

—— (2007a). 'Reply to Künne'. In Auxier and Hahn 2007, pp. 345–50.

—— (2007b). 'Reply to Putnam'. In Auxier and Hahn 2007, pp. 168–84.

—— (2009). 'Fitch's Paradox of Knowability'. In Salerno 2009, pp. 51–2.

Ebbs, G. (1992a). 'Realism and Rational Inquiry'. *Philosophical Topics* 20.1, pp. 1–33.

—— (1992b). 'Skepticism, Objectivity, and Brains in Vats'. *Pacific Philosophical Quarterly* 73, pp. 239–66.

—— (1996). 'Can We Take Our Words at Face Value?' *Philosophy and Phenomenological Research* 56.3, pp. 499–530.

—— (2000). 'The Very Idea of Sameness of Extension Across Time'. *American Philosophical Quarterly* 37.3, pp. 245–68.

—— (2012). 'The dialectical context of Putnam's argument that we are not brains in vats'. In Brueckner and Ebbs 2012, pp. 66–82.

Edgington, D. (1985). 'The Paradox of Knowability'. *Mind* 94, pp. 557–68.

Eklund, M. (2006). 'Neo-Fregean Ontology'. *Philosophical Perspectives* 20, pp. 95–121.

—— (2008a). 'Putnam on Ontology'. In Monroy et al. 2008, pp. 203–22.

—— (2008b). 'The Picture of Reality as an Amorphous Lump'. In Hawthorne et al. 2008, pp. 382–96.

—— (2009). 'Carnap and Ontological Pluralism'. In Chalmers et al. 2009, pp. 130–56.

Evans, G. (1973). 'The Causal Theory of Names'. *Proceedings of the Aristotelian Society, Supplementary Volume* 47, pp. 187–208.

Falvey, K. and J. Owens (1994). 'Externalism, Self-Knowledge, and Skepticism'. *The Philosophical Review* 103.1, pp. 107–37.

Farrell, F. B. (1986). 'Putnam and the Vat-People'. *Philosophia* 16.2, pp. 147–60.

Feyerabend, P. (1993). *Against Method,* 3rd edn. London: Verso.

Field, H. (1975). 'Conventionalism and Instrumentalism in Semantics'. *Noûs* 9.4, pp. 375–405.

—— (1982). 'Realism and Relativism'. *The Journal of Philosophy* 79.10, pp. 553–67.

Fitch, F. B. (1963). 'A Logical Analysis of Some Value Concepts'. *The Journal of Symbolic Logic* 28.2, pp. 135–42.

Folina, J. (1995). 'Putnam, Realism and Truth'. *Synthese* 103.2, pp. 141–52.

Foot, P. (1967). 'The Problem of Abortion and the Doctrine of Double Effect'. *Oxford Review* 5, pp. 5–15.

Forbes, G. (1995). 'Realism and Skepticism: Brains in a vat revisited'. *The Journal of Philosophy* 92.4, pp. 205–22.

Frege, G. (1884). *Die Grundlagen der Arithmetik: Eine logisch mathematische Unter- suchung über den Begriff der Zahl.* Trans. by J. L. Austin (1953, Oxford: Blackwell). I have departed slightly from Austin's translation. Breslau: Wilhelm Koebner.

—— (1893). *Grundgesetze der Arithmetik: Begriffsschriftlich abgeleitet.* Vol. 1. Jena: H. Pohle.

French, P. et al., eds. (1988). *Realism and Antirealism.* Midwest Studies in Philosophy 12. Minneapolis: University of Minnesota Press.

Friedman, M. (1992). 'Epistemology in the *Aufbau*'. *Synthese* 93, pp. 15–57.

Glymour, C. (1982). 'Conceptual Scheming or Confessions of a Metaphysical Realist'. *Synthese* 51.2, pp. 169–80.

Goldberg, S. C. (2008). 'Metaphysical Realism and Thought'. *American Philosophical Quarterly* 45.2, pp. 149–63.

Goodman, N. (1978). *Ways of Worldmaking.* Indianapolis: Hackett.

Groves, C. P. and C. H. Bell (2004). 'New Investigations on the Taxonomy of the Zebras Genus *Equus*, Subgenus *Hippotigris*'. *Mammalian Biology* 69.3, pp. 182–96.

Hacking, I. (2007). 'The Contingencies of Ambiguity'. *Analysis* 67.4, pp. 269–77.

Haddock, A. and F. Macpherson, eds. (2008). *Disjunctivism: Perception, action, knowledge.* Oxford: Oxford University Press.

Hale, B. and C. Wright (1997). 'Putnam's Model-Theoretic Argument against Metaphysical Realism'. In *A Companion to the Philosophy of Language.* Ed. by B. Hale and C. Wright. Oxford: Blackwell, pp. 427–57.

Han, X. (2010). 'A Butterfly Dream in a Brain in a Vat'. *Philosophia* 38, pp. 157–67.

Hansen, C. (1987). 'Putnam's Indeterminacy Argument: The Skolemization of absolutely everything'. *Philosophical Studies* 51.1, pp. 77–99.

Hawthorne, J. (2006). 'Plenitude, Convention, and Ontology'. In *Metaphysical Essays.* Oxford: Oxford University Press, pp. 53–69.

Hawthorne, J. (2009). 'Superficialism in Ontology'. In Chalmers et al. 2009, pp. 213–30.

—— et al., eds. (2008). *Contemporary Debates in Metaphysics*. Oxford: Blackwell.

Heller, M. (1988). 'Putnam, Reference, and Realism'. In French et al. 1988, pp. 113–27.

Hill, C. S. (1990). 'Review of *Subject, Thought, and Context* by Philip Pettit and John McDowell'. *The Journal of Philosophy* 87.2, pp. 106–12.

Hinton, J. M. (1967). 'Visual Experiences'. *Mind* 76.392, pp. 217–27.

Hirsch, E. (2002). 'Quantifier Variance and Realism'. In *Realism and Relativism*. Ed. by E. Sosa and E. Villanueva. *Philosophical Issues 12*. Oxford: Blackwell, pp. 51–73.

—— (2005). 'Physical-Object Ontology, Verbal Disputes, and Common Sense'. *Philosophy and Phenomenological Research* 70.1, pp. 67–97.

—— (2008). 'Ontological Arguments: Interpretive charity and quantifier variance'. In Hawthorne et al. 2008, pp. 367–81.

—— (2009). 'Ontology and Alternative Languages'. In Chalmers et al. 2009, pp. 231–58.

Hylton, P. (2006). 'Quine on Reference and Ontology'. In *The Cambrdige Companion to Quine*. Ed. by R. F. Gibson Jr. Cambridge: Cambridge University Press, pp. 115–50.

Jackman, H. (1999). 'We Live Forwards but Understand Backwards: Linguistic practices and future behavior'. *Pacific Philosophical Quarterly* 80, pp. 157–77.

—— (2001). 'Semantic Pragmatism and "A Priori" Knowledge (Or "Yes We Could All Be Brains in a Vat")'. *Canadian Journal of Philosophy* 31.4, pp. 455–80.

—— (2005). 'Temporal Externalism, Deference, and Our Ordinary Linguistic Practice'. *Pacific Philosophical Quarterly* 86, pp. 365–80.

James, W. (1904). 'Humanism and Truth'. *Mind* 13.52, pp. 457–75.

—— (1907). *Pragmatism: A new name for some old ways of thinking*. Ed. by B. Kuklick. 1981 edition. Indianapolis: Hackett.

Jeffrey, R. C. (1964). 'Review of *Logic, Methodology, and Philosophy of Science*'. *The Journal of Philosophy* 61.2, pp. 76–94.

Kamm, F. M. (2007). *Intricate Ethics: Rights, Responsibilities, and Permissible Harm*. Oxford: Oxford University Press.

Kant, I. (1787). *Kritik der reinen Vernunft*. Trans. by N. Kemp Smith. Revised (2003) edition. Basingstoke: Palgrave Macmillan.

Kelp, C. and D. Pritchard (2009). 'Two Deflationary Approaches to Fitch-Style reasoning'. In Salerno 2009, pp. 324–38.

Kripke, S. A. (1972). *Naming and Necessity*. Cambridge, MA: Harvard University Press.

—— (1979). 'A Puzzle About Belief'. In Margalit 1979, pp. 239–83.

Künne, W. (2002). 'From Alethic Anti-Realism to Alethic Realism'. In Conant and Żegleń 2002, pp. 144–65.

—— (2007). 'Two Principles Concerning Truth'. In Auxier and Hahn 2007, pp. 315–44.

Leitgeb, H. and J. Ladyman (2008). 'Criteria of Identity and Structuralist Ontology'. *Philosophia Mathematica* 16.3, pp. 388–96.

LePore, E. and B. Loewer (1988). 'A Putnam's Progress'. In French et al. 1988, pp. 459–73.

Lewis, C. I. (1934). 'Experience and Meaning'. *The Philosophical Review* 43.2, pp. 125–46.

Lewis, D. (1984). 'Putnam's Paradox'. *Australasian Journal of Philosophy* 62.3, pp. 221–36.

—— (1986). *On the Plurality of Worlds*. Oxford: Basil Blackwell.

Lillehammer, H. (2008). 'Review of Kamm 2007'. *Journal of Moral Philosophy* 5, pp. 455–7.

—— (2011). 'The Epistemology of Ethical Intuitions'. *Philosophy* 86, pp. 175–200.

Lipton, P. (1991). *Inference to the Best Explanation*. London: Routledge.

Longuenesse, B. (2008). 'Cassam and Kant on "How Possible" Questions and Categorial Thinking'. *Philosophy and Phenomenological Research* 77.2, pp. 510–7.

Lorenzen, E. D. et al. (2008). 'High Variation and Very Low Differentiation in Wide Ranging Plains Zebra (*Equus quagga*): Insights from mtDNA and microsatellites'. *Molecular Ecology* 17, pp. 2812–24.

MacFarlane, J. (2004). 'McDowell's Kantianism'. *Theoria* 70.2–3, pp. 250–65.

Madden, R. (2010). 'Could a Brain in a Vat Self-Refer?' *European Journal of Philosophy* 21.1, pp. 74–93.

Maddy, P. (1990). *Realism in Mathematics*. Corrected 1992 edition. Oxford: Clarendon Press.

Malchowski, A. (1986). 'Metaphysical Realist Semantics: Some moral desiderata'. *Philosophia* 16.2, pp. 167–74.

Malcolm, N. (1963). 'Memory and the Past'. *The Monist* 47.2, pp. 247–66.

Margalit, A., ed. (1979). *Meaning and Use: Papers presented at the second Jerusalem Philosophical Encounter, April 1976*. Vol. 3. London: D. Reidel.

Marker, D. (2002). *Model Theory: An introduction*. New York: Springer.

Maxwell, G. (1962). 'The Ontological Status of Theoretical Entities'. In *Scientific Explanation, Space, and Time*. Ed. by H. Feigl and G. Maxwell. Vol. 3. *Minnesota studies in the philosophy of science*. Minneapolis: University of Minnesota Press, pp. 3–15.

McDowell, J. (1992). 'Putnam on Mind and Meaning'. *Philosophical Topics* 20.1, pp. 35–48.

McDowell, J. (1994). *Mind and World*. Cambridge, MA: Havard University Press.

—— (1998). 'Having the World in View: Sellars, Kant, and intentionality'. *The Journal of Philosophy* 95.9, pp. 431–91.

—— (2008). 'The Disjunctive Conception of Experience as Material for a Transcendental Argument'. In Haddock and Macpherson 2008, pp. 376–89.

McGee, V. (2005). 'Inscrutability and its Discontents'. *Noûs* 39.3, pp. 397–425.

McLeish, C. (2009). 'Empty Threats'. PhD thesis. Cambridge University.

McManus, D., ed. (2004). *Wittgenstein and Scepticism*. New York: Routledge.

Merrill, G. H. (1980). 'The Model-Theoretic Argument against Realism'. *Philosophy of Science* 47.1, pp. 69–81.

Monroy, M. U. R. et al., eds. (2008). *Following Putnam's Trail*. Amsterdam: Rodopi.

Moore, A. W. (1994). 'Solipsism and Subjectivity'. *European Journal of Philosophy* 4.2, pp. 220–33.

—— (1997). *Points of View*. Oxford: Clarendon Press.

—— (2011). 'Vats, Sets, and Tits'. In *Transcendental Philosophy and Naturalism*. Ed. by P. Sullivan and J. Smith. Oxford: Oxford University Press, pp. 42–54.

Moore, G. E. (1939). 'Proof of an External World'. *Proceedings of the British Academy* 25, p. 273–300.

—— (1942). 'Reply to My Critics'. In *The Philosophy of G. E. Moore*. Ed. by P. A. Schilpp. Open Court, pp. 535–677.

Moretti, L. (2000). 'Putnam's Internal Realism'. PhD thesis. King's College London.

Nagel, T. (1986). *The View from Nowhere*. Oxford: Oxford University Press.

Newman, M. (1928). 'Mr. Russell's "Causal Theory of Perception"'. *Mind* 37.146, pp. 137–48.

Nozick, R. (1974). *Anarchy, State, and Utopia*. Oxford: Blackwell.

O'Hear, A., ed. (2002). *Logic, Thought and Language*. Cambridge: Cambridge University Press.

Okasha, S. (2002). 'Underdetermination, Holism and the Theory/Data Distinction'. *The Philosophical Quarterly* 52.208, pp. 303–19.

Patton, M. F., Jr. (1988). 'Can Bad Men make Good Brains do Bad Things?' *Proceedings and Addresses of the American Philosophical Association* 61.3, pp. 555–6.

Pearce, D. and V. Rantala (1982). 'Realism and Formal Semantics'. *Synthese* 52.1, pp. 39–53.

Peirce, C. S. (1868). 'Some Consequences of Four Incapacities'. *The Journal of Speculative Philosophy* 2.3, pp. 140–57.

—— (1877). 'Illustrations of the Logic of Science: The fixation of belief'. *The Popular Science Monthly* 12.1, pp. 1–15.

—— (1878). 'Illustrations of the Logic of Science: How to make Our Ideas Clear'. *The Popular Science Monthly* 13, pp. 287–302.

Potter, M. (2000). *Reason's Nearest Kin: Philosophy of mathematics from Kant to Carnap.* Oxford: Oxford University Press.

Price, H. (2009). 'Metaphysics After Carnap: The ghost who walks?' In Chalmers et al. 2009, pp. 320–46.

Priest, G. (2008). *An Introduction to Non-Classical Logic: From if to is.* 2nd edn. Cambridge: Cambridge University Press.

Putnam, H. (1967). 'Mathematics without Foundations'. *The Journal of Philosophy* 64.1, pp. 5–22.

—— (1969). 'Logical Positivism and the Philosophy of Mind'. In Putnam 1975a, pp. 441–51.

—— (1973). 'Meaning and Reference'. *The Journal of Philosophy* 70.19, pp. 699–711.

—— (1974). 'The Refutation of Conventionalism'. *Noûs* 8.1, pp. 25–40.

—— (1975a). *Mind, Language and Reality.* Cambridge: Cambridge University Press.

—— (1975b). 'The Meaning of "Meaning"'. In Putnam 1975a, pp. 215–71.

—— (1975c). 'What is Mathematical Truth?' In *Mathematics, Matter and Method.* Cambridge: Cambridge University Press, pp. 60–78.

—— (1977). 'Realism and Reason'. *Proceedings and Addresses of the American Philosophical Association* 50.6, pp. 483–98.

—— (1978a). 'Equivalence'. In Putnam 1983a, pp. 26–45.

—— (1978b). 'Reference and Understanding'. In *Meaning and the Moral Sciences.* London: Routledge & Kegan Paul, pp. 95–119.

—— (1979a). 'Comments'. In Margalit 1979, pp. 284–8.

—— (1979b). 'Reflections on Goodman's *Ways of Worldmaking*'. *The Journal of Philosophy* 76.11, pp. 603–18.

—— (1979c). 'Reply to Dummett's Comment'. In Margalit 1979, pp. 226–8.

—— (1980a). 'How to be an Internal Realist and a Transcendental Idealist (at the Same Time)'. In *Language, Logic, and Philosophy.* Ed. by R. Haller and W. Grassl. Vol. 4. *Proceedings of the International Wittgenstein Symposium.* Vienna: Hölder-Pichler-Tempsky, pp. 100–8.

—— (1980b). 'Models and Reality'. *Journal of Symbolic Logic* 45.3, pp. 464–82.

—— (1981a). 'Philosophers and Human Understanding'. In Putnam 1983a, pp. 184–204.

—— (1981b). 'Quantum Mechanics and the Observer'. *Erkenntnis* 16.2, pp. 193–219.

—— (1981c). *Reason, Truth and History.* Cambridge: Cambridge University Press.

—— (1982a). 'A Defense of Internal Realism'. In Putnam 1990b, pp. 30–42.

—— (1982b). 'Beyond the Fact–Value Dichotomy'. *Crítica* 14.41, pp. 3–12.

—— (1982c). 'Why There isn't a Ready-Made World'. In Putnam 1983a, pp. 205–28.

Putnam, H. (1983a). *Realism and Reason*. Cambridge: Cambridge University Press.

—— (1983b). 'Reference and Truth'. In Putnam 1983a, pp. 69–86.

—— (1983c). 'Why Reason Can't Be Naturalized'. In Putnam 1983a, pp. 229–47.

—— (1984a). 'Is the Causal Structure of the Physical Itself Something Physical?' In Putnam 1990b, pp. 80–95.

—— (1984b). 'The Craving for Objectivity'. *New Literary History* 15.2, pp. 229–39.

—— (1985). 'After Empiricism'. In Putnam 1990b, pp. 43–53.

—— (1986a). 'Meaning Holism'. In Putnam 1990b, pp. 278–302.

—— (1986b). 'Why Is a Philosopher?' In Putnam 1990b, pp. 105–19.

—— (1987a). 'Realism with a Human Face'. In Putnam 1990b, pp. 3–29.

—— (1987b). *The Many Faces of Realism*. La Salle, IL: Open Court.

—— (1987c). 'Truth and Convention'. *Dialectica* 40.1–2, pp. 69–77.

—— (1988). *Representation and Reality*. London: MIT Press.

—— (1989). 'Model Theory and the "Factuality" of Semantics'. In Putnam 1994d, pp. 351–75.

—— (1990a). 'Is Water Necessarily H$_2$O?' In Putnam 1990b, pp. 54–79.

—— (1990b). *Realism with a Human Face*. Ed. by J. Conant. London: Harvard University Press.

—— (1991a). 'Does the Disquotational Theory of Truth Solve All Philosophical Problems?' In Putnam 1994d, pp. 264–78.

—— (1991b). 'Logical Positivism and Intentionality'. In Putnam 1994d, pp. 85–98.

—— (1991c). 'Replies and Comments'. *Erkenntnis* 34.3, pp. 401–24.

—— (1992a). *Renewing Philosophy*. Cambridge, MA: Harvard University Press.

—— (1992b). 'Replies'. *Philosophical Topics* 20.1, pp. 347–408.

—— (1993a). 'Aristotle after Wittgenstein'. In Putnam 1994d, pp. 62–81.

—— (1993b). 'Realism without Absolutes'. *International Journal of Philosophical Studies* 1.2, pp. 179–92.

—— (1993c). 'The Question of Realism'. In Putnam 1994d, pp. 295–312.

—— (1994a). 'Comments and Replies'. In Clark and Hale 1994, pp. 242–95.

—— (1994b). 'Interview mit Hilary Putnam'. In *Hilary Putnam*. Ed. by A. Burri. Interview conducted by Alex Burri. Frankfurt: Campus Verlag GmbH, pp. 170–89.

—— (1994c). 'Sense, Nonsense, and the Senses: An inquiry into the powers of the human mind'. *The Journal of Philosophy* 91.9, pp. 445–517.

—— (1994d). *Words and Life*. Ed. by J. Conant. Cambridge, MA: Harvard University Press.

—— (1995a). 'Pragmatism'. *Proceedings of the Aristotelian Society* 95, pp. 291–306.

—— (1995b). *Pragmatism: An open question*. Oxford: Blackwell.

—— (1997). 'Functionalism: Cognitive science or science fiction?' In Putnam 2012d, pp. 608–23.

Putnam, H. (1998). 'Skepticism and Occasion-Sensitive Semantics'. In Putnam 2012d, pp. 514–34.

—— (1999). *The Threefold Cord: Mind, Body, and World*. New York: Columbia University Press.

—— (2000). 'Das modelltheoretische Argument und die Suche nach dem Realismus des Common sense'. In *Realismus*. Ed. by M. Willaschek. Trans. by B. Brinkmeier. English quotations from a manuscript supplied to me by Putnam. Paderbon: Ferdinand Schöningh Verlag, pp. 125–42.

—— (2001a). 'Reply to Jennifer Case'. *Revue Internationale de Philosophie* 218.4, pp. 431–8.

—— (2001b). 'Reply to Michael Devitt'. *Revue Internationale de Philosophie* 218.4, pp. 495–502.

—— (2001c). 'When "Evidence Transcendence" is not Malign: A reply to Crispin Wright'. *The Journal of Philosophy* 98.11, pp. 594–600.

—— (2002a). 'Comments'. In Conant and Żegleń 2002.

—— (2002b). *The Collapse of the Fact/Value Dichotomy*. Cambridge, MA: Harvard University Press.

—— (2002c). 'Travis on Meaning, Thought and the Ways the World Is'. *The Philosophical Quarterly* 52.206, pp. 96–106.

—— (2004). *Ethics Without Ontology*. Cambridge, MA: Harvard University Press.

—— (2005). 'The Depths and Shallows of Experience'. In Putnam 2012d, pp. 567–83.

—— (2007). 'Beween Scylla and Charybdis: Does Dummett have a way through?' In Auxier and Hahn 2007, pp. 155–67.

—— (2008). 'What Makes Pragmatism so Different?' In Monroy et al. 2008, pp. 19–34.

—— (2012a). 'Corresponding with Reality'. In Putnam 2012d, pp. 72–90.

—— (2012b). 'From Quantum Mechanics to Ethics and Back Again'. In Putnam 2012d, pp. 51–71.

—— (2012c). 'How to be a Sophisticated "Naïve Realist"'. In Putnam 2012d, pp. 624–39.

—— (2012d). *Philosophy in an Age of Science*. Ed. by M. D. Caro and D. Macarthur. Cambridge, MA: Harvard University Press.

Quine, W. v. O. (1948). 'On What There Is'. *Review of Metaphysics* 2.5, pp. 21–36.

—— (1951a). 'On Carnap's Views on Ontology'. *Philosophical Studies* 2.5, pp. 65–72.

—— (1951b). 'Ontology and Ideology'. *Philosophical Studies* 2.1, pp. 11–15.

—— (1957). 'The Scope and Language of Science'. *British Journal for the Philosophy of Science* 8.29, pp. 1–17.

Quine, W. v. O. (1960). *Word and Object*. Cambridge, MA: MIT Press.

—— (1964). 'Ontological Reduction and the World of Numbers'. *The Journal of Philosophy* 61.7, pp. 209–16.

—— (1968). 'Ontological Relativity'. *The Journal of Philosophy* 65.7, pp. 185–212.

—— (1970). 'On the Reasons for the Indeterminacy of Translation'. *The Journal of Philosophy* 67.6, pp.178–83.

—— (1987). 'Indeterminacy of Translation Again'. *The Journal of Philosophy* 84.1, pp. 5–10.

Resnik, M. D. (1987). 'You Can't Trust an Ideal Theory to Tell the Truth'. *Philosophical Studies* 52.2, pp. 151–60.

Rorty, R. (1979). 'Transcendental Arguments, Self-Reference, and Pragmatism'. In *Transcendental Arguments and Science* (1979). Ed. by P. Bieri et al. Dordrecht: D. Reidel, pp. 77–103.

Russell, B. (1921). *The Analysis of Mind*. London: George Allen & Unwin.

Sainsbury, R. M. (1991). 'Cartesian Possibilities and the Externality and Extrinsicness of Content'. *Synthese* 89.3, pp. 407–24.

Salerno, J., ed. (2009). *New Essays on the Knowability Paradox*. Oxford: Oxford University Press.

Schilpp, P. A., ed. (1963). *The Philosophy of Rudolf Carnap*. La Salle, IL: Open Court.

Schlick, M. (1936). 'Meaning and Verification'. *The Philosophical Review* 45.4, pp. 339–69.

Shapiro, S. (1991). *Foundations without Foundationalism*. Oxford: Oxford University Press.

—— (1997). *Philosophy of Mathematics: Structure and Ontology*. New York: Oxford University Press.

Silva, C. C. (2008). 'Introduction: Putnam and the Notion of "Reality"'. In Monroy et al. 2008, pp. 9–16.

Singer, P. (2005). 'Ethics and Intuitions'. *The Journal of Ethics* 9, pp. 331–52.

Skolem, T. (1922). 'Einige Bemerkungen zur axiomatischen Begründung der Mengenlehre'. In *Selected Works in Logic* (1970). Ed. by E. J. Fenstad. Oslo: Universitetsforlaget, pp. 137–52.

Smart, J. J. C. (1995). 'A Form of Metaphysical Realism'. *The Philosophical Quarterly* 45.180, pp. 301–15.

Smith, P. (1984). 'Could We Be Brains in a Vat?' *Canadian Journal of Philosophy* 14.1, pp. 115–23.

Sprevak, M. and C. McLeish (2004). 'Magic, Semantics, and Putnam's Vat Brains'. *Studies in History and Philosophy of Biological and Biomedical Sciences* 35, pp. 227–36.

Stephens, J. and L.-M. Russow (1985). 'Brains in Vats and the Internalist Perspective'. *Australasian Journal of Philosophy* 63.2, pp. 205–12.

Stern, R., ed. (1999). *Transcendental Arguments: Problems and Prospects.* Oxford: Clarendon Press.

Strawson, P. F. (1959). *Individuals.* London: Methuen.

—— (1966). *The Bounds of Sense: An Essay on Kant's* Critique of Pure Reason. London: Methuen.

Stroud, B. (1994). 'Kantian Argument, Conceptual Capacities, and Invulnerability'. In *Kant and Contemporary Epistemology.* Ed. by P. Parrini. Dordrecht: Kluwer Academic, pp. 231–51.

Taylor, B. (2006). *Models, Truth and Realism.* Oxford: Clarendon Press.

Thomson, J. J. (1976). 'Killing, Letting Die, and the Trolley Problem'. *The Monist* 59, pp. 204–17.

Tymoczko, T. (1989). 'In Defense of Putnam's Brains'. *Philosophical Studies* 57.3, pp. 281–97.

Van Cleve, J. (1992). 'Semantic Supervenience and Referential Indeterminacy'. *The Journal of Philosophy* 89.7, pp. 344–61.

Van Inwagen, P. (1988). 'On Always Being Wrong'. In French et al. 1988, pp. 95–111.

—— (2009). 'The New Anti-Metaphysicians'. *Proceedings and Addresses of the American Philosophical Association* 83.2, pp. 45–61.

Wallace, J. (1979). 'Only in the Context of a Sentence do Words have any Meaning'. In *Contemporary Perspectives in the Philosophy of Language.* Ed. by P. A. French et al. Minneapolis: University of Minnesota Press, pp. 305–25.

Warfield, T. A. (1998). 'A Priori Knowledge of the World: Knowing the world by knowing our minds'. *Philosophical Studies* 92.1/2, pp. 127–47.

Whorf, B. L. (1956). *Language, Thought, and Reality.* Ed. by J. B. Carroll. Cambridge, MA: MIT Press.

Williams, J. R. G. (2007). 'Eligibility and Inscrutability'. *Philosophical Review* 116.3, pp. 361–99.

—— (2015). 'Lewis on Reference and Eligibility'. In *A Companion to David Lewis.* Ed. by B. Loewer and J. Schaffer. Oxford: Wiley Blackwell, pp. 367–81.

Williamson, T. (2002). 'Necessary Existents'. In O'Hear 2002, pp. 233–51.

Wilson, M. (1982). 'Predicate Meets Property'. *The Philosophical Review* 91.4, pp. 549–89.

Winnie, J. A. (1967). 'The Implicit Definition of Theoretical Terms'. *British Journal for the Philosophy of Science* 18.3, pp. 223–9.

Wittgenstein, L. (1921). *Tractatus Logico-Philosophicus.* Trans. by D. F. Pears and B. F. McGuinness. Revised 2002 edition. London: Routledge.

Wittgenstein, L. (1953). *Philosophical Investigations.* Trans. by Elizabeth Anscombe. I have departed slightly from Anscombe's translation. Chichester: Blackwell.

—— (1969). *On Certainty.* Ed. by G. E. M. Anscombe and G. H. von Wright. Trans. by D. Paul and G. E. M. Anscombe. Oxford: Basil Blackwell.

Wright, C. (1992a). 'On Putnam's Proof that We Are Not Brains in a Vat'. *Proceedings of the Aristotelian Society* 92,pp. 67–94.

—— (1992b). *Truth and Objectivity.* Cambridge, MA: Harvard University Press.

—— (2000). 'Truth as Sort of Epistemic: Putnam's peregrinations'. *The Journal of Philosophy* 97.6, pp. 335–64.

—— (2002). '(Anti-)Sceptics Simple and Subtle'. *Philosophy and Phenomenological Research* 65.2, pp. 330–48.

—— (2008). 'Comment on John McDowell's "The Disjunctive Conception of Experience as Material for a Transcendental Argument"'. In Haddock and Macpherson 2008, pp. 390–404.

Index

Printed and bound by CPI Group (UK) Ltd, Croydon, CR0 4YY